Efficient MySQL Performance

Best Practices and Techniques

Daniel Nichter

Beijing · Boston · Farnham · Sebastopol · Tokyo

Efficient MySQL Performance

by Daniel Nichter

Copyright © 2022 Daniel Nichter. All rights reserved.

Published by O'Reilly Media, Inc., 1005 Gravenstein Highway North, Sebastopol, CA 95472.

O'Reilly books may be purchased for educational, business, or sales promotional use. Online editions are also available for most titles (*http://oreilly.com*). For more information, contact our corporate/institutional sales department: 800-998-9938 or *corporate@oreilly.com*.

Acquisitions Editor: Andy Kwan
Development Editor: Corbin Collins
Production Editor: Katherine Tozer
Copyeditor: Justin Billing
Proofreader: Piper Editorial Consulting, LLC

Indexer: Amnet Systems LLC
Interior Designer: David Futato
Cover Designer: Karen Montgomery
Illustrator: Kate Dullea

December 2021:   First Edition

Revision History for the First Edition
2021-11-30:   First Release

See *http://oreilly.com/catalog/errata.csp?isbn=9781098105099* for release details.

The O'Reilly logo is a registered trademark of O'Reilly Media, Inc. *Efficient MySQL Performance*, the cover image, and related trade dress are trademarks of O'Reilly Media, Inc.

978-1-098-10509-9

[LSI]

Table of Contents

Preface

A gap in MySQL literature exists between basic MySQL knowledge and advanced MySQL performance. There are several books about the former, and one book about the latter: *High Performance MySQL*, 4th Edition, by Silvia Botros and Jeremy Tinley (O'Reilly). This is the first book to bridge the gap.

The gap exists because MySQL is complex, and it's difficult to teach performance without addressing that complexity—the proverbial elephant in the room. But engineers using (not managing) MySQL should not need to become MySQL experts to achieve remarkable MySQL performance. To bridge the gap, this book is unapologetically efficient—pay no attention to the elephant; it's friendly.

Efficient MySQL performance means *focus*: learning and applying only the best practices and techniques that directly affect remarkable MySQL performance. Focus dramatically narrows the scope of MySQL complexity and allows me to show you a much simpler and faster path through the vast and complex field of MySQL performance. The journey begins with the first sentence of Chapter 1, "Performance is query response time." From there, we move fast through indexes, data, access patterns, and a lot more.

On a scale of one to five—where one is an introduction for anyone, and five is a deep dive for aspiring experts—this book ranges from three to four: deep, but far from the bottom. I presume that you're an experienced engineer who has basic knowledge of and experience with a relational database (MySQL or otherwise), so I do not explain SQL or database fundamentals. I presume that you're an accomplished programmer who is responsible for one or more applications that use MySQL, so I continually reference *the application* and trust that you know the details of *your application*. I also presume that you're familiar with computers in general, so I talk freely about hardware, software, networks, and so forth.

Since this book focuses on MySQL performance for engineers using MySQL, not managing it, a few references to MySQL configuration are made when necessary but not explained. For help configuring MySQL, ask a DBA where you work. If you don't have a DBA, hire a MySQL consultant—there are many great consultants with affordable contract options. You can also learn by reading the *MySQL Reference Manual* (*https://oreil.ly/Y1W2r*). The MySQL manual is superb and experts use it all the time, so you're in good company.

Conventions Used in This Book

The following typographical conventions are used in this book:

Italic
> Indicates new terms, URLs, email addresses, filenames, and file extensions.

`Constant width`
> Used for program listings, as well as within paragraphs to refer to program elements such as variable or function names, databases, data types, environment variables, statements, and keywords.

`Constant width bold`
> Shows commands or other text that should be typed literally by the user.

`Constant width italic`
> Shows text that should be replaced with user-supplied values or by values determined by context.

This element signifies a tip or suggestion.

This element signifies a general note.

This element indicates a warning or caution.

Using Code Examples

Supplemental material (code examples, exercises, etc.) is available for download at *https://github.com/efficient-mysql-performance*.

If you have a technical question or a problem using the code examples, please email *bookquestions@oreilly.com*.

This book is here to help you get your job done. In general, if example code is offered with this book, you may use it in your programs and documentation. You do not need to contact us for permission unless you're reproducing a significant portion of the code. For example, writing a program that uses several chunks of code from this book does not require permission. Selling or distributing examples from O'Reilly books does require permission. Answering a question by citing this book and quoting example code does not require permission. Incorporating a significant amount of example code from this book into your product's documentation does require permission.

We appreciate, but generally do not require, attribution. An attribution usually includes the title, author, publisher, and ISBN. For example: "*Efficient MySQL Performance* by Daniel Nichter (O'Reilly). Copyright 2022 Daniel Nichter, 978-1-098-10509-9*."

If you feel your use of code examples falls outside fair use or the permission given above, feel free to contact us at *permissions@oreilly.com*.

O'Reilly Online Learning

 For more than 40 years, *O'Reilly Media* has provided technology and business training, knowledge, and insight to help companies succeed.

Our unique network of experts and innovators share their knowledge and expertise through books, articles, and our online learning platform. O'Reilly's online learning platform gives you on-demand access to live training courses, in-depth learning paths, interactive coding environments, and a vast collection of text and video from O'Reilly and 200+ other publishers. For more information, visit *http://oreilly.com*.

How to Contact Us

Please address comments and questions concerning this book to the publisher:

O'Reilly Media, Inc.
1005 Gravenstein Highway North
Sebastopol, CA 95472
800-998-9938 (in the United States or Canada)
707-829-0515 (international or local)
707-829-0104 (fax)

We have a web page for this book, where we list errata, examples, and any additional information. You can access this page at *https://oreil.ly/efficient-mysql-performance*.

Email *bookquestions@oreilly.com* to comment or ask technical questions about this book.

For news and information about our books and courses, visit *http://oreilly.com*.

Follow us on Twitter: *http://twitter.com/oreillymedia*

Watch us on YouTube: *http://youtube.com/oreillymedia*

Acknowledgments

Thank you to the MySQL experts who reviewed this book: Vadim Tkachenko, Frédéric Descamps, and Fernando Ipar. Thank you to the MySQL experts who reviewed parts of this book: Marcos Albe, Jean-François Gagné and Kenny Gryp. Thank you to many other MySQL experts who have helped me, taught me, and provided opportunities over the years: Peter Zaitsev, Baron Schwartz, Ryan Lowe, Bill Karwin, Emily Slocombe, Morgan Tocker, Shlomi Noach, Jeremy Cole, Laurynas Biveinis, Mark Callaghan, Domas Mituzas, Ronald Bradford, Yves Trudeau, Sveta Smirnova, Alexey Kopytov, Jay Pipes, Stewart Smith, Aleksandr Kuzminsky, Alexander Rubin, Roman Vynar, and—again—Vadim Tkachenko.

Thank you to O'Reilly and my editors: Corbin Collins, Katherine Tozer, Andy Kwan, and all the people behind the scenes.

And thank you to my wife, Moon, who supported me during the time-consuming process of writing this book.

## CHAPTER 1

Query Response Time

Performance is query response time.

This book explores that idea from various angles with a single intent: to help you achieve remarkable MySQL performance. *Efficient* MySQL performance means *focusing* on the best practices and techniques that directly affect MySQL performance—no superfluous details or deep internals required by DBAs and experts. I presume that you're a busy professional who is using MySQL, not managing it, and that you need the most results for the least effort. That's not laziness, that's efficiency. To that end, this book is direct and to the point. And by the end, you will be able to achieve remarkable MySQL performance.

MySQL performance is a complex and multifaceted subject, but you do not need to become an expert to achieve remarkable performance. I narrow the scope of MySQL complexity by focusing on the essentials. MySQL performance begins with query response time.

Query response time is how long it takes MySQL to execute a query. Synonymous terms are: *response time*, *query time*, *execution time*, and (inaccurately) *query latency*.[1] Timing starts when MySQL receives the query and ends when it has sent the result set to the client. Query response time comprises many stages (steps during query execution) and waits (lock waits, I/O waits, and so on), but a complete and detailed breakdown is neither possible nor necessary. As with many systems, basic troubleshooting and analysis reveal the majority of problems.

---

1 Latency is delay inherent in the system. Query response time is not a delay inherent in MySQL; it comprises various latencies: network, storage, and so on.

Performance increases as query response time decreases. *Improving* query response time is synonymous with *reducing* query response time.

This chapter is the foundation. It expounds query response time so that, in subsequent chapters, you can learn how to improve it. There are seven major sections. The first is a true story to motivate and amuse. The second discusses why query response time is the North Star of MySQL performance. The third outlines how query metrics are transformed into meaningful reports: query reporting. The fourth addresses query analysis: using query metrics and other information to understand query execution. The fifth maps out the journey of improving query response time: query optimization. The sixth gives an honest and modest schedule for optimizing queries. The seventh discusses why MySQL cannot simply go faster—why query optimization is necessary.

A True Story of False Performance

In 2004, I was working the night shift at a data center—2 p.m. to midnight. It was a great job for two reasons. First, the only employees in the data center after 5 p.m. were a handful of engineers monitoring and managing thousands of physical servers for an undisclosed number of customers and websites—probably tens of thousands of websites. It was an engineer's dream. Second, there were countless MySQL servers that always had problems to fix. It was a gold mine of learning and opportunity. But at the time, there were few books, blogs, or tools about MySQL. (Though that same year, O'Reilly published the first edition of *High Performance MySQL*.) Consequently, the state of the art for "fixing" MySQL performance problems was "sell the customer more RAM." For sales and management it always worked, but for MySQL the results were inconsistent.

One night I decided not to sell the customer more RAM and, instead, to do a technical deep dive to find and fix the true root cause of their MySQL performance problem. Their database was powering a bulletin board which had slowed to a crawl under the weight of its success—still a common problem today, almost 20 years later. To make a long story short, I found a single query missing a critical index. After properly indexing the query, performance improved dramatically and the website was saved. It cost the customer zero dollars.

Not all performance problems and solutions are that straightforward and glamorous. But just shy of 20 years' experience with MySQL has taught me (and many others) that MySQL performance problems are very often solved by the best practices and techniques in this book.

North Star

I'm a MySQL DBA *and* a software engineer, so I know what it's like working with MySQL as the latter. Especially when it comes to performance, we (software engineers) just want it (MySQL) to work. Between shipping features and putting out fires, who has time for MySQL performance? And when MySQL performance is poor—or worse: when it suddenly becomes poor—the way forward can be difficult to see because there are many considerations: where do we begin? Do we need more RAM? Faster CPUs? More storage IOPS? Is the problem a recent code change? (Fact: code changes deployed in the past can cause performance problems in the future, sometimes days in the future.) Is the problem a noisy neighbor? Are the DBAs doing something to the database? Has the app has gone viral and it's the good kind of problem to have?

As an engineer whose expertise is the application, not MySQL, that situation can be overwhelming. To move forward confidently, start by looking at query response time because it is *meaningful* and *actionable*. These are powerful qualities that lead to real solutions:

Meaningful

    Query response time is the only metric anyone truly cares about because, let's be honest, when the database is fast, nobody looks at it or asks questions. Why? Because query response time is the only metric we *experience*. When a query takes 7.5 seconds to execute, we experience 7.5 seconds of impatience. That same query might examine a million rows, but we don't experience a million rows examined. Our time is precious.

Actionable

    There's so much you can do to improve query response time and make everyone happy again that you're holding a book about it. (Do people still hold books in the future? I hope so.) Query response time is directly actionable because you own the code, so you can change the queries. Even if you don't own the code (or have access to it), you can still indirectly optimize query response time. "Improving Query Response Time" on page 27 addresses direct and indirect query optimization.

Focus on improving query response time—the North Star of MySQL performance. Do not begin by throwing hardware at the problem. Begin by using query metrics to determine what MySQL is doing, then analyze and optimize slow queries to reduce response time, and repeat. Performance *will* improve.

Query Reporting

Query metrics provide invaluable insights into query execution: response time, lock time, rows examined, and so on. But query metrics, like all metrics, are raw values that need to be collected, aggregated, and reported in a way that's meaningful to (and readable for) engineers. That's what this section outlines: how query metric tools transform query metrics into query reports. But query reporting is only a means to an end, as discussed in "Query Analysis" on page 11.

Looking ahead, query analysis is the real work: analyzing query metrics (as reported) and other information with the goal of understanding query execution. To improve MySQL performance, you must optimize queries. To optimize queries, you must understand how they execute. And to understand that, you must analyze them with pertinent information, including query reports and metadata.

But first you need to understand query reporting, since it represents the trove of query metrics that provide invaluable insights into query execution. The next three sections teach you about the following:

- Sources: query metrics originate from two sources and vary by MySQL distribution and version
- Aggregation: query metric values are grouped and aggregated by normalized SQL statements
- Reporting: query reports are organized by a high-level profile and a query-specific report

Then you're ready for "Query Analysis" on page 11.

This is not a book about database administration, so this section does not discuss the setup and configuration of query metrics in MySQL. I presume this is already done or will be done. If not, don't worry: ask your DBA, hire a consultant, or learn how by reading the MySQL manual.

Sources

Query metrics originate from the slow query log (*https://oreil.ly/Glss3*) or the Performance Schema (*https://oreil.ly/FNXRq*). As the names indicate, the former is a log file on disk, and the latter is a database with the same name: performance_schema. Although completely different in nature (log file on disk as opposed to tables in a database), both provide query metrics. The important difference is how many metrics they provide: apart from query response time, which both provide, the number of metrics ranges from 3 to more than 20.

The name *slow query log* is historical. Long ago, MySQL logged only queries that took greater than N *seconds* to execute, and the minimum value for N was 1. Old versions of MySQL would not log a query that took 900 milliseconds to execute because that was "fast." The slow query log really earned its name. Today, the minimum value is zero with a resolution of microseconds. When set to zero, MySQL logs every query executed. Therefore, the name is a little misleading, but now you know why.

All things considered, the Performance Schema is the best source of query metrics because it exists in every current version and distribution of MySQL, it works locally and in the cloud, it provides all nine metrics covered in "Query Metrics" on page 11, and it's the most consistent. Plus, the Performance Schema contains a wealth of other data for deep MySQL analysis, so its usefulness extends far beyond query metrics. The slow query log is a good source, too, but it varies considerably:

MySQL

As of MySQL 8.0.14, enable system variable `log_slow_extra` (*https://oreil.ly/ibfRK*) and the slow query log provides six of the nine metrics in "Query Metrics" on page 11, lacking only `Rows_affected`, `Select_scan`, and `Select_full_join`. It's still a good source, but use the Performance Schema if possible.

Before MySQL 8.0.14, which includes MySQL 5.7, the slow query log is bare bones, providing only `Query_time`, `Lock_time`, `Rows_sent`, and `Rows_examined`. You can still analyze queries with only these four metrics, but the analysis is much less insightful. Consequently, avoid the slow query log before MySQL 8.0.14 and instead use the Performance Schema.

Percona Server

Percona Server (*https://oreil.ly/ILyh2*) provides a significantly greater number of metrics in the slow query log when system variable `log_slow_verbosity` is configured: all nine metrics covered in "Query Metrics" on page 11 and more. It also supports query sampling (logging a percentage of queries) when system variable `log_slow_rate_limit` is configured, which is helpful for busy servers. These features make the Percona Server slow query log a great source. See "Slow Query Log" (*https://oreil.ly/5JQ06*) in the Percona Server manual for details.

MariaDB Server

MariaDB Server (*https://oreil.ly/oeGJO*) 10.x uses the Percona Server slow query log enhancements, but there are two notable differences: system variable `log_slow_verbosity` is configured differently in MariaDB, and it does not provide metric `Rows_affected`. Otherwise, it's essentially the same and a great source, too. See "Slow Query Log Extended Statistics" (*https://oreil.ly/oOVe7*) in the MariaDB knowledge base for details.

The slow query log is disabled by default, but you can enable it dynamically (without restarting MySQL). The Performance Schema should be enabled by default, though some cloud providers disable it by default. Unlike the slow query log, the Performance Schema cannot be enabled dynamically—you must restart MySQL to enable it.

Make sure the best query metric source is used and properly configured. Ask your DBA, hire a consultant, or learn how by reading the MySQL manual.

 The slow query log can log *all* queries when `long_query_time` (*https://oreil.ly/NUmuA*) is set to zero, but be careful: on a busy server, this can increase disk I/O and use a significant amount of disk space.

Aggregation

Query metrics are grouped and aggregated by query. That sounds obvious since they're called *query* metrics, but some query metric tools can group by username, hostname, database, and so on. These alternate groupings are exceptionally rare and yield a different type of query analysis, so I don't address them in this book. Since query response time is the North Star of MySQL performance, grouping query metrics by query is the best way to see which queries have the slowest response time, which forms the basis of query reporting and analysis.

There's one little problem: how do you uniquely identify queries to determine the groups to which they belong? For example, system metrics (CPU, memory, storage, and so on) are grouped by hostname because hostnames are unique and meaningful. But queries don't have any uniquely identifying properties like hostname. The solution: a SHA-256 hash of the normalized SQL statement. Example 1-1 shows how a SQL statement is normalized.

Example 1-1. SQL statement normalization

```
SELECT col FROM tbl WHERE id=1 ❶
```

```
SELECT `col` FROM `tbl` WHERE `id` = ? ❷
```

```
f49d50dfab1c364e622d1e1ff54bb12df436be5d44c464a4e25a1ebb80fc2f13 ❸
```

❶ SQL statement (sample)

❷ Digest text (normalized SQL statement)

❸ Digest hash (SHA-256 of digest text)

MySQL normalizes SQL statements to digest texts, then computes the SHA-256 hash of the digest text to yield the digest hash. (It's not necessary to understand the full process of normalization; it's sufficient to know that normalization replaces all values with ? and collapses multiple whitespaces to a single space.) Since the digest text is unique, the digest hash is also unique (hash collisions notwithstanding).

> The MySQL manual uses the term *digest* equivocally to mean either *digest text* or *digest hash*. Since the digest hash is computed from the digest text, the equivocation is only a language ambiguity, not a technical error. Please allow me to equivocate, too, and use *digest* to mean either *digest text* or *digest hash* when the technical difference doesn't matter.

There is an important shift in terminology in the context of query metrics: the term *query* changes to be synonymous with *digest text*. The shift in terminology aligns with the shift in focus: grouping metrics by query. To group by query, *query* must be unique, which is only true of digests.

SQL statements are also called *query samples* (or *samples* for short), and they may or may not be reported. For security, most query metric tools discard samples by default (because they contain real values) and report only digest texts and hashes. Samples are required for query analysis because you can EXPLAIN (*https://oreil.ly/YSnio*) them, which produces metadata necessary for understanding query execution. Some query metric tools EXPLAIN a sample, then discard it, and report the EXPLAIN plan (the output of EXPLAIN). Others only report the sample, which is still very convenient: copy-paste to EXPLAIN. If you have neither, then manually extract samples from the source or manually write them when needed.

Two more clarifications about terminology and then I promise we'll move on to more exciting material. First, terminology varies widely depending on the query metric tool, as shown in Table 1-1.

Table 1-1. Query metric terminology

Official (MySQL)	Alternatives
SQL statement	Query
Sample	Query
Digest text	Class, family, fingerprint, query
Digest hash	Class ID, query ID, signature

Second, another term that originated from Percona (*https://www.percona.com*) is *query abstract*: a SQL statement highly abstracted to its SQL command and table list. Example 1-2 is the query abstract for SELECT col FROM tbl WHERE id=1.

Example 1-2. Query abstract

```
SELECT tbl
```

Query abstracts are not unique, but they are useful because they're succinct. Usually, developers only need to see a query abstract to know the full query that it represents.

> Brevity is the soul of wit.
>
> —William Shakespeare

It's important to understand that SQL statements are normalized because the queries you write are not the queries you see. Most of the time, this is not a problem because digest texts closely resemble SQL statements. But the process of normalization raises another important point: do not dynamically generate the same logical query with different syntax, else it will normalize to different digests and be reported as different queries. For example, in the case of a programmatically-generated query that changes the WHERE clause based on user input:

```
SELECT name FROM captains WHERE last_name = 'Picard'
SELECT name FROM captains WHERE last_name = 'Picard' AND first_name = 'Jean-Luc'
```

Those two queries may be logically the same to you and the application, but they're different queries with respect to reporting because they normalize to different digests. To my knowledge, no query metric tool allows you to combine queries. And it's technically correct to report those queries separately because every condition—especially in the WHERE clause—affects query execution and optimization.

One point about query normalization: values are removed, so the following two queries normalize to the same digest:

```
-- SQL statements
SELECT `name` FROM star_ships WHERE class IN ('galaxy')
SELECT `name` FROM star_ships WHERE class IN ('galaxy', 'intrepid')

-- Digest text
SELECT `name` FROM `star_ships` WHERE `class` IN (...)
```

Since the digest is the same for both queries, the metrics for both queries are grouped, aggregated, and reported as one query.

Enough about terminology and normalization. Let's talk about reporting.

Reporting

Reporting is a challenge and an art form because a single application can have hundreds of queries. Each query has many metrics and each metric has several statistics: minimum, maximum, average, percentile, and so forth. On top of that, each query has metadata: samples, EXPLAIN plans, table structures, on so on. It's challenging to store, process, and present all this data. Almost every query metric tool presents the data in a two-level hierarchy: *query profile* and *query report*. Those terms vary by query metric tool, but you will easily recognize each when you see them.

Query profile

A *query profile* shows slow queries. It is the top-level organization for query reporting, usually the first thing you see in a query metric tool. It presents query digests and a limited subset of query metrics, which is why it's called a profile.

Slow is relative to the *sort metric*: the aggregate value of a query metric by which queries are ordered. The first ordered query is called *the slowest*, even if the sort metric is not query time (or any time). For example, if the sort metric is average rows sent, the first ordered query is still called the slowest.

Although any query metric can be the sort metric, query time is the universal default sort metric. When you reduce query execution time, you free up time that allows MySQL to do more work, or possibly do other work more quickly. Sorting queries by query time shows you where to begin: the slowest, most time-consuming queries.

What's not universal is how query time is aggregated. The most common aggregate values are:

Total query time
> *Total query time* is the sum of execution time (per query). This is the most common aggregate value because it answers an important question: *which query does MySQL spend the most time executing?* To answer that, a query metric tool adds up all the time MySQL spends executing each query. The query with the greatest total time is the slowest, most time-consuming query. Here's an example of why this is important. Suppose query *A* has a 1-second response time and executes 10 times, while query *B* has a 0.1-second response time and executes 1,000 times. Query *A* has a much slower response time, but query *B* is 10 times more time-consuming: 10 seconds in total versus 100 seconds in total, respectively. In a query profile sorted by total query time, query *B* is the slowest query. This is important because you free up the most time for MySQL by optimizing query *B*.

Percentage execution time
> *Percentage execution time* is total query time (per query) divided by grand total execution time (all queries). For example, if query *C* has a total query time of 321 ms and query *D* has a total query time of 100 ms, then grand total execution time is 421 ms. Individually, query *C* is (321 ms / 421 ms) × 100 = 76.2% of grand total execution time, and query *D* is (100 ms / 421 ms) × 100 = 23.8% of grand total execution time. In other words, MySQL spent 421 ms executing queries, 76.2% of which was spent executing query *C*. In a query profile sorted by percentage execution time, query *C* is the slowest query. Percentage execution time is used by some query metric tools, but not all.

Query load

> *Query load* is total query time (per query) divided by clock time, where *clock time* is the number of seconds in the time range. If the time range is 5 minutes, then clock time is 300 seconds. For example, if query *E* has a total query time 250.2 seconds, then its load is 250.2 s / 300 s = 0.83; and if query *F* has a total query time of 500.1 seconds, then its load is 500.1 s / 300 s = 1.67. In a query profile sorted by query load, query *F* is the slowest query because its load is the greatest.

> Load is relative to time but also subtly indicative of *concurrency*: multiple instances of a query executing at the same time. Query load less than 1.0 means that, on average, the query does not execute concurrently. Query load greater than 1.0 indicates query concurrency. For example, a query load of 3.5 means that, any time you look, you're likely to see 3.5 instances of the query executing. (In reality, 3 or 4 instances of the query since there cannot be 0.5 instances of a query.) The higher the query load, the greater the possibility of contention if the query accesses the same or nearby rows. Query load greater than 10 is high and likely to be a slow query, but there are exceptions. As I write this, I'm looking at a query with a load of 5,962. How is that possible? I reveal the answer in "Data Access" on page 97.

When the sort metric uses a nontemporal query metric, like rows sent, a different aggregate value (average, maximum, and so on) might make sense depending on what you're trying to diagnose. This is far less common than total query time, but it occasionally reveals interesting queries worth optimizing.

Query report

A *query report* shows you everything there is to know about one query. It is the second-level organization for query reporting, usually accessed by selecting a slow query in the query profile. It presents all query metrics and metadata. Whereas the query profile tells you something just by looking at it (which queries are the slowest), a query report is an organized information dump used for query analysis. As such, the more information, the better because it helps you understand query execution.

Query reports vary dramatically depending on the query metric tool. A bare minimum report includes all query metrics from the source and the basic statistics for those metrics: minimum, maximum, average, percentile, and so forth. A thorough report includes metadata: query samples, EXPLAIN plans, table structures, and more. (Samples may be disabled for security purposes because they contain real values.) A few query metric tools go further by adding additional information: metric graphs, histograms (distributions), anomaly detection, time shift comparison (now versus last week), developer notes, SQL comment key-value extraction, and so on.

Query analysis only requires query metrics in the report. Metadata can be collected manually. If the query metric tool you use reports only query metrics, don't worry:

that's a start, but you will need to manually collect EXPLAIN plans and table structures, at the very least.

With a query report figuratively in hand, you're equipped for query analysis.

Query Analysis

The goal of query analysis is understanding query execution, not solving slow response time. That might surprise you, but solving slow response time happens *after* query analysis, during query optimization. First, you need to understand what you're trying to change: query execution.

Query execution is like a story with a beginning, middle, and end: you read all three to understand the story. Once you understand how MySQL executes a query, then you will understand how to optimize it. Understanding through analysis, then action through optimization.

 I have helped many engineers analyze queries, and the primary difficulty is not understanding the metrics but getting stuck in the analysis: staring deeply into the numbers, waiting for a revelation. Don't get stuck. Carefully review all the metrics and metadata—read the whole story—then turn your attention to query optimization with the goal of improving response time.

The following sections address key aspects to an efficient and insightful query analysis. Sometimes the cause of slow response time is so obvious that the analysis reads more like a tweet than a story. But when it's not—when the analysis reads like a graduate thesis on French existentialism—understanding these aspects will help you find the cause and determine a solution.

Query Metrics

From "Sources" on page 4, you know that query metrics vary depending on the source, MySQL distribution, and MySQL version. All query metrics are important because they help you understand query execution, but the nine metrics detailed in the following sections are essential to every query analysis.

The Performance Schema provides all nine essential query metrics.

 Query metric names also vary by source. In the slow query log, query time is `Query_time`; but in the Performance Schema, it's `TIMER_WAIT`. I don't use either convention. Instead, I use human-friendly names like *query time* and *rows sent*. Query reporting almost always uses human-friendly names, too.

Query time

Query time is the most important metric—you knew that already. What you may not know is that query time includes another metric: lock time.

Lock time is an inherent part of query time, so it's not surprising that the latter includes the former. What's surprising is that query time and lock time are the only two time-based query metrics, with one exception: the Percona Server slow query log has metrics for InnoDB read time, row lock wait time, and queue wait time. Lock time is important, but there's an unfortunate technical gotcha: it's accurate only in the slow query log. More on this later.

Using the Performance Schema, you can see many (but not all) parts of query execution. This is off-topic and beyond the scope of this book, but it's good awareness so you know where to look if you need to dig deeper. MySQL instruments a bewildering number of *events* that the manual defines as, "anything the server does that takes time and has been instrumented so that timing information can be collected." Events are organized in a hierarchy:

```
transactions
└─ statements
   └─ stages
      └─ waits
```

Transactions
> Transactions are the top-level event because every query executes in a transaction (Chapter 8 covers transactions).

Statements
> Statements are queries, to which query metrics apply.

Stages
> Stages are "steps during the statement-execution process, such as parsing a statement, opening a table, or performing a filesort operation."

Waits
> Waits are "events that take time." (This definition amuses me. It's tautological and oddly satisfying in its simplicity.)

Example 1-3 shows the stages for a single UPDATE statement (as of MySQL 8.0.22).

Example 1-3. Stages for a single UPDATE statement

```
+-------------------------------+-------------------------------+-----------+
| stage                         | source:line                   | time (ms) |
+-------------------------------+-------------------------------+-----------+
| stage/sql/starting            | init_net_server_extension.cc:101 |  0.109 |
| stage/sql/Executing hook on trx | rpl_handler.cc:1120         |    0.001 |
| stage/sql/starting            | rpl_handler.cc:1122           |    0.008 |
| stage/sql/checking permissions | sql_authorization.cc:2200    |    0.004 |
| stage/sql/Opening tables      | sql_base.cc:5745              |    0.102 |
| stage/sql/init                | sql_select.cc:703             |    0.007 |
| stage/sql/System lock         | lock.cc:332                   |    0.072 |
| stage/sql/updating            | sql_update.cc:781             | 10722.618 |
| stage/sql/end                 | sql_select.cc:736             |    0.003 |
| stage/sql/query end           | sql_parse.cc:4474             |    0.002 |
| stage/sql/waiting handler commit | handler.cc:1591            |    0.034 |
| stage/sql/closing tables      | sql_parse.cc:4525             |    0.015 |
| stage/sql/freeing items       | sql_parse.cc:5007             |    0.061 |
| stage/sql/logging slow query  | log.cc:1640                   |    0.094 |
| stage/sql/cleaning up         | sql_parse.cc:2192             |    0.002 |
+-------------------------------+-------------------------------+-----------+
```

The real output is more complex; I simplified it for easy reading. The UPDATE state-ment executed in 15 stages. The actual execution of the UPDATE was the eighth stage: stage/sql/updating. There were 42 waits, but I removed them from the output because they're too far off topic.

Performance Schema events (transactions, statements, stages, and waits) are the fine details of query execution. Query metrics apply to statements. If you need to dig deeper in a query, look in the Performance Schema.

Efficiency is our modus operandi, so don't get lost in the Performance Schema until you need to, which may be never. Query time is sufficient.

Lock time

Lock time is time spent acquiring locks during query execution. Ideally, lock time is a minuscule percentage of query time, but values are relative (see "Relative Values" on page 24). For example, on one extremely optimized database that I manage, lock time is 40% to 50% of query time for the slowest query. Sounds terrible, right? But it's not: the slowest query has a maximum query time of 160 microseconds and a maximum lock time of 80 microseconds—and the database executes over 20,000 queries per second (QPS).

Although values are relative, I can safely say that lock time greater than 50% of query time is a problem because MySQL should spend the vast majority of its time doing work, not waiting. A theoretically perfect query execution would have zero wait time, but that's impossible due to shared resources, concurrency, and latency inherent in the system. Still, we can dream.

MySQL Storage Engines and Data Locking

Before I explain more about lock time and locks in general, let me clarify some background information.

MySQL has many storage engines—and a history of storage engines, but I won't bore you with that. The default storage engine is InnoDB. Other storage engines include: MyISAM, MEMORY, TempTable (*https://oreil.ly/Ubz65*), Aria (*https://oreil.ly/VVAjG*) with MariaDB, MyRocks (*https://myrocks.io*) with Percona Server and MariaDB, XtraDB (*https://oreil.ly/jrGlq*) with Percona Server, and more. (Fun fact: the Performance Schema is implemented as a storage engine.) In this book, InnoDB is implied unless stated otherwise.

There are table locks and row locks. The server (MySQL) manages tables and table locks. Tables are created using a storage engine (InnoDB by default) but are storage engine agnostic, meaning you can convert a table from one storage engine to another. Row-level locking is managed by the storage engine if supported. MyISAM does not support row-level locking, so it manages data access with table locks. InnoDB supports row-level locking, so it manages data access with row locks. Since InnoDB is the default storage engine, row-level locking is implied unless stated otherwise.

> InnoDB also has table locks called *intention locks* (*https://oreil.ly/XYLnq*), but they're not important for this discussion.

There are metadata locks managed by the server that control access to schemas, tables, stored programs, and more. Whereas table locks and row locks control access to table data, metadata locks control access to table structures (columns, indexes, and so on) to prevent changes while queries are accessing the tables. Every query acquires a metadata lock on every table that it accesses. Metadata locks are released at the end of the transaction, not the query.

> Remember: InnoDB and row-level locking are implied unless stated otherwise.

Remember the unfortunate technical gotcha mentioned earlier? Here it is: lock time from the Performance Schema does *not* include row lock waits, only table and metadata lock waits. Row lock waits are the most important part of lock time, which makes lock time from the Performance Schema nearly useless. By contrast, lock time from the slow query log includes all lock waits: metadata, table, and row. Lock time from either source does not indicate which type of lock wait. From the Performance Schema, it's certainly metadata lock wait; and from the slow query log, it's probably row lock wait, but metadata lock wait is a possibility, too.

Lock time from the Performance Schema does not include row lock waits.

Locks are primarily used for writes (INSERT, UPDATE, DELETE, REPLACE) because rows must be locked before they can be written. Response time for writes depends, in part, on lock time. The amount of time needed to acquire row locks depends on concurrency: how many queries are accessing the same (or nearby) rows at the same time. If a row has zero concurrency (accessed by only one query at a time), then lock time is vanishingly small. But if a row is *hot*—jargon for *very frequently accessed*—then lock time could account for a significant percentage of response time. Concurrency is one of several data access patterns (see "Data Access Patterns" in Chapter 4).

For reads (SELECT), there are nonlocking and locking reads (*https://oreil.ly/WcyD3*). The distinction is easy because there are only two locking reads: SELECT...FOR UPDATE and SELECT...FOR SHARE. If not one of those two, then SELECT is nonlocking, which is the normal case.

Although SELECT...FOR UPDATE and SELECT...FOR SHARE are the only locking reads, don't forget about writes with an optional SELECT. In the following SQL statements, the SELECT acquires shared row locks on table s:

- INSERT...SELECT FROM s
- REPLACE...SELECT FROM s
- UPDATE...WHERE...(SELECT FROM s)
- CREATE TABLE...SELECT FROM s

Strictly speaking, those SQL statements are writes, not reads, but the optional SELECT acquires shared row locks on table s. See "Locks Set by Different SQL Statements in InnoDB" (*https://oreil.ly/SJXcq*) in the MySQL manual for details.

Locking reads should be avoided, especially SELECT...FOR UPDATE, because they don't scale, they tend to cause problems, and there is usually a nonlocking solution to achieve the same result. With respect to lock time, a locking read is like a write: it depends on concurrency. Be careful with SELECT...FOR SHARE: shared locks are compatible with other shared locks, but they're incompatible with exclusive locks, which means shared locks block writes on the same (or nearby) rows.

For nonlocking reads, even though row locks are not acquired, lock time will not be zero because metadata and table locks are acquired. But acquiring these two should be very fast: less than 1 millisecond. For example, another database I manage executes over 34,000 QPS but the slowest query is a nonlocking SELECT that does a full table scan, reading six million rows every execution, with very high concurrency: 168 query load. Despite these large values, its maximum lock time is 220 microseconds, and average lock time is 80 microseconds.

Nonlocking read does *not* mean non-blocking. SELECT queries must acquire shared metadata locks (MDL) on all tables accessed. As usual with locks, shared MDL are compatible with other shared MDL, but one exclusive MDL blocks all other MDL. ALTER TABLE is the common operation that acquires an exclusive MDL. Even using ALTER TABLE...ALGORITHM=INPLACE, LOCK=NONE or third-party online schema change tools like pt-online-schema-change (*https://oreil.ly/EzcrU*) and gh-ost (*https://oreil.ly/TeHjG*), an exclusive MDL must be acquired at the end to swap the old table structure for the new one. Although the table swap is very quick, it can cause a noticeable disruption when MySQL is heavily loaded because *all* table access is blocked while the exclusive MDL is held. This problem shows up as a blip in lock time, especially for SELECT statements.

SELECT can block waiting for metadata locks.

Locking might be the most complex and nuanced aspect of MySQL. To avoid going down the proverbial rabbit hole, let me state five points but defer explanation for now. Merely being aware of these points greatly increases your MySQL prowess:

- Lock time can be significantly greater than innodb_lock_wait_timeout (*https://oreil.ly/HlWwX*) because this system variable applies to *each row lock*.
- Locking and transaction isolation levels are related.
- InnoDB locks every row it accesses *including rows it does not write*.

- Locks are released on transaction commit or rollback, and sometimes during query execution.
- InnoDB has different types of locks: record, gap, next-key, and more.

"Row Locking" on page 260 goes into detail. For now, let's put it all together and visualize how query time includes lock time. Figure 1-1 shows locks acquired and released during query execution.

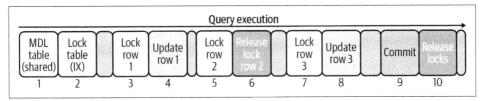

Figure 1-1. Lock time during query execution

Labels 1 to 10 mark events and details with respect to locking:

1. Acquire shared metadata lock on table
2. Acquire intention exclusive (IX) table lock
3. Acquire row lock 1
4. Update (write) row 1
5. Acquire row lock 2
6. Release row lock 2
7. Acquire row lock 3
8. Update (write) row 3
9. Commit transaction
10. Release all locks

Two points of interest:

- Lock time from the Performance Schema includes only labels 1 and 2. From the slow query log it includes labels 1, 2, 3, 5, and 7.
- Although row 2 is locked (label 5), it's not written and its lock is released (label 6) before the transaction commits (label 9). This can happen, but not always. It depends on the query and transaction isolation level.

That was a lot of information about lock time and locking, but now you are well-equipped to understand lock time in your query analysis.

Rows examined

Rows examined is the number of rows that MySQL accessed to find matching rows. It indicates the selectivity of the query and the indexes. The more selective both are, the less time MySQL wastes examining non-matching rows. This applies to reads and writes, except INSERT unless it's an INSERT...SELECT statement.

To understand rows examined, let's look at two examples. First, let's use the following table, t1, and three rows:

```
CREATE TABLE `t1` (
  `id` int NOT NULL,
  `c` char(1) NOT NULL,
  PRIMARY KEY (`id`)
) ENGINE=InnoDB;
```

```
+----+---+
| id | c |
+----+---+
|  1 | a |
|  2 | b |
|  3 | c |
+----+---+
```

Column id is the primary key, and column c is not indexed.

The query SELECT c FROM t1 WHERE c = 'b' matches one row but examines three rows because there is no unique index on column c. Therefore, MySQL has no idea how many rows match the WHERE clause. We can see that only one row matches, but MySQL doesn't have eyes, it has indexes. By contrast, the query SELECT c FROM t1 WHERE id = 2 matches and examines only one row because there is a unique index on column id (the primary key) and the table condition uses the entire index. Now MySQL can figuratively see that only one row matches, so that's all it examines. Chapter 2 teaches indexes and indexing, which explain table conditions and a lot more.

For the second example, let's use the following table, t2, and seven rows:

```
CREATE TABLE `t2` (
  `id` int NOT NULL,
  `c` char(1) NOT NULL,
  `d` varchar(8) DEFAULT NULL,
  PRIMARY KEY (`id`),
  KEY `c` (`c`)
) ENGINE=InnoDB;
```

```
+----+------+--------+
| id | c    | d      |
+----+------+--------+
|  1 | a    | apple  |
|  2 | a    | ant    |
|  3 | a    | acorn  |
|  4 | a    | apron  |
|  5 | b    | banana |
|  6 | b    | bike   |
|  7 | c    | car    |
+----+------+--------+
```

Column id is the same as before (primary key). Column c has a *nonunique* index. Column d is not indexed.

How many rows will query SELECT d FROM t2 WHERE c = 'a' AND d = 'acorn' examine? The answer is: four. MySQL uses the nonunique index on column c to look up rows matching the condition c = 'a', and that matches four rows. And to match the other condition, d = 'acorn', MySQL examines each of those four rows. As a result, the query examines four rows but matches (and returns) only one row.

It's not uncommon to discover that a query examines more rows than expected. The cause is usually the selectivity of the query or the indexes (or both), but sometimes it's because the table has grown a lot larger than expected, so there are a lot more rows to examine. Chapter 3 examines this further (pun intended).

Rows examined only tells half the story. The other half is rows sent.

Rows sent

Rows sent is the number of rows returned to the client—the result set size. Rows sent is most meaningful in relation to rows examined.

Rows sent = Rows examined
> The ideal case is when rows sent and rows examined are equal and the value is relatively small, especially as a percentage of total rows, and query response time is acceptable. For example, 1,000 rows from a table with one million rows is a reasonable 0.1%. This is ideal if response time is acceptable. But 1,000 rows from a table with only 10,000 rows is a questionable 10% even if response time is acceptable. Regardless of the percentage, if rows sent and rows examined are equal and the value is suspiciously high, it strongly indicates that the query is causing a table scan, which is usually terrible for performance—"Table scan" on page 48 explains why.

Rows sent < Rows examined
> Fewer rows sent than examined is a reliable sign of poor query or index selectivity. If the difference is extreme, it likely explains slow response time. For example, 1,000 rows sent and 100,000 rows examined aren't large values, but they mean

99% of rows did not match—the query caused MySQL to waste a lot of time. Even if response time is acceptable, an index could dramatically reduce the wasted time.

Rows sent > Rows examined

It's possible, but rare, to send more rows than were examined. This happens under special conditions, like when MySQL can "optimize away" the query. For example, `SELECT COUNT(id) FROM t2` on the table in the previous section sends one row for the value of `COUNT(id)` but examines zero rows.

Rows sent is rarely a problem by itself. Modern networks are fast and the MySQL protocol is efficient. If your distribution and version of MySQL have the *bytes sent* metric in the slow query log (the Performance Schema does not provide this query metric), you can use it two ways. First, the minimum, maximum, and average values reveal the result set size in bytes. This is usually small, but it can be large if the query returns `BLOB` or `JSON` columns. Second, total bytes sent can be converted to a network throughput (Mbps or Gbps) to reveal the network utilization of the query, which is also usually very small.

Rows affected

Rows affected is the number of rows inserted, updated, or deleted. Engineers are very careful to affect only the correct rows. It's a serious bug when the wrong rows are changed. Viewed this way, the value of rows affected is always correct. But a surprisingly large value could indicate a new or modified query that affects more rows than intended.

Another way to view rows affected is as the batch size of bulk operations. Bulk `INSERT`, `UPDATE`, and `DELETE` are a common source of several problems: replication lag, history list length, lock time, and overall performance degradation. Equally common is the question, "How large should the batch size be?" There's no universally correct answer. Instead, you must determine the batch size *and* rate that MySQL and the application can sustain without impacting query response time. I explain in "Batch Size" on page 115, which focuses on `DELETE` but is also applicable to `INSERT` and `UPDATE`.

Select scan

Select scan is the number of full table scans on the first table accessed. (If the query accesses two or more tables, the next metric applies: select full join.) This is usually bad for performance because it means the query isn't using an index. After Chapter 2, which teaches indexes and indexing, it should be easy to add an index to fix a table scan. If select scan is not zero, query optimization is strongly advised.

It's possible, but *very* rare, that a query causes a table scan sometimes but not always. To determine why, you need a query sample and EXPLAIN plan for both: a query sample that causes a table scan, and a query sample that does not. One likely reason is how many rows MySQL estimates the query will examine relative to index cardinality (the number of unique values in the index), total rows in the table, and other costs. (The MySQL query optimizer uses a cost model.) Estimates aren't perfect and sometimes MySQL is wrong, resulting in a table scan or suboptimal execution plan, but again: this is *very* rare.

More than likely, select scan is either all zero or all one (it's a binary value). Be happy if it's zero. Optimize the query if it's not zero.

Select full join

Select full join is the number of full table scans on tables joined. This is similar to select scan but worse—I explain why in a moment. Select full join should always be zero; if not, query optimization is practically required.

When you EXPLAIN a query with multiple tables (*https://oreil.ly/sRswS*), MySQL prints the table join order from top (first table) to bottom (last table). Select scan applies only to the first table. Select full join applies only to the second and subsequent tables.

Table join order is determined by MySQL, not the query.[2] Example 1-4 shows the EXPLAIN plan for SELECT...FROM t1, t2, t3: MySQL determines a different join order than the implicit three-table join in the query.

Example 1-4. EXPLAIN plan for three tables joined

```
*************************** 1. row ***************************
           id: 1
  select_type: SIMPLE
        table: t3
   partitions: NULL
         type: ALL
possible_keys: NULL
          key: NULL
      key_len: NULL
          ref: NULL
         rows: 3
     filtered: 100.00
        Extra: NULL
*************************** 2. row ***************************
           id: 1
```

---

2 Unless STRAIGHT_JOIN is used—but don't use this. Let the MySQL query optimizer choose the join order for the best query execution plan. It's almost always right, so trust it unless you can prove it wrong.

```
   select_type: SIMPLE
         table: t1
    partitions: NULL
          type: range
 possible_keys: PRIMARY
           key: PRIMARY
       key_len: 4
           ref: NULL
          rows: 2
      filtered: 100.00
         Extra: Using where
*************************** 3. row ***************************
            id: 1
   select_type: SIMPLE
         table: t2
    partitions: NULL
          type: ALL
 possible_keys: NULL
           key: NULL
       key_len: NULL
           ref: NULL
          rows: 7
      filtered: 100.00
         Extra: NULL
```

MySQL reads table t3 first, then joins table t1, then joins table t2. That join order is different than the query (FROM t1, t2, t3), which is why you must EXPLAIN a query to see its join order.

 Always EXPLAIN a query to see its join order.

Select scan applies to table t3 because it's the first table in the join order and it causes a table scan (indicated by type: ALL). Select full join would apply to table t1 if it caused a table scan, but it doesn't: MySQL joins the table using a range scan on the primary key (indicated by type: range and key: PRIMARY, respectively). Select full join applies to table t2 because MySQL joins it using a full table scan (indicated by type: ALL).

The table scan on t2 is called a *full join* because MySQL scans the full table on join. Select full join is worse than select scan because the number of full joins that occur on a table during query execution is equal to the product of rows from the preceding tables. MySQL estimates three rows from table t3 (indicated by rows: 3) and two rows from table t1 (indicated by rows: 2). Therefore, 3 × 2 = 6 full joins on table t2 during query execution. But the select full join metric value will be 1 because it counts full joins in the execution plan, not during query execution, which is sufficient because even one full join is too many.

 As of MySQL 8.0.18, the hash join optimization (*https://oreil.ly/zf7Rs*) improves performance for certain joins, but avoiding full joins remains the best practice. See "Table Join Algorithms" on page 87 for a brief overview of hash join.

Created tmp disk tables

Created tmp disk tables is the number of temporary tables created on disk. It's normal for queries to create temporary tables in memory; but when an in-memory temporary table becomes too large, MySQL writes it to disk. That can affect response time because disk access is orders of magnitude slower than memory access.

However, temporary tables on disk is not a common problem because MySQL tries to avoid them. Excessive "tmp disk tables" indicates a query that can be optimized, or (perhaps) the system variable `tmp_table_size` (*https://oreil.ly/8exZw*) is too small. Always optimize queries first. Change system variables as a last resort—especially ones that affect memory allocation.

See "Internal Temporary Table Use in MySQL" (*https://oreil.ly/CeCSv*) in the MySQL manual for more information.

Query count

Query count is the number of query executions. The value is arbitrary unless extremely low and the query is slow. "Low and slow" is an odd combination worth investigating.

As I write this, I'm looking at a query profile that's a perfect example: the slowest query executed *once* but took 44% of execution time. Other metrics are:

- Response time: 16 s
- Lock time: 110 µs
- Rows examined: 132,000
- Rows sent: 13

Not your everyday query. It looks like an engineer manually executed the query, but I can tell from the digest text that it was programmatically generated. What's the story behind this query? To find out, I'll have to ask the application developers.

Metadata and the Application

There's more to query analysis than query metrics: metadata. In fact, you can't complete a query analysis without at least two pieces of metadata: the EXPLAIN plan (also called the *query execution plan*), and the table structure for each table. A few query metric tools automatically collect metadata and show it in the query report. If your query metric tool does not, don't worry: it's easy to collect metadata. EXPLAIN (*https://oreil.ly/AZvGt*) and SHOW CREATE TABLE (*https://oreil.ly/Wwp8f*) report the EXPLAIN plan and table structures, respectively.

Metadata is indispensable for query analysis, query optimization, and MySQL performance in general. EXPLAIN is a vital tool in your MySQL repertoire. I explain it in "EXPLAIN: Query Execution Plan" on page 51 and use it extensively throughout this book.

There's even more to query analysis than query metrics and metadata: the application. Metrics and metadata are must-have for any query analysis, but the story is only complete when you know what purpose the query serves: *why* does the application execute the query? Knowing this allows you to evaluate changes to the application, which is the focus of Chapter 4. More than once, I've seen engineers realize that a query can be a lot simpler—or completely removed.

Query metrics, metadata, and the application should complete the story. But I'd be remiss not to mention that, sometimes, issues outside MySQL and the application influence the story—and usually not for the better. "Noisy Neighbors" on page 301 is a classic case. If response time is slow but a thorough query analysis doesn't reveal why, then consider outside issues. But don't be too quick to jump to this conclusion; outside issues should be the exception, never the norm.

Relative Values

For each query metric, the only objectively good value is zero because, as the saying goes, the fastest way to do something is to not do it. Nonzero values are always relative to the query and application. For example, one thousand rows sent is fine in general, but it could be terrible if the query is supposed to return only one row. Relative values are meaningful when considering the full story: metrics, metadata, and the application.

Here's another true story to illustrate that values are relative and meaningful with the full story. I inherited an application that became slower and slower over the years. It was an internal application—not used by customers—so fixing it wasn't a priority until it became unbearably slow. In the query profile, the slowest query was examining and returning over ten thousand rows—not a full table scan, just a lot of rows. Instead of fixating on the values, I went spelunking in the source code and discovered that the function executing the query was only counting the number of rows, not using the rows. It was slow because it needlessly accessed and returned thousands of rows, and it became slower over time because the number of rows increased as the database grew. With the full story, the optimization was glaringly obvious and simple: `SELECT COUNT(*)`.

Average, Percentile, and Maximum

It's standard to talk about query response time as if it's a single value, but it's not. From "Aggregation" on page 6 you know that query metrics are grouped and aggregated by query. As a result, query metrics are reported as single, statistical values: minimum, maximum, average, and percentile. You are undoubtedly familiar with these ubiquitous "stats," but with respect to query response time, the following points may surprise you:

- Average is overly optimistic
- Percentile is an assumption
- Maximum is the best representation

Let me explain:

Average
Don't be fooled by the average: if query count is small, a few very large or small values can skew the average response time (or any metric). Moreover, without knowing the distribution of values, we cannot know what percentage of values the average represents. For example, if the average equals the median, then the average represents the bottom 50% of values, which are the better (faster) response times. In that case, the average is overly optimistic. (Most values are overly optimistic if you ignore the worst half.) The average only tells you, at a glance, if the query typically executes in a matter of microseconds, milliseconds, or seconds. Don't read more into it than that.

Percentile
Percentiles solve the problem of averages. Without going into a full explanation of percentiles, P95 is the value that 95% of samples are less than or equal to.[3] For example, if P95 equals 100 ms, then 95% of values are less than or equal to 100 ms, and 5% of values are greater than 100 ms. Consequently, P95 represents 95% of values, which is objectively more representative—and less optimistic—than the average. There's another reason percentiles are used: the small percentage of values ignored are considered outliers. For example, network jitter and flukes can cause a small percentage of query executions to take longer than normal. Since that's no fault of MySQL, we ignore those execution times as outliers.

---

3 For a full explanation of percentiles, see HackMySQL (*https://hackmysql.com/p95*).

Percentiles are standard practice, but they're also an assumption. Yes, there can be outliers, but they should be *proven*, not assumed. Until the top N% are proven *not* to be outliers, they are the most interesting values precisely because they're not normal. *What's causing them?* That's difficult to answer, which is why percentiles are standard practice: it's easier to ignore the top N% of values than to dig deep and find the answer.

The best percentile is P999 (99.9%) because discarding 0.1% of values is an acceptable tradeoff between assuming that they're outliers and the reality that outliers do exist.[4]

Maximum

Maximum query time solves the problem of percentiles: don't discard any values. The maximum value is not a myth or statistical apparition like the average. Somewhere in the world, some application user experienced the maximum query response time—or gave up after a few seconds and left. You should want to know why, and you can find the answer. Whereas explaining the top N% of values is difficult because there are many values and, thus, many potentially different answers, explaining the maximum is a single value and answer. Query metric tools often use the query with the maximum response time as the sample, which makes explaining it almost trivial because you have the proverbial smoking gun. With that sample, one of two things will happen: either it reproduces the problem, in which case you continue with the analysis; or, it does not reproduce the problem, in which case you have proven that it's an outlier that can be ignored.

Here's another true story of the former case. An otherwise good application would randomly respond very slowly. Minimum, average, and P99 query time were all milliseconds, but maximum query time was seconds. Instead of ignoring the maximum, I collected query samples of normal and maximum execution time. The difference was the size of the IN list in the WHERE clause: hundreds of values for normal query time, and several thousand values for maximum query time. Fetching more values takes longer to execute, but milliseconds to seconds is not normal even for thousands of values. EXPLAIN provided the answer: normal query time used an index, but maximum query time caused a full table scan. MySQL can switch query execution plans (see "It's a Trap! (When MySQL Chooses Another Index)" on page 87), which explains MySQL, but what explains the application? Long story short, the query was used to look up data for fraud detection, and occasionally a big case would look up several thousand rows at once, which caused MySQL to switch query execution plans. Normally, the query was perfectly fine, but digging into the maximum response time revealed not

---

4 P95, P99, and P999 are conventional. I've never seen other percentiles used with MySQL—median (P50) and maximum (P100) notwithstanding.

only a MySQL gotcha but also an opportunity to improve the application and user experience by handling large lookups more efficiently.

Average, percentile, and maximum are useful, just be aware of what they do and do not represent.

Also consider the distribution of values between the minimum and maximum. If you're lucky, the query report includes histograms, but don't count on it: calculating histograms for an arbitrary time range is difficult, so almost no query metric tool does it. The basic statistics (minimum, maximum, average, and percentile) indicate enough of the distribution to determine if the query is *stable*: metrics are roughly the same for every execution. (In Chapter 6, I return to the idea of stability. See "Normal and Stable: The Best Database Is a Boring Database" on page 180.) Unstable queries complicate the analysis: what causes the query to execute differently? The cause is likely outside MySQL, which makes it more difficult to find, but it's necessary to find because stable queries are easier to analyze, understand, and optimize.

Improving Query Response Time

Improving query response time is a journey called *query optimization*. I call it a journey to set the proper expectations. Query optimization takes time and effort, and there is a destination: faster query response time. To make the journey efficient—not a waste of time and effort—there are two parts: direct query optimization and indirect query optimization.

Direct Query Optimization

Direct query optimization is changes to queries and indexes. These changes solve *a lot* of performance problems, which is why the journey begins with direct query optimization. And because these changes are so powerful, the journey often ends here, too.

Let me use an analogy that's a little simplistic now but will be more insightful later. Think of a query as a car. Mechanics have tools to fix a car when it's not running well. Some tools are common (like a wrench), and others are specialized (like a dual overhead cam lock). Once a mechanic pops the hood and finds the problem, they know which tools are needed to fix it. Likewise, engineers have tools to fix a query when it's running slowly. The common tools are query analysis, EXPLAIN (*https:// oreil.ly/oB3q9*), and indexes. The specialized tools are query-specific optimizations. To name only a few from "Optimizing SELECT Statements" (*https://oreil.ly/dqEWw*) in the MySQL manual:

- Range Optimization
- Index Merge Optimization

- Hash Join Optimization
- Index Condition Pushdown Optimization
- Multi-Range Read Optimization
- Constant-Folding Optimization
- `IS NULL` Optimization
- `ORDER BY` Optimization
- `GROUP BY` Optimization
- `DISTINCT` Optimization
- `LIMIT` Query Optimization

In this book, I do not explain query-specific optimizations because Chapter 8, "Optimization" (*https://oreil.ly/03htc*) in the MySQL manual already explains them in detail, and it's authoritative and regularly updated. Plus, query-specific optimizations vary by MySQL version and distribution. Instead, I teach indexes and indexing in Chapter 2: the foundation for knowing which query-specific optimizations to use—and how—when fixing a slow query. After Chapter 2, you will wield specialized tools like the "Index Condition Pushdown Optimization" (*https://oreil.ly/5CEbX*) like a master mechanic wields a dual overhead cam lock.

Every so often I talk with an engineer who is surprised and a little unhappy when the query optimizations they so assiduously applied do not solve the problem. Direct query optimization is necessary but not always sufficient. An optimized query can be or become a problem under different circumstances. When you can't optimize a query any further (or you can't optimize it at all because you don't have access to the source code), you can optimize *around* the query, which leads to part two of the journey: indirect query optimization.

Indirect Query Optimization

Indirect query optimization is changes to data and access patterns. Instead of changing a query, you change what the query accesses and how: its data and access patterns, respectively. These changes indirectly optimize the query because query, data, and access patterns are inextricable with respect to performance. Changes to one influence the others. It's easy to prove.

Suppose you have a slow query. Data size and access patterns don't matter for this proof, so imagine whatever you like. I can reduce query response time to near-zero. (Let's say near-zero is 1 microsecond. For a computer that's a long time, but for a human it's imperceptible.) The indirect "optimization" is: `TRUNCATE TABLE`. With no data, MySQL can execute any query in near-zero time. That's cheating, but it nonetheless proves the point: reducing data size improves query response time.

Let's revisit the car analogy. Indirect query optimization is analogous to changing major design elements of the car. For example, weight is a factor in fuel efficiency: decreasing weight increases fuel efficiency. (Data is analogous to weight, which is why TRUNCATE TABLE dramatically increases performance—but don't use this "optimization.") Reducing weight is not a straightforward (direct) change because engineers can't magically make parts weigh less. Instead, they have to make significant changes, such as switching from steel to aluminum, which can affect many other design elements. Consequently, these changes require a greater level of effort.

A greater level of effort is why indirect query optimization is part two of the journey. If direct query optimization solves the problem, then stop—be efficient. (And congratulations.) If it doesn't and you're certain the query cannot be further optimized, then it's time to change data and access patterns, which Chapters 3 and 4 cover.

When to Optimize Queries

When you fix a slow query, another one takes its place. There will always be slow queries, but you should not always optimize them because it's not an efficient use of your time. Instead, recall "North Star" on page 3 and ask: is query response time acceptable? If not, then please continue optimizing queries. If yes, then you're done for now because when the database is fast, nobody looks or asks questions.

As a DBA, I would like you to review query metrics (starting with the "Query profile" on page 9) every week and optimize the slowest queries *if needed*, but as a software engineer I know that's not practical and almost never happens. Instead, here are three occasions when you should optimize queries.

Performance Affects Customers

When performance affects customers, it is the duty of engineers to optimize queries. I don't think any engineer would disagree; rather, engineers are eager to improve performance. Some might say this is bad advice because it's reactive, not proactive, but my overwhelming experience is that engineers (and even DBAs) don't look at query metrics until customers report that the application is too slow or timing out. As long as query metrics are always on and at the ready, this is an objectively good time to optimize queries because the need for better performance is as real as your customers.

Before and After Code Changes

Most engineers don't argue against prioritizing query optimization before and after code changes, but my experience is that they don't do it, either. I implore you to avoid this common pattern: seemingly innocent changes are made to code, vetted in staging, deployed to production, then performance starts to "swirl the bowl" (a colorful metaphor related to toilets that means "become worse"). What happened? The cause is usually changes to queries and access patterns, which are closely related. Chapter 2 begins to explain why; Chapters 3 and 4 complete the explanation. For now, the point is: you will be a hero if you review query metrics before and after code changes.

Once a Month

Even if your code and queries do not change, at least two things around them are changing: data and access patterns. I hope your application is wildly successful and stores ever more data as the number of users climbs "up and to the right." Query response time changes over time as data and access patterns change. Fortunately, these changes are relatively slow, usually on the order of weeks or months. Even for an application experiencing hyper-growth (for example, adding thousands of new users every day to millions of existing users), MySQL is really good at scaling up so that query response time remains stable—but nothing lasts forever (even the stars die). There is always a point at which good queries go bad. This reality becomes clear after Chapters 3 and 4. For now, the point is: you will rise from hero to legend— possibly with song and story written about you—if you review query metrics once a month.

MySQL: Go Faster

There is no magic or secret to make MySQL significantly faster without changing queries or the application. Here's another true story to illustrate what I mean.

A team of developers learned that their application was going to be mentioned by a celebrity. They expected a flood of traffic, so they planned ahead to ensure that MySQL and the application would survive. An engineer on the team asked me to help increase MySQL throughput (QPS). I asked, "By how much?" She said, "By 100x". I said, "Sure. Do you have a year and a willingness to rearchitect the application?" She said, "No, we have one day."

I understand what the engineer was thinking: how much throughput could MySQL handle if we *significantly* upgraded the hardware—more CPU cores, more memory, more IOPS? There's no simple or single answer because it depends on many factors that this book explores in the coming chapters. But one thing is certain: *time is a hard limit.*

There are 1,000 milliseconds in 1 second—no more, no less. If a query takes 100 milliseconds to execute, then its worst-case throughput is 10 QPS per CPU core: 1,000 ms / 100 ms/query = 10 QPS. (Its real throughput is likely higher—more on this in a moment.) If nothing changes, then there's simply no more time to execute the query with greater throughput.

To make MySQL do more work in the same amount of time, you have three options:

- Change the nature of time
- Decrease response time
- Increase load

Option one is beyond the scope of this book, so let's focus on options two and three.

Decreasing response time frees time that MySQL can use to do more work. It's simple math: if MySQL is busy 999 milliseconds out of every second, then it has one free millisecond to do more work. If that's not enough free time, then you must decrease the time that the current work is consuming. The best way to accomplish that: direct query optimization. Failing that: indirect query optimization. And finally: better, faster hardware. The following chapters teach you how.

Increasing load—the number of queries executing concurrently—tends to happen first because it doesn't require any query or application changes: simply execute more queries at once (concurrently), and MySQL responds by using more CPU cores. This happens because one CPU core executes one thread, which executes one query. Worst case, MySQL uses N CPU cores to execute N queries concurrently. But the worst case is practically nonexistent because response time is not CPU time. A nonzero amount of response time is CPU time, and the rest is off-CPU (*https://oreil.ly/drw2d*). For example, response time might be 10 ms of CPU time and 90 ms of disk I/O wait. Therefore, the worst-case throughput for a query that takes 100 milliseconds to execute is 10 QPS per CPU core, but its real throughput should be higher since the worst case is practically nonexistent. Sounds great, right? Just push MySQL harder and voilà: more performance. But you know how the story ends: push MySQL too hard and it stops working because every system has finite capacity. MySQL can easily push most modern hardware to its limits, but don't try it until you've read "Performance Destabilizes at the Limit" on page 125.

Bottom line: MySQL cannot simply *go faster*. To make MySQL go faster, you must embark on the journey of direct and indirect query optimization.

Summary

This chapter expounded query time so that, in subsequent chapters, you can learn how to improve it. The central takeaway points are:

- Performance is *query response time*: how long it takes MySQL to execute a query.
- Query response time is the North Star of MySQL performance because it is *meaningful* and *actionable*.
- Query metrics originate from the slow query log or the Performance Schema.
- The Performance Schema is the best source of query metrics.
- Query metrics are grouped and aggregated by *digest*: normalized SQL statements.
- A *query profile* shows slow queries; *slow* is relative to the sort metric.
- A *query report* shows all available information for one query; it's used for query analysis.
- The goal of *query analysis* is understanding query execution, not solving slow response time.
- Query analysis uses query metrics (as reported), metadata (EXPLAIN plans, table structures, and so on), and knowledge of the application.
- Nine query metrics are essential to every query analysis: query time, lock time, rows examined, rows sent, row affected, select scan, select full join, created tmp disk tables, and query count.
- Improving query response time (query optimization) is a two-part journey: direct query optimization, then indirect query optimization.
  - *Direct query optimization* is changes to queries and indexes.
  - *Indirect query optimization* is changes to data and access patterns.
- At the very least, review the query profile and optimize slow queries when performance affects customers, before and after code changes, and once a month.
- To make MySQL go faster, you must decrease response time (free time to do more work) or increase load (push MySQL to work harder).

The next chapter teaches MySQL indexes and indexing—direct query optimization.

Practice: Identify Slow Queries

The goal of this practice is to identify slow queries using pt-query-digest (*https://oreil.ly/KU0hj*): a command-line tool that generates a query profile and query reports from a slow query log.

Use a development or staging MySQL instance—do not use production unless you are confident that it will not cause problems. The slow query log is inherently safe, but enabling it on a busy server can increase disk I/O.

If you have DBAs who manage MySQL, ask them to enable and configure the slow query log. Or, you can learn how by reading "The Slow Query Log" (*https://oreil.ly/Hz0Sz*) in the MySQL manual. (You need a MySQL user account with SUPER privileges to configure MySQL.) If you're using MySQL in the cloud, read the cloud provider documentation to learn how to enable and access the slow query log.

MySQL configurations vary, but the simplest way to configure and enable the slow query log is:

```
SET GLOBAL long_query_time=0;

SET GLOBAL slow_query_log=ON;

SELECT @@GLOBAL.slow_query_log_file;
+------------------------------+
| @@GLOBAL.slow_query_log_file |
+------------------------------+
| /usr/local/var/mysql/slow.log |
+------------------------------+
```

Zero in the first statement, SET GLOBAL long_query_time=0;, causes MySQL to log *every query*. Be careful: on a busy server, this can increase disk I/O and use gigabytes of disk space. If needed, use a slightly larger value like 0.0001 (100 microseconds) or 0.001 (1 millisecond).

Percona Server and MariaDB Server support slow query log sampling: set system variable log_slow_rate_limit to log every Nth query. For example, log_slow_rate_limit = 100 logs every 100th query, which equals 1% of all queries. Over time, this creates a representative sample when combined with long_query_time = 0. When using this feature, be sure that the query metric tool accounts for sampling, else it will under report values. pt-query-digest accounts for sampling.

The last statement, SELECT @@GLOBAL.slow_query_log_file;, outputs the slow query log filename that you need as the first command line argument to pt-query-digest. You can dynamically change this variable if you want to log to a different file.

Second, run pt-query-digest with the slow query log filename as the first command line argument. The tool will print a lot of output; but for now, look at the Profile near the top of the output:

```
# Profile
# Rank Query ID                           Response time    Calls
# ==== ================================== ================ =====
#    1 0x95FD3A847023D37C95AADD230F4EB56A 1000.0000 53.8%    452  SELECT tbl
#    2 0xBB15BFCE4C9727175081E1858C60FD0B  500.0000 26.9%     10  SELECT foo bar
#    3 0x66112E536C54CE7170E215C4BFED008C   50.0000  2.7%      5  INSERT tbl
# MISC 0xMISC                              310.0000 16.7%    220  <2 ITEMS>
```

The preceding output is a text-based table listing the slowest queries from the slow query log. In this example, SELECT tbl (a query abstract) is the slowest query, accounting for 53.8% of total execution time. (By default, pt-query-digest sorts queries by percentage execution time.) Below the query profile, a query report is printed for each query.

Explore the pt-query-digest output. Its manual documents the output, and there is a trove of information on the internet because the tool is widely used. Also check out Percona Monitoring and Management (*https://oreil.ly/rZSx2*): a comprehensive database monitoring solution that uses Grafana (*https://grafana.com*) to report query metrics. Both tools are free, open source, and supported by Percona (*https://percona.com*).

By reviewing slow queries, you know exactly which queries to optimize for the most efficient performance gains. More importantly, you've begun to practice MySQL performance like an expert: with a focus on queries, because performance is query response time.

CHAPTER 2
Indexes and Indexing

Many factors determine MySQL performance, but indexes are special because performance cannot be achieved without them. You can remove other factors—queries, schemas, data, and so on—and still achieve performance, but removing indexes limits performance to brute force: relying on the speed and capacity of hardware. If this book were titled *Brute Force MySQL Performance*, the contents would be as long as the title: "Buy better, faster hardware." You laugh, but just a few days ago I met with a team of developers who had been improving performance in the cloud by purchasing faster hardware until stratospheric costs compelled them to ask, "How else can we improve performance?"

MySQL leverages hardware, optimizations, and indexes to achieve performance when accessing data. Hardware is an obvious leverage because MySQL runs on hardware: the faster the hardware, the better the performance. Less obvious and perhaps more surprising is that hardware provides the *least* leverage. I explain why in a moment. *Optimizations* refer to the numerous techniques, algorithms, and data structures that enable MySQL to utilize hardware efficiently. Optimizations bring the power of hardware into focus. And focus is the difference between a light bulb and a laser. Consequently, optimizations provide more leverage than hardware. If databases were small, hardware and optimizations would be sufficient. But increasing data size *deleverages* the benefits of hardware and optimizations. Without indexes, performance is severely limited.

To illustrate these points, think of MySQL as a fulcrum that leverages hardware, optimizations, and indexes to figuratively lift data, as shown in Figure 2-1.

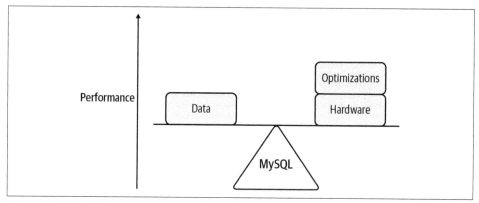

Figure 2-1. MySQL performance without indexes

Without indexes (on the right side), MySQL achieves limited performance with relatively small data. But add indexes to the balance, as shown in Figure 2-2, and MySQL achieves high performance with large data.

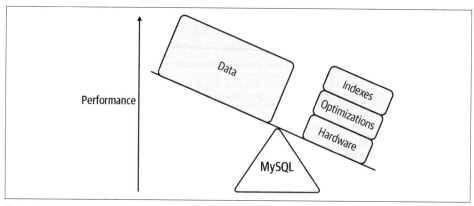

Figure 2-2. MySQL performance with indexes

Indexes provide the most *and the best* leverage. They are required for any nontrivial amount of data. MySQL performance requires proper indexes and indexing, both of which this chapter teaches in detail.

Several years ago, I designed and implemented an application that stores a lot of data. Originally, I estimated the largest table not to exceed a million rows. But there was a bug in the data archiving code that allowed the table to reach one *billion* rows. For years, nobody noticed because response time was always great. Why? Good indexes.

It's commonly said that MySQL uses only one index per table, but that's not entirely true. The index merge optimization, for example, can use two indexes. In this book, however, I focus on the normal case: one query, one table, one index.

This chapter teaches MySQL indexes and indexing. There are five major sections. The first argues why you should not be distracted by hardware or MySQL tuning. It's a necessary digression in order to fully understand why hardware and MySQL tuning are not efficient solutions for improving MySQL performance. The second is a visual introduction to MySQL indexes: what they are and how they work. The third teaches indexing—applying indexes for maximum leverage—by thinking like MySQL. The fourth covers common reasons why indexes lose effectiveness (leverage). The fifth is a brief overview of MySQL table join algorithms because effective joins rely on effective indexes.

Red Herrings of Performance

Red herring is an idiom that refers to a distraction from a goal. When tracking down solutions to improve MySQL performance, two red herrings commonly distract engineers: faster hardware and MySQL tuning.

Better, Faster Hardware!

When MySQL performance isn't acceptable, do *not* begin by scaling up (using better, faster hardware) to "see if that helps." It probably will help if you scale up significantly, but you learn nothing because it only proves what you already know: computers run faster on faster hardware. Better, faster hardware is a red herring of performance because you miss learning the real causes of, and solutions to, slow performance.

There are two reasonable exceptions. First, if the hardware is blatantly insufficient, then scale up to reasonable hardware. For example, using 1 GB of memory with 500 GB of data is blatantly insufficient. Upgrading to 32 GB or 64 GB of memory is reasonable. By contrast, upgrading to 384 GB of memory is sure to help but is unreasonable. Second, if the application is experiencing *hyper-growth* (a massive increase in users, usage, and data) and scaling up is a stopgap solution to keep the application running, then do it. Keeping the application running is always reasonable.

Otherwise, scaling up to improve MySQL performance happens *last*. Experts agree: *first* optimize queries, data, access patterns, and the application. If all those optimizations do not yield sufficient performance, then scale up. Scaling up happens last for the following reasons.

You don't learn anything by scaling up, you simply clobber the problem with faster hardware. Since you're an engineer, not a cave-dwelling protohuman, you *solve* problems by learning and understanding—you don't clobber them. Admittedly, learning and understanding is more difficult and time-consuming, but it's far more effective and sustainable, which leads to the next reason.

Scaling up is not a sustainable approach. Upgrading physical hardware is nontrivial. Some upgrades are relatively quick and easy, but it depends on many factors outside the scope of this book. Sufficient to say, however, that you will drive yourself or the hardware engineers crazy if you frequently change hardware. Crazy engineers are not sustainable. Moreover, companies often use the same hardware for several years because the purchasing process is long and complicated. As a result, easy hardware scalability is one allure of the cloud. In the cloud, you can scale up (or down) CPU cores, memory, and storage in a few minutes. But this ease is *significantly* more expensive than physical hardware. Cloud costs can increase exponentially. The cost of Amazon RDS, for example, doubles from one instance size to the next—double the hardware, double the price. Exponentially increasing costs are not sustainable.

Generally speaking, MySQL can fully utilize all the hardware that it's given. (There are limits, which I address in Chapter 4.) The real question is: can the application fully utilize MySQL? The presumptive answer is yes, but it's not guaranteed. Faster hardware helps MySQL but it does not change how the application uses MySQL. For example, increasing memory might not improve performance if the application causes table scans. Scaling up is only effective at increasing performance when the application workload can scale up, too. Not all workloads can scale up.

 Workload is the combination of queries, data, and access patterns.

But let's imagine that you successfully scale up the workload to fully utilize MySQL on the fastest hardware available. What happens as the application continues to grow, and its workload continues to increase? This reminds me of a Zen proverb: "When you reach the top of the mountain, keep climbing." While I do encourage you to meditate on that, it presents a less enlightening dilemma for your application. With nowhere else to go, the only option is doing what should have been done first: optimize queries, data, access patterns, and the application.

MySQL Tuning

In the television series *Star Trek*, engineers are able to modify the ship to increase power to engines, weapons, shields, sensors, transporters, tractor beams—everything. MySQL is more difficult to operate than a starship because no such modifications are possible. But that does not stop engineers from trying.

First, let's clarify three terms.

Tuning
> Tuning is adjusting MySQL system variables for research and development (R&D). It's laboratory work with specific goals and criteria. Benchmarking is common: adjusting system variables to measure the effect on performance. The blog post "MySQL Challenge: 100k Connections" (*https://oreil.ly/CGvrU*) by renowned MySQL expert Vadim Tkachenko is an example of extreme tuning. Since tuning is R&D, the results are not expected to be generally applicable; rather, the goal is to expand our collective knowledge and understanding of MySQL, especially with respect to its current limits. Tuning influences future MySQL development and best practices.

Configuring
> Configuring is setting system variables to values that are appropriate for the hardware and environment. The goal is a reasonable configuration with respect to a few default values that need to be changed. Configuring MySQL is usually done when the MySQL instance is provisioned or when hardware changes. It's also necessary to reconfigure when data size increases by an order of magnitude, for example from 10 GB to 100 GB. Configuring influences how MySQL runs in general.

Optimizing
> Optimizing is improving MySQL performance by reducing the workload or making it more efficient—usually the latter since application usage tends to increase. The goal is faster response time and more capacity with the existing hardware. Optimizing influences MySQL and application performance.

You will undoubtedly encounter these terms in MySQL literature, videos, conferences, and so forth. The descriptions are more important than the terms. If, for example, you read a blog post that uses *optimizing* but describes what is defined here as *tuning*, then it's tuning as defined here.

The distinction of these terms is important because engineers do all three, but only optimizing (as defined here) is an efficient use of your time.[1]

---

[1] Unless you're Vadim Tkachenko, in which case: please keep tuning.

MySQL tuning is a red herring of performance for two reasons. First, it's often not done as a controlled laboratory experiment, which makes the results dubious. In totality, MySQL performance is complex; experiments must be carefully controlled. Second, results are unlikely to have a significant effect on performance because MySQL is already highly optimized. Tuning MySQL is akin to squeezing blood from a turnip.

Going back to the first paragraph of this section, I realize that we all admire Lieutenant Commander Geordi La Forge, the Chief Engineer in *Star Trek: The Next Generation*. When the captain calls for more power, we feel obligated to make it so by applying arcane server parameters. Or, on Earth, when the application needs more power, we want to save the day by applying an ingenious reconfiguration of MySQL that boosts throughput and concurrency by 50%. Good work, La Forge! Unfortunately, MySQL 8.0 introduced automatic configuration by enabling `innodb_dedica ted_server` (*https://oreil.ly/niPGL*). Since MySQL 5.7 will be end-of-life (EOL) soon after this book is published, let's keep looking to and building the future. Good work nevertheless, La Forge.

Optimizing is all you need to do because tuning is a red herring and configuration is automatic as of MySQL 8.0. This book is all about optimizing.

MySQL Indexes: A Visual Introduction

Indexes are the key to performance and, if you recall "Direct Query Optimization" on page 27, changes to queries and indexes solve *a lot* of performance problems. The journey of query optimization requires a solid understanding of MySQL indexes, and that's what this section presents—in detail with copious illustrations.

Although this section is detailed and relatively long, I call it an *introduction* because there is more to learn. But this section is the key that unlocks the treasure chest of MySQL query optimizations.

The following nine sections apply only to standard indexes on InnoDB tables—the type of index created by a simple PRIMARY KEY or [UNIQUE] INDEX table definition. MySQL supports other specialized index types, but I don't cover them in this book because standard indexes are the basis of performance.

Before we dive into the details of MySQL indexes, I begin with a revelation about InnoDB tables that will change the way you see not only indexes but most of MySQL performance.

InnoDB Tables Are Indexes

Example 2-1 is the structure of table elem (short for *elements*) and the 10 rows that it contains. All examples in this chapter refer to table elem—with one clearly noted exception—so take a moment to study it.

Example 2-1. Table elem

```
CREATE TABLE `elem` (
  `id` int unsigned NOT NULL,
  `a` char(2) NOT NULL,
  `b` char(2) NOT NULL,
  `c` char(2) NOT NULL,
  PRIMARY KEY (`id`),
  KEY `idx_a_b` (`a`,`b`)
) ENGINE=InnoDB;
```

```
+----+------+------+------+
| id | a    | b    | c    |
+----+------+------+------+
|  1 | Ag   | B    | C    |
|  2 | Au   | Be   | Co   |
|  3 | Al   | Br   | Cr   |
|  4 | Ar   | Br   | Cd   |
|  5 | Ar   | Br   | C    |
|  6 | Ag   | B    | Co   |
|  7 | At   | Bi   | Ce   |
|  8 | Al   | B    | C    |
|  9 | Al   | B    | Cd   |
| 10 | Ar   | B    | Cd   |
+----+------+------+------+
```

Table elem has two indexes: the primary key on column id and a nonunique secondary index on columns a, b. The value for column id is a monotonically increasing integer. The values for columns a, b, and c are atomic symbols corresponding to the column name letter: "Ag" (silver) for column a, "B" (boron) for column b, and so on. The row values are random and meaningless; it's just a simple table used for examples.

Figure 2-3 shows a typical view of table elem—just the first four rows for brevity.

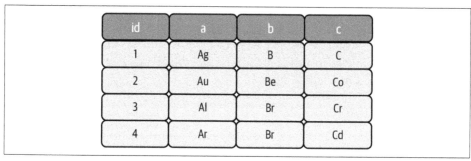

Figure 2-3. Table elem: visual model

Nothing special about table elem, right? It's so simple, one might say it's elementary. But what if I told you that it's not really a table, it's an index? Get the "F" (fluorine) out of here! Figure 2-4 shows the true structure of table elem as an InnoDB table.

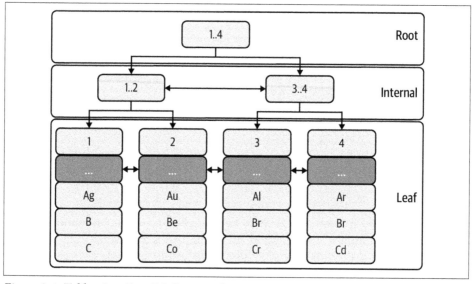

Figure 2-4. Table elem: InnoDB B-tree index

InnoDB tables are B-tree indexes organized by the primary key. Rows are index records stored in leaf nodes of the index structure. Each index record has metadata (denoted by "…") used for row locking, transaction isolation, and so on.

Figure 2-4 is a highly simplified depiction of the B-tree index that is table elem. Four index records (at bottom) correspond to the first four rows. Primary key column values (1, 2, 3, and 4) are shown at the top of each index record. Other column values ("Ag," "B," "C," and so forth) are shown below the metadata for each index record.

You don't need to know the technical details of InnoDB B-tree indexes to understand or achieve remarkable MySQL performance. Only two points are important:

- Primary key lookups are extremely fast and efficient
- The primary key is pivotal to MySQL performance

The first point is true because B-tree indexes are inherently fast and efficient, which is one reason why many database servers use them. The second point becomes increasingly clear in the coming sections—and chapters.

To learn about the fascinating world of database internals, including indexes, read *Database Internals* (*https://oreil.ly/TDsCc*) by Alex Petrov (O'Reilly, 2019). For a deep dive into InnoDB internals, including its B-tree implementation, cancel all your meetings and check out the website of renowned MySQL expert Jeremy Cole (*https://oreil.ly/9sH9m*).

An InnoDB primary key is a clustered index. The MySQL manual occasionally refers to the primary key as *the clustered index*.

Indexes provide the most and the best leverage because the table *is* an index. The primary key is pivotal to performance. This is especially true because secondary indexes include primary key values. Figure 2-5 shows the secondary index on columns a, b.

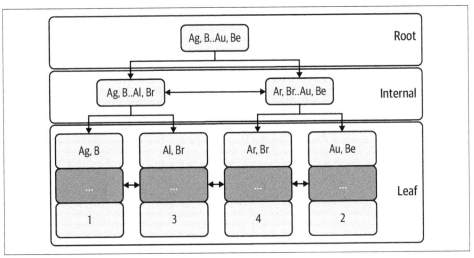

Figure 2-5. Secondary index on columns a, b

Secondary indexes are B-tree indexes, too, but leaf nodes store primary key values. When MySQL uses a secondary index to find a row, it does a second lookup on the primary key to read the full row. Let's put the two together and walk through a secondary index lookup for query SELECT * FROM elem WHERE a='Au' AND b='Be':

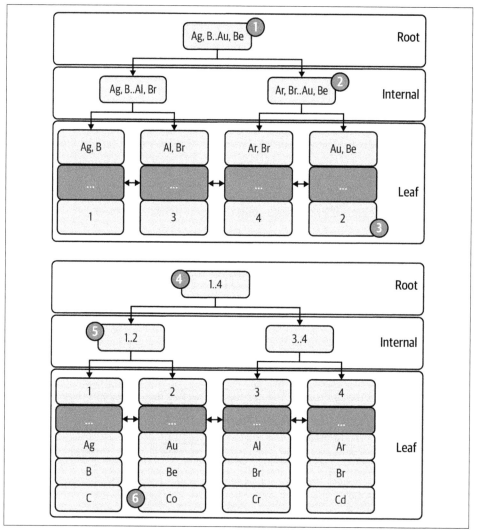

Figure 2-6. Secondary index lookup for value "Au, Be"

Figure 2-6 shows the secondary index (columns a, b) on top and the primary key (column id) on bottom. Six callouts (numbered circles) show the lookup for value "Au, Be" using the secondary index:

1. Index lookups begin at the root node; branch right to an internal node for value "Au, Be."

2. At an internal node, branch right to the leaf node for value "Au, Be."

3. Leaf node for secondary index value "Au, Be" contains the corresponding primary key value: 2.

4. Begin primary key lookup at the root node; branch left to an internal node for value 2.

5. At an internal node, branch right to the leaf node for value 2.

6. Leaf node for primary key value 2 contains the full row matching "Au, Be."

A table has only one primary key. All other indexes are secondary indexes.

This section is short but incredibly important because the correct model provides the foundation for understanding indexes *and more*. For example, if you think back to "Lock time" on page 13, you might see it in a new light since rows are actually leaf nodes in the primary key. Knowing that an InnoDB table is its primary key is akin to knowing that heliocentrism, not geocentrism, is the correct model of the solar system. In the world of MySQL, everything revolves around the primary key.

Table Access Methods

Using an index to look up rows is one of three table access methods. Since tables are indexes, an *index lookup* is the best and most common access method. But sometimes, depending on the query, an index lookup is not possible and the only recourse is an *index scan* or a *table scan*—the other access methods. Knowing which access method MySQL uses for a query is imperative because performance requires an index lookup. Avoid index scans and table scans. "EXPLAIN: Query Execution Plan" on page 51 shows how to see the access method. But first, let's clarify and visualize each one.

The MySQL manual uses the terms *access method*, *access type*, and *join type*. And EXPLAIN uses a field called type or access_type to refer to those terms. In MySQL, the terms are closely related but used equivocally.

In this book, for precision and consistency I use only two terms: *access method* and *access type*. There are three access methods: index lookup, index scan, and table scan. For an index lookup, there are several access types: ref, eq_ref, range, and so forth.

Index lookup

An index lookup finds specific rows—or ranges of rows—by leveraging the ordered structure and algorithmic access of an index. This is the fastest access method because it's precisely what indexes are designed for: fast and efficient access to large amounts of data. Consequently, index lookups are essential for direct query optimization. Performance requires that practically every query uses an index lookup for every table. There are several access types for an index lookup that I cover in forthcoming sections such as "WHERE" on page 54.

Figure 2-6 in the previous section shows an index lookup using a secondary index.

Index scan

When an index lookup is not possible, MySQL must use brute force to find rows: read all rows and filter out non-matching ones. Before MySQL resorts to reading every row using the primary key, it tries to read rows using a secondary index. This is called an index scan.

There are two types of index scan. The first is a *full* index scan, meaning MySQL reads all rows in index order. Reading all rows is usually terrible for performance, but reading them in index order can avoid sorting rows when the index order matches the query ORDER BY.

Figure 2-7 shows a full index scan for query SELECT * FROM elem FORCE INDEX (a) ORDER BY a, b. The FORCE INDEX clause is required because, since table elem is tiny, it's more efficient for MySQL to scan the primary key and sort the rows rather than scan the secondary index and fetch the rows in order. (Sometimes bad queries make good examples.)

Figure 2-7 has eight callouts (numbered circles) that show the order of row access:

1. Read first value of secondary index (SI): "Ag, B."

2. Look up corresponding row in primary key (PK).

3. Read second value of SI: "Al, Br."

4. Look up corresponding row in PK.

5. Read third value of SI: "Ar, Br."

6. Look up corresponding row in PK.

7. Read fourth value of SI: "Au, Be."

8. Look up corresponding row in PK.

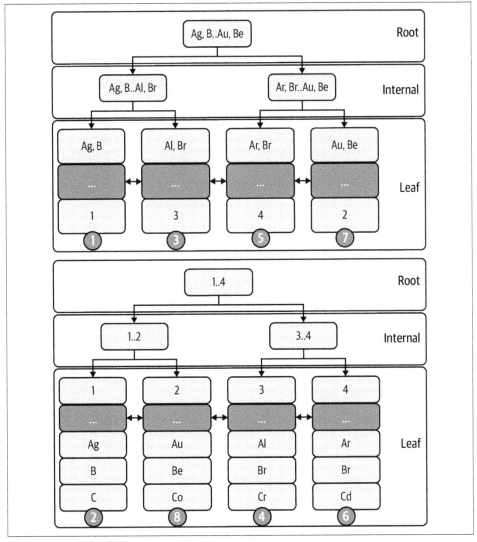

Figure 2-7. Full index scan on secondary index

There is a subtle but important detail in Figure 2-7: scanning the secondary index in order might be sequential reads, but the primary key lookups are almost certainly random reads. Accessing rows in index order does not guarantee sequential reads; more than likely, it incurs random reads.

 Sequential access (reads and writes) is faster than random access.

The second type of index scan is an *index-only scan*: MySQL reads column values (not full rows) from the index. This requires a covering index, which is covered later (pun intended) in "Covering Indexes" on page 71. It should be faster than a full index scan because it doesn't require primary key lookups to read full rows; it only reads column values from the secondary index, which is why it requires a covering index.

Don't optimize for an index scan unless the only alternative is a full table scan. Otherwise, avoid index scans.

Table scan

A (full) table scan reads *all* rows in primary key order. When MySQL cannot do an index lookup or an index scan, a table scan is the only option. This is usually terrible for performance, but it's also usually easy to fix because MySQL is adept at using indexes and has many index-based optimizations. Essentially every query with a WHERE, GROUP BY, or ORDER BY clause can use an index—even if just an index scan—because those clauses use columns and columns can be indexed. Consequently, there are nearly zero reasons for an unfixable table scan.

Figure 2-8 shows a full table scan: reading *all* rows in primary key order. It has four callouts that show the order of row access. Table elem is tiny and only four rows are shown here, but imagine MySQL slogging through thousands or millions of rows in a real table.

The general advice and best practice is to avoid table scans. But for a complete and balanced discussion, there are two cases when a table scan might be acceptable or (surprisingly) better:

- When the table is tiny and infrequently accessed
- When the table selectivity is very low (see "Extreme Selectivity" on page 86)

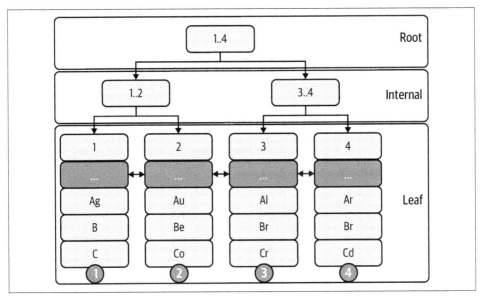

Figure 2-8. Full table scan

But don't take any table scan for granted: they're usually bad for performance. In very rare cases, MySQL can incorrectly choose a table scan when an index lookup is possible, as explained in "It's a Trap! (When MySQL Chooses Another Index)" on page 87.

Leftmost Prefix Requirement

To use an index, a query must use a *leftmost prefix* of the index: one or more index columns starting with the leftmost index column as specified by the index definition. A leftmost prefix is required because the underlying index structure is ordered by the index column order, and it can only be traversed (searched) in that order.

> Use SHOW CREATE TABLE (*https://oreil.ly/cwQZy*) or SHOW INDEX (*https://oreil.ly/5wBhH*) to see index definitions.

Figure 2-9 shows an index on columns a, b, c and a WHERE clause using each leftmost prefix: column a; columns a, b; and columns a, b, c.

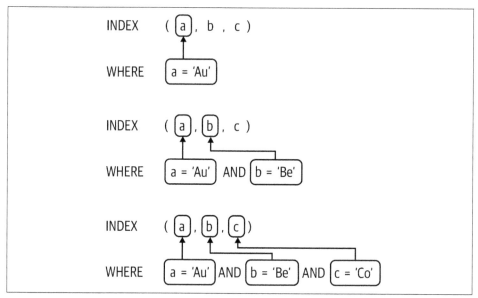

Figure 2-9. Leftmost prefixes of a three-column index

The top WHERE clause in Figure 2-9 uses column a, which is the leftmost column of the index. The middle WHERE clause uses columns a and b that, together, form a leftmost prefix of the index. And the bottom WHERE clause uses the entire index: all three columns. It's ideal to use all columns of an index, but it's not required; only a leftmost prefix is required. Index columns can be used in other SQL clauses, as illustrated by many examples in the following sections.

To use an index, a query must use a *leftmost prefix* of the index.

The leftmost prefix requirement has two logical consequences:

1. Indexes (a, b) and (b, a) are different indexes. They index the same columns but in a different order, which results in different leftmost prefixes. However, a query that uses both columns (for example, WHERE a = 'Au' AND b = 'Be') can use either index, but that does not mean the indexes are equivalent in terms of performance. MySQL will choose the better of the two by calculating many factors.

2. MySQL can most likely use index (a, b, c) in place of indexes (a) and (a, b) because the latter two are leftmost prefixes of the first. In this case, indexes

(a) and (a, b) are duplicates and can be dropped. Use pt-duplicate-key-checker (*https://oreil.ly/EqtfV*) to find and report duplicate indexes.

Lurking at the end (rightmost) of every secondary index is the primary key. For table elem (Example 2-1), the secondary index is effectively (a, b, id), but the rightmost id is hidden. MySQL doesn't show the primary key appended to secondary indexes; you have to imagine it.

> The primary key is appended to every secondary index: (S, P) where S are secondary index columns and P are primary key columns.

In MySQL lingo we say, "The primary key is appended to secondary indexes" even though it's not literally appended. (You can literally append it by creating index (a, b, id), but don't do that.) "Appended to" really means that secondary index leaf nodes contain primary key values, as shown earlier in Figure 2-5. This is important because it increases the size of every secondary index: primary key values are duplicated in secondary indexes. Larger indexes require more memory, which means fewer indexes can fit in memory. Keep the size of the primary key small and the number of secondary indexes reasonable. Just the other day, my colleagues were helping a team whose database has 693 GB of secondary indexes on 397 GB of data (primary key).

The leftmost prefix requirement is a blessing and a restriction. The restriction is relatively easy to work around with additional secondary indexes, but wait until you read "Excessive, Duplicate, and Unused" on page 85. Joining tables is a particular challenge given the restriction, but I address it in "Join Tables" on page 71. I encourage you to see the leftmost prefix requirement as a blessing. Query optimization with respect to indexing is not trivial, but the leftmost prefix requirement is a simple and familiar starting point on the journey.

EXPLAIN: Query Execution Plan

The MySQL EXPLAIN (*https://oreil.ly/M99Gp*) command shows a *query execution plan* (or, *EXPLAIN plan*) that describes how MySQL plans to execute the query: table join order, table access method, index usage, and other important details.

EXPLAIN output is vast and varied. Moreover, it's completely dependent on the query. Changing a single character in a query can significantly change its EXPLAIN plan. For example, WHERE id = 1 verses WHERE id > 1 yields a significantly different EXPLAIN plan. And to complicate the matter further, EXPLAIN continues to evolve. "EXPLAIN Output Format" (*https://oreil.ly/IMCOJ*) in the MySQL manual is required reading—even for experts. Fortunately for the sake of our sanity, the fundamentals have remained the same for decades.

To illustrate index usage, the next five sections explain queries for each case that MySQL can use an index:

- Find matching rows: "WHERE" on page 54
- Group rows: "GROUP BY" on page 60
- Sort rows: "ORDER BY" on page 65
- Avoid reading rows: "Covering Indexes" on page 71
- Join tables: "Join Tables" on page 71

There are other specific cases like MIN() and MAX(), but these five cases are the bread and butter of index usage.

But first I need to set the stage by reviewing the meaning of the EXPLAIN output fields shown in Example 2-2.

Example 2-2. EXPLAIN output (traditional format)

```
EXPLAIN SELECT * FROM elem WHERE id = 1\G

*************************** 1. row ***************************
           id: 1
  select_type: SIMPLE
        table: elem
   partitions: NULL
         type: const
possible_keys: PRIMARY
          key: PRIMARY
      key_len: 4
          ref: const
         rows: 1
     filtered: 100.00
        Extra: NULL
```

For this introduction, we ignore fields id, select_type, partitions, key_len, and filtered; but the examples include them to habituate you to the output. The remaining seven fields convey a wealth of information that constitutes the query execution plan:

table

The table field is the table name (or alias) or subquery reference. Tables are listed in the join order determined by MySQL, not the order they appear in the query. The top table is the first table, and the bottom table is the last table.

type

They type field is the table access method or index lookup access type—see the first note in "Table Access Methods" on page 45 for clarification. ALL means a full table scan (see "Table scan" on page 48). index means an index scan (see "Index scan" on page 46). Any other value—const, ref, range, and so on—is an access type for an index lookup (see "Index lookup" on page 46).

possible_keys

The possible_keys field lists indexes that MySQL could use because the query uses a leftmost prefix. If an index is not listed in this field, then the leftmost prefix requirement is not met.

key

The key field is the name of the index that MySQL will use, or NULL if no index can be used. MySQL chooses the best index based on many factors, some of which are indicated in the Extra field. It's a safe bet that MySQL will use this index when executing the query (EXPLAIN does not execute the query), but see "It's a Trap! (When MySQL Chooses Another Index)" on page 87.

ref

The ref field lists the source of values used to look up rows in the index (the key field).

For single-table queries or the first table in a join, ref is often const, which refers to a constant condition on one or more index columns. A *constant condition* is equality (= or <=> [NULL-safe equal]) to a literal value. For example, a = 'Au' is a constant condition that equals only one value.

For queries that join multiple tables, ref is a column reference from the preceding table in the join order. MySQL joins the current table (the table field) using the index to look up rows that match values from column ref in the preceding table. "Join Tables" on page 71 shows this in action.

rows

The rows field is the estimated number of rows that MySQL will examine to find matching rows. MySQL uses index statistics to estimate rows, so expect the real number—"Rows examined" on page 18—to be close but different.

Extra

The Extra field provides additional information about the query execution plan. This field is important because it indicates query optimizations that MySQL can apply, if any.

All EXPLAIN output in this book is *traditional format*: tabular output (EXPLAIN query;) or list output (EXPLAIN query\G). Other formats are *JSON* (EXPLAIN FORMAT=JSON query) and, as of MySQL 8.0.16, *tree* (EXPLAIN FORMAT=TREE query). JSON and tree formats are completely different than traditional format, but all formats convey the query execution plan.

Don't expect to glean much information from those fields without context: tables, indexes, data, and a query. In the following sections, all illustrations refer to table elem (Example 2-1), its two indexes, and its ten rows.

WHERE

MySQL can use an index to find rows that match table conditions in a WHERE clause. I'm careful to say that MySQL *can* use an index, not that MySQL *will* use an index, because index usage depends on several factors, primarily: table conditions, indexes, and the leftmost prefix requirement (see "Leftmost Prefix Requirement" on page 49). (There are other factors, like index statistics and optimizer costs, but they're beyond the scope of this book.)

A *table condition* is a column and its value (if any) that matches, groups, aggregates, or orders rows. (For brevity, I use the term *condition* when it's unambiguous.) In a WHERE clause, table conditions are also called *predicates*.

Figure 2-10 shows the primary key on column id and a WHERE clause with a single condition: id = 1.

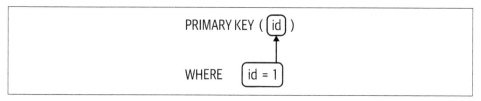

Figure 2-10. WHERE: primary key lookup

A solid box delineates a table condition and an index column (also called an *index part*) that MySQL can use because the former (table condition) is a leftmost prefix of the latter (index). An arrow points from the table condition to the index column that it uses. Later, we'll see examples of table conditions and index columns that MySQL cannot use.

In Figure 2-10, MySQL can find rows that match condition id = 1 using primary key column id. Example 2-3 is the EXPLAIN plan for the full query.

Example 2-3. EXPLAIN plan for primary key lookup

```
EXPLAIN SELECT * FROM elem WHERE id = 1\G

*************************** 1. row ***************************
           id: 1
  select_type: SIMPLE
        table: elem
   partitions: NULL
         type: const
possible_keys: PRIMARY
          key: PRIMARY
      key_len: 4
          ref: const
         rows: 1
     filtered: 100.00
        Extra: NULL
```

In Example 2-3, key: PRIMARY confirms that MySQL will use the primary key—an index lookup. Correspondingly, the access type (the type field) is not ALL (table scan) or index (index scan), which is expected given a simple primary key lookup. The secondary index is not listed in the possible_keys field because MySQL cannot use it for this query: column id is not a leftmost prefix of the secondary index on columns a, b.

Access type const is a special case that occurs only when there are constant conditions (ref: const) on all index columns of the primary key or a unique secondary index. The result is a *constant row*. This is a little too in-depth for an introduction, but since we're here, let's keep learning. Given the table data (Example 2-1) and the fact that column id is the primary key, the row identified by id = 1 can be treated as constant because, when the query is executed, id = 1 can match only one row (or no row). MySQL reads that one row and treats its values as constant, which is great for response time: const access is extremely fast.

Extra: NULL is somewhat rare because real queries are more complex than these examples. But here, Extra: NULL means that MySQL does not need to match rows. Why? Because the constant row can match only one row (or no row). But matching rows is the norm, so let's see a more realistic example by changing the table conditions to id > 3 AND id < 6 AND c = 'Cd', as shown in Figure 2-11 and the corresponding EXPLAIN plan in Example 2-4.

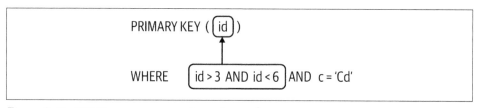

Figure 2-11. WHERE: range access using primary key

Example 2-4. EXPLAIN plan for range access using primary key

```
EXPLAIN SELECT * FROM elem WHERE id > 3 AND id < 6 AND c = 'Cd'\G

*************************** 1. row ***************************
            id: 1
   select_type: SIMPLE
         table: elem
    partitions: NULL
>          type: range
 possible_keys: PRIMARY
           key: PRIMARY
       key_len: 4
>           ref: NULL
>          rows: 2
      filtered: 10.00
>         Extra: Using where
```

 To highlight EXPLAIN plan changes, I prepend > characters to the pertinent fields that changed. These highlights are not part of EXPLAIN.

By changing the table conditions to id > 3 AND id < 6 AND c = 'Cd', the EXPLAIN plan changes from Example 2-3 to Example 2-4, which is more realistic for a single-table query. The query still uses the primary key (key: PRIMARY), but the access type changes to a *range scan* (type: range): using an index to read rows between a range of values. In this case, MySQL uses the primary key to read rows where the value of column id is between 3 and 6. The ref field is NULL because the conditions on column id are not constant (and this is a single-table query, so there's no preceding table to reference). The condition c = 'Cd' is constant, but it's not used for the index lookup (the range scan), so ref does not apply. MySQL estimates that it will examine two rows in the range (rows: 2). That's correct for this trivial example, but remember: rows is an estimate.

"Using where" in the Extra field is so common that it's expected. It means that MySQL will find *matching rows* using the WHERE conditions: for each row read, a row matches if all WHERE conditions are true. Since the conditions on column id define the range, it's really just the condition on column c that MySQL will use to match rows in the range. Glancing back at Example 2-1, one row matches all the WHERE conditions:

```
+----+------+------+------+
| id | a    | b    | c    |
+----+------+------+------+
|  4 | Ar   | Br   | Cd   |
+----+------+------+------+
```

The row with id = 5 is in the range, so MySQL examines the row, but its column c value ("Cd") does not match the WHERE clause, so MySQL does not return the row.

To illustrate other query execution plans, let's use both leftmost prefixes of the secondary index, as shown in Figure 2-12 and the corresponding EXPLAIN plans in Example 2-5.

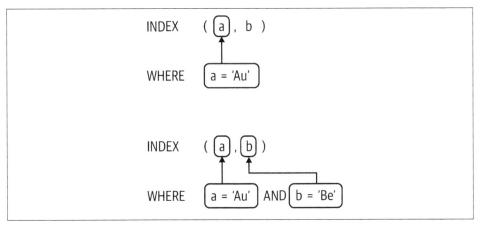

Figure 2-12. WHERE: secondary index lookups

Example 2-5. EXPLAIN plans for secondary index lookups

```
EXPLAIN SELECT * FROM elem WHERE a = 'Au'\G

*************************** 1. row ***************************
            id: 1
   select_type: SIMPLE
         table: elem
    partitions: NULL
>          type: ref
 possible_keys: idx_a_b
>           key: idx_a_b
       key_len: 3
           ref: const
          rows: 1
      filtered: 100.00
```

```
          Extra: NULL


EXPLAIN SELECT * FROM elem WHERE a = 'Au' AND b = 'Be'\G

*************************** 1. row ***************************
            id: 1
   select_type: SIMPLE
         table: elem
    partitions: NULL
>          type: ref
 possible_keys: idx_a_b
>           key: idx_a_b
       key_len: 6
           ref: const,const
          rows: 1
      filtered: 100.00
         Extra: NULL
```

For each EXPLAIN plan in Example 2-5, key: idx_a_b confirms that MySQL uses the secondary index because the conditions meet the leftmost prefix requirement. The first WHERE clause uses only the first index part: column a. The second WHERE clause uses both index parts: columns a and b. Using only column b would not meet the leftmost prefix requirement—I show this in a moment.

What's new and important from previous EXPLAIN plans is the access type: ref. In simplest terms, the ref access type is an equality (= or <=>) lookup on a leftmost prefix of the index (the key field). Like any index lookup, ref access is very fast as long as the estimated number of rows to examine (the rows field) is reasonable.

Although the conditions are constant, the const access type is not possible because the index (key: idx_a_b) is nonunique, so the lookup can match more than one row. And even though MySQL estimates that each WHERE clause will examine only one row (rows: 1), that could change when the query is executed.

Extra: NULL occurs again because MySQL can find matching rows using only the index since there are no conditions on non-indexed columns—so let's add one. Figure 2-13 shows a WHERE clause with conditions on columns a and c, and Example 2-6 is the corresponding EXPLAIN plan.

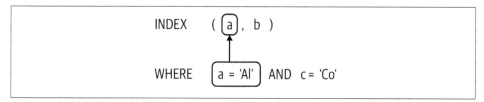

Figure 2-13. WHERE: index lookup and non-indexed column

Example 2-6. EXPLAIN plan for index lookup and non-indexed column

```
EXPLAIN SELECT * FROM elem WHERE a = 'Al' AND c = 'Co'\G

*************************** 1. row ***************************
           id: 1
  select_type: SIMPLE
        table: elem
   partitions: NULL
         type: ref
possible_keys: idx_a_b
          key: idx_a_b
      key_len: 3
          ref: const
>         rows: 3
     filtered: 10.00
>       Extra: Using where
```

In Figure 2-13, there is no box around condition c = 'Co' because the index does not cover column c. MySQL still uses the secondary index (key: idx_a_b), but the condition on column c prevents MySQL from matching rows using only the index. Instead, MySQL uses the index to look up and read rows for the condition on column a, then it matches rows for the condition on column c (Extra: Using where).

Glancing back at Example 2-1 again, you'll notice that zero rows match this WHERE clause, but EXPLAIN reports rows: 3. Why? The index lookup on column a matches three rows where a = 'Al' is true: row id values 3, 8, and 9. But none of these rows also matches c = 'Co'. The query examines three rows but matches zero rows.

 EXPLAIN output rows is an estimate of the number of rows that MySQL will examine when it executes the query, not the number of rows that will match all table conditions.

As a final example of indexes, WHERE, and EXPLAIN, let's *not* meet the leftmost prefix requirement, as shown in Figure 2-14 and Example 2-7.

INDEX   (a , b)

WHERE   b = 'Be'

Figure 2-14. WHERE without leftmost prefix

Example 2-7. EXPLAIN plan for WHERE without leftmost prefix

```
EXPLAIN SELECT * FROM elem WHERE b = 'Be'\G

*************************** 1. row ***************************
            id: 1
   select_type: SIMPLE
         table: elem
    partitions: NULL
>          type: ALL
 possible_keys: NULL
>           key: NULL
       key_len: NULL
           ref: NULL
          rows: 10
      filtered: 10.00
         Extra: Using where
```

A dotted box outline (and lack of arrow) delineates a table condition and an index column that MySQL cannot use because they do not meet the leftmost prefix requirement.

In Figure 2-14, there is no condition on column a, therefore the index cannot be used for the condition on column b. The EXPLAIN plan (Example 2-7) confirms this: possible_keys: NULL and key: NULL. Without an index, MySQL is forced to do a full table scan: type: ALL. Likewise, rows: 10 reflects the total number of rows, and Extra: Using where reflects that MySQL reads and then filters rows not matching b = 'Be'.

Example 2-7 is an example of the worst possible EXPLAIN plan. Whenever you see type: ALL, possible_keys: NULL, or key: NULL, stop what you're doing and analyze the query.

As simple as these examples have been, they represent the fundamentals of EXPLAIN with respect to indexes and WHERE clauses. Real queries have more indexes and WHERE conditions, but the fundamentals don't change.

GROUP BY

MySQL can use an index to optimize GROUP BY because values are implicitly grouped by index order. For the secondary index idx_a_b (on columns a, b), there are five distinct groups of column a values, as shown in Example 2-8.

Example 2-8. Distinct groups of column a values

```
SELECT a, b FROM elem ORDER BY a, b;
```

```
+------+------+
| a    | b    |
+------+------+
| Ag   | B    | -- Ag group
| Ag   | B    |
|      |      |
| Al   | B    | -- Al group
| Al   | B    |
| Al   | Br   |
|      |      |
| Ar   | B    | -- Ar group
| Ar   | Br   |
| Ar   | Br   |
|      |      |
| At   | Bi   | -- At group
|      |      |
| Au   | Be   | -- Au group
+------+------+
```

I separated the groups in Example 2-8 with blank lines and annotated the first row in each group. A query with GROUP BY a can use index idx_a_b because column a is a leftmost prefix and the index is implicitly grouped by column a values. Example 2-9 is a representative EXPLAIN plan for the simplest type of GROUP BY optimization.

Example 2-9. EXPLAIN plan for GROUP BY a

```
EXPLAIN SELECT a, COUNT(*) FROM elem GROUP BY a\G

*************************** 1. row ***************************
           id: 1
  select_type: SIMPLE
        table: elem
   partitions: NULL
>        type: index
possible_keys: idx_a_b
          key: idx_a_b
      key_len: 6
          ref: NULL
         rows: 10
     filtered: 100.00
>       Extra: Using index
```

key: idx_a_b confirms that MySQL uses the index to optimize the GROUP BY. Since the index is ordered, MySQL is assured that each new value for column a is a new group. For example, after reading the last "Ag" value, the index order assures that no more "Ag" values will be read, so the "Ag" group is complete.

"Using index" in the Extra field indicates that MySQL is reading column a values only from the index; it's not reading full rows from the primary key. I cover this optimization in "Covering Indexes" on page 71.

This query uses an index, but not for an index lookup: type: index denotes an index scan (see "Index scan" on page 46). And since there's no WHERE clause to filter rows, MySQL reads all rows. If you add a WHERE clause, MySQL can still use the index for the GROUP BY, but the leftmost prefix requirement still applies. In this case, the query is using the leftmost index part (column a), so the WHERE condition must be on column a or b to meet the leftmost prefix requirement. Let's first add a WHERE condition on column a, as shown in Figure 2-15 and Example 2-10.

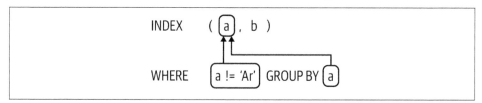

Figure 2-15. GROUP BY and WHERE on same index column

Example 2-10. EXPLAIN plan for GROUP BY and WHERE on same index column

```
EXPLAIN SELECT a, COUNT(a) FROM elem WHERE a != 'Ar' GROUP BY a\G

*************************** 1. row ***************************
            id: 1
   select_type: SIMPLE
         table: elem
    partitions: NULL
>          type: range
 possible_keys: idx_a_b
           key: idx_a_b
       key_len: 3
           ref: NULL
          rows: 7
      filtered: 100.00
>         Extra: Using where; Using index
```

"Using where" in the Extra field refers to WHERE a != 'Ar'. The interesting change is type: range. The range access type works with the not-equal operator (!= or <>). You can think of it like WHERE a < 'Ar' AND a > 'Ar', as shown in Figure 2-16.

A condition on column b in the WHERE clause can still use the index because the conditions, regardless of being in different SQL clauses, meet the leftmost prefix requirement. Figure 2-17 shows this, and Example 2-11 shows the EXPLAIN plan.

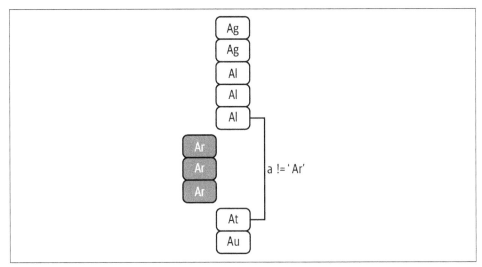

Figure 2-16. Range for not-equal

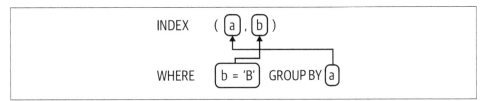

Figure 2-17. GROUP BY and WHERE on different index columns

Example 2-11. EXPLAIN plan for GROUP BY and WHERE on different index columns

```
EXPLAIN SELECT a, b FROM elem WHERE b = 'B' GROUP BY a\G

*************************** 1. row ***************************
           id: 1
  select_type: SIMPLE
        table: elem
   partitions: NULL
         type: range
possible_keys: idx_a_b
          key: idx_a_b
      key_len: 6
          ref: NULL
         rows: 6
     filtered: 100.00
>       Extra: Using where; Using index for group-by
```

The query in Example 2-11 has two important details: an equality condition on column b in the WHERE clause, and selecting columns a and b in the SELECT clause.

These details enable the special "Using index for group-by" optimization revealed in the Extra field. If, for example, the equality (=) is changed to not-equal (!=), the query optimization is lost. When it comes to query optimizations like this, details are critical. You must read the MySQL manual to learn and apply the details. "GROUP BY Optimization" (*https://oreil.ly/ZknLf*) in the MySQL manual elaborates.

The final GROUP BY example in Figure 2-18 and Example 2-12 might surprise you.

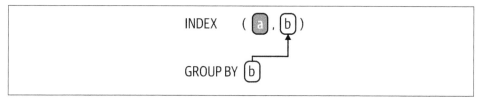

Figure 2-18. GROUP BY without leftmost prefix

Example 2-12. EXPLAIN plan for GROUP BY without leftmost prefix

```
EXPLAIN SELECT b, COUNT(*) FROM elem GROUP BY b\G

*************************** 1. row ***************************
            id: 1
   select_type: SIMPLE
         table: elem
    partitions: NULL
>        type: index
 possible_keys: idx_a_b
           key: idx_a_b
       key_len: 6
           ref: NULL
          rows: 10
      filtered: 100.00
>        Extra: Using index; Using temporary
```

Notice key: idx_a_b: MySQL uses the index despite the query having no condition on column a. What happened to the leftmost prefix requirement? It's being met because MySQL is scanning the index (type: index) on column a. You can imagine a condition on column a that's always true, like a = a.

Would MySQL still index scan on column a for GROUP BY c? No, it would not; it would do a full table scan. Figure 2-18 works because the index has column b values; it does not have column c values.

"Using temporary" in the Extra field is a side effect of not having a strict set of leftmost prefix conditions. As MySQL reads column a values from the index, it collects column b values in a temporary table (in memory). After reading all column a values, it table scans the temporary table to group and aggregate for COUNT(*).

There is a lot more to learn about GROUP BY with respect to indexes and query optimizations, but these examples are the fundamentals. Unlike WHERE clauses, GROUP BY clauses tend to be simpler. The challenge is creating an index to optimize GROUP BY plus other SQL clauses. MySQL has the same challenge when formulating the query execution plan, so it might not optimize GROUP BY even when possible. MySQL almost always chooses the best query execution plan, but if you want to experiment with different ones, read "Index Hints" (*https://oreil.ly/mbBof*) in the MySQL manual.

ORDER BY

Unsurprisingly, MySQL can use an ordered index to optimize ORDER BY. This optimization avoids sorting rows, which takes a little more time, by accessing rows in order. Without this optimization, MySQL reads all matching rows, sorts them, then returns the sorted result set. When MySQL sorts rows, it prints "Using filesort" in the Extra field of the EXPLAIN plan. *Filesort* means *sort rows*. It's a historical (and now misleading) term but still the prevalent term in MySQL lingo.

Filesort is a consternation for engineers because it has a reputation for being slow. Sorting rows is extra work, so it does not improve response time, but it's usually not the root cause of slow response time. At the end of this section, I use EXPLAIN ANALYZE, which is new as of MySQL 8.0.18, to measure the real-time penalty of filesort. (Spoiler: sorting rows is very fast.) But first, let's examine how to use indexes to optimize ORDER BY.

There are three ways to use an index to optimize ORDER BY. The first and simplest way is using a leftmost prefix of an index for the ORDER BY clause. For table elem, that means:

- ORDER BY id
- ORDER BY a
- ORDER BY a, b

The second way is to hold a leftmost part of the index constant and order by the next index columns. For example, holding column a constant and ordering by column b, as shown in Figure 2-19 with corresponding EXPLAIN plan in Example 2-13.

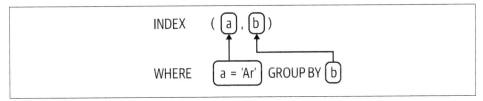

Figure 2-19. ORDER BY and WHERE on different index columns

Example 2-13. EXPLAIN plan for ORDER BY and WHERE on different index columns

```
EXPLAIN SELECT a, b FROM elem WHERE a = 'Ar' ORDER BY b\G

*************************** 1. row ***************************
           id: 1
  select_type: SIMPLE
        table: elem
   partitions: NULL
         type: ref
possible_keys: idx_a_b
          key: idx_a_b
      key_len: 3
          ref: const
         rows: 3
     filtered: 100.00
        Extra: Using index
```

WHERE a = 'Ar' ORDER BY b can use index (a, b) because the WHERE condition on the first index part (column a) is constant, so MySQL jumps to a = 'Ar' in the index and, from there, reads column b values in order. Example 2-14 is the result set, and although it's nothing fancy, it shows that column a is constant (value "Ar") and column b is sorted.

Example 2-14. Result set of WHERE a = 'Ar' ORDER BY b

```
+------+------+
| a    | b    |
+------+------+
| Ar   | B    |
| Ar   | Br   |
| Ar   | Br   |
+------+------+
```

If table elem had an index on columns a, b, c, a query like WHERE a = 'Au' AND b = 'Be' ORDER BY c could use the index because the conditions on columns a and b hold the leftmost part of the index.

The third way is a special case of the second. Before showing the figure that explains it, see if you can determine why the query in Example 2-15 does *not* cause a filesort (why "Using filesort" is not reported in the Extra field).

Example 2-15. EXPLAIN plan for ORDER BY id

```
EXPLAIN SELECT * FROM elem WHERE a = 'Al' AND b = 'B' ORDER BY id\G

*************************** 1. row ***************************
           id: 1
```

```
  select_type: SIMPLE
        table: elem
   partitions: NULL
         type: ref
possible_keys: idx_a_b
          key: idx_a_b
      key_len: 16
          ref: const,const
         rows: 2
     filtered: 100.00
>        Extra: Using index condition
```

It's understandable that the query uses index idx_a_b because the WHERE conditions are a leftmost prefix, but shouldn't ORDER BY id cause a filesort? Figure 2-20 reveals the answer.

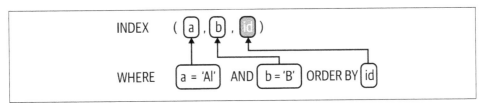

Figure 2-20. ORDER BY using primary key appended to secondary index

"Leftmost Prefix Requirement" on page 49 has a paragraph that begins with, "Lurking at the end (rightmost) of every secondary index is the primary key." That's what's happening in Figure 2-20: the dark box around index column id reveals the "hidden" primary key appended to the secondary index. This ORDER BY optimization might not seem useful with a little table like elem, but with real tables it can be very useful—worth remembering.

To prove that the "hidden" primary key allows the ORDER BY to avoid a filesort, let's remove the condition on column b to invalidate the optimization, as shown in Figure 2-21 and followed by the resulting EXPLAIN plan in Example 2-16.

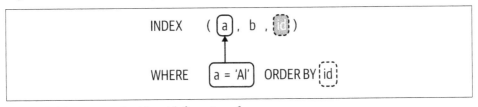

Figure 2-21. ORDER BY without leftmost prefix

Example 2-16. EXPLAIN plan for ORDER BY without leftmost prefix

```
EXPLAIN SELECT * FROM elem WHERE a = 'Al' ORDER BY id\G

*************************** 1. row ***************************
           id: 1
  select_type: SIMPLE
        table: elem
   partitions: NULL
         type: ref
possible_keys: idx_a_b
          key: idx_a_b
      key_len: 8
          ref: const
         rows: 3
     filtered: 100.00
>       Extra: Using index condition; Using filesort
```

By removing the condition on column b, there's no longer a leftmost prefix on the secondary index that allows MySQL to use the "hidden" primary key to optimize ORDER BY. Therefore, for this particular query, "Using filesort" appears in the Extra field.

The new optimization is "Using index condition," which is called index condition pushdown. *Index condition pushdown* means the storage engine uses an index to matches rows for WHERE conditions. Normally, storage engines only read and write rows, and MySQL handles the logic of matching rows. This is a clean separation of concerns (which is a virtue for software design), but it's inefficient when rows don't match: both MySQL and the storage engine waste time reading non-matching rows. For the query in Example 2-16, index condition pushdown means the storage engine (InnoDB) uses index idx_a_b to match condition a = 'Al'. Index condition pushdown helps improve response time, but don't exert yourself trying to optimize for it because MySQL uses it automatically when possible. To learn more, read "Index Condition Pushdown Optimization" (*https://oreil.ly/L3Nzm*) in the MySQL manual.

There's an important detail that affects all ORDER BY optimizations: index order is ascending by default, and ORDER BY col implies ascending: ORDER BY col ASC. Optimizing ORDER BY works in only one direction for all columns: ASC (ascending) or DESC (descending). Consequently, ORDER BY a, b DESC does not work because column a is an implicit ASC sort, which is different than b DESC.

 MySQL 8.0 supports descending indexes (*https://oreil.ly/FDTsN*).

What is the real time penalty of filesort? Prior to MySQL 8.0.18, it was neither measured nor reported. But as of MySQL 8.0.18, EXPLAIN ANALYZE (*https://oreil.ly/DFPiF*) measures and reports it. For only Example 2-17, I must use a different table.

Example 2-17. Sysbench table sbtest

```
CREATE TABLE `sbtest1` (
  `id` int NOT NULL AUTO_INCREMENT,
  `k` int NOT NULL DEFAULT '0',
  `c` char(120) NOT NULL DEFAULT '',
  `pad` char(60) NOT NULL DEFAULT '',
  PRIMARY KEY (`id`),
  KEY `k_1` (`k`)
) ENGINE=InnoDB;
```

That's a standard sysbench table (*https://oreil.ly/XAYX2*); I loaded it with one million rows. Let's use a random, meaningless query with a large result set and ORDER BY:

```
SELECT c FROM sbtest1 WHERE k < 450000 ORDER BY id;
-- Output omitted
68439 rows in set (1.15 sec)
```

The query takes 1.15 seconds to sort and return a little over 68,000 rows. But it's not a bad query; check out its EXPLAIN plan:

```
EXPLAIN SELECT c FROM sbtest1 WHERE k < 450000 ORDER BY id\G

*************************** 1. row ***************************
           id: 1
  select_type: SIMPLE
        table: sbtest1
   partitions: NULL
         type: range
possible_keys: k_1
          key: k_1
      key_len: 4
          ref: NULL
         rows: 133168
     filtered: 100.00
        Extra: Using index condition; Using MRR; Using filesort
```

The only new information in that EXPLAIN plan is "Using MRR" in the Extra field, which refers to the "Multi-Range Read Optimization" (*https://oreil.ly/QX1wJ*). Otherwise, that EXPLAIN plan reports information already covered in this chapter.

Does filesort make this query slow? EXPLAIN ANALYZE reveals the answer, albeit cryptically:

```
EXPLAIN ANALYZE SELECT c FROM sbtest1 WHERE k < 450000 ORDER BY id\G

*************************** 1. row ***************************
1 -> Sort: sbtest1.id  (cost=83975.47 rows=133168)
2    (actual time=1221.170..1229.306 rows=68439 loops=1)
3    -> Index range scan on sbtest1 using k_1, with index condition: (k<450000)
4        (cost=83975.47 rows=133168) (actual time=40.916..1174.981 rows=68439)
```

The real output of EXPLAIN ANALYZE is wider, but I wrapped and numbered the lines for print legibility and reference. EXPLAIN ANALYZE output is dense and requires practice to grok; for now, let's go straight to the point—or as straight as possible since the output does not read sequentially. On line 4, 1174.981 (milliseconds) means the index range scan (line 3) took 1.17 seconds (rounded). On line 2, 1221.170..1229.306 means the filesort (line 1) *started* after 1,221 milliseconds and ended after 1,229 milliseconds, which means the filesort took 8 milliseconds. Total execution time is 1.23 seconds: 95% reading rows and less than 1% sorting rows. The remaining 4%—roughly 49 milliseconds—is spent in other stages: preparing, statistics, logging, cleaning up, and so forth.

The answer is no: filesort does *not* make this query slow. The problem is data access: 68,439 rows is not a small result set. Sorting 68,439 values is practically zero work for a CPU that does *billions* of operations per second. But reading 68,439 rows is appreciable work for a relational database that must traverse indexes, manage transactions, etc. To optimize a query like this, focus on "Data Access" on page 97.

One last question to address: why does filesort have a reputation for being slow? Because MySQL uses temporary files on disk when sorting data exceeds the sort_buffer_size (*https://oreil.ly/x5mbN*), and hard drives are orders of magnitude slower than memory. This was especially true decades ago when spinning disks were the norm; but today, SSD is the norm, and storage in general is quite fast. Filesort might be an issue for a query at high throughput (QPS), but use EXPLAIN ANALYZE to measure and verify.

 EXPLAIN ANALYZE executes the query. To be safe, use EXPLAIN ANALYZE on a read-only replica, not the source.

Now back to table elem (Example 2-1) and the next case for which MySQL can use an index: covering indexes.

Covering Indexes

A *covering index* includes all columns referenced in a query. Figure 2-22 shows a covering index for a SELECT statement.

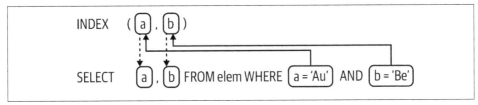

Figure 2-22. Covering indexes

The WHERE conditions on columns a and b point to the corresponding index columns as usual, but these index columns also point back to the corresponding columns in the SELECT clause to signify that the values for these columns are read from the index.

Normally, MySQL reads full rows from the primary key (recall "InnoDB Tables Are Indexes" on page 41). But with a covering index, MySQL can read only column values from the index. This is most helpful with secondary indexes because it avoids the primary key lookup.

MySQL uses the covering index optimization automtically, and EXPLAIN reports it as "Using index" in the Extra field. "Using index for group-by" is a similar optimization specific to GROUP BY and DISTINCT, as demonstrated in "GROUP BY" on page 60. But "Using index condition" and "Using index for skip scan" are completely different and unrelated optimizations.

An index scan (type: index) plus a covering index (Extra: Using index) is an index-only scan (see "Index scan" on page 46). There are two examples in "GROUP BY" on page 60: Example 2-9 and Example 2-12.

Covering indexes are glamorous but rarely practical because realistic queries have too many columns, conditions, and clauses for one index to cover. Do not spend time trying to create covering indexes. When designing or analyzing simple queries that use very few columns, take a moment to see if a covering index might work. If it does, then congratulations. If not, that's okay; no one expects covering indexes.

Join Tables

MySQL uses an index to join tables, and this usage is fundamentally the same as using an index for anything else. The main difference is the source of values used in join conditions for each table. This becomes more clear when visualized, but first we need a second table to join. Example 2-18 shows the structure of table elem_names and the 14 rows that it contains.

Example 2-18. Table `elem_names`

```
CREATE TABLE `elem_names` (
  `symbol` char(2) NOT NULL,
  `name` varchar(16) DEFAULT NULL,
  PRIMARY KEY (`symbol`)
) ENGINE=InnoDB;
```

```
+--------+-----------+
| symbol | name      |
+--------+-----------+
| Ag     | Silver    |
| Al     | Aluminum  |
| Ar     | Argon     |
| At     | Astatine  |
| Au     | Gold      |
| B      | Boron     |
| Be     | Beryllium |
| Bi     | Bismuth   |
| Br     | Bromine   |
| C      | Carbon    |
| Cd     | Cadmium   |
| Ce     | Cerium    |
| Co     | Cobalt    |
| Cr     | Chromium  |
+--------+-----------+
```

Table `elem_name` has one index: the primary key on column `symbol`. The values in column `symbol` match the values in table `elem` columns a, b, and c. Therefore, we can join tables `elem` and `elem_names` on these columns.

Figure 2-23 shows a SELECT statement that joins tables `elem` and `elem_names`, and a visual representation of the conditions and indexes for each table.

In previous figures, there's only one index and SQL clause pair because there's only one table. But Figure 2-23 has two pairs—one for each table—delineated by large rightward-pointing chevrons with the table name commented in each: /* elem */ and /* elem_names */. Like EXPLAIN, these figures list tables in join order: top to bottom. Table `elem` (at top) is the first table in the join order and table `elem_names` (at bottom) is the second table.

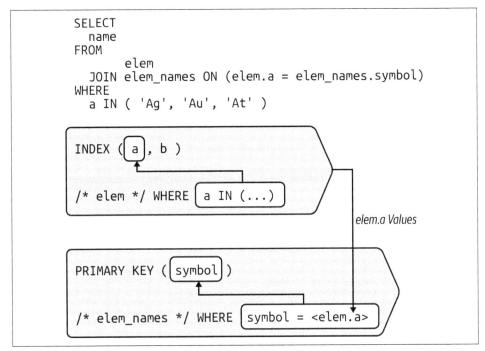

Figure 2-23. Join table on primary key lookup

Index usage on table elem is nothing new or special: MySQL uses the index for the condition a IN (…). So far, so good.

Index usage on table elem_names, which is joined to the preceding table, is fundamentally the same with two minor differences. First, the WHERE clause is a rewrite of the JOIN…ON clause—more on this later. Second, values for the condition on column symbol come from the preceding table: elem. To represent this, an arrow points from the preceding table to a column reference in angle brackets: <elem.a>. On join, MySQL looks up rows in table elem_names using column a values from matching rows in table elem for the join condition on column symbol. In MySQL vernacular we'd say, "symbol is equal to column a from table elem." Given a value from the preceding table, the primary key lookup on column symbol is nothing new or special: if a row matches, it's returned and joined with the row from the preceding table.

Example 2-19 shows the EXPLAIN plan for the SELECT statement in Figure 2-23.

Example 2-19. EXPLAIN plan for join table on primary key lookup

```
EXPLAIN SELECT name
       FROM elem JOIN elem_names ON (elem.a = elem_names.symbol)
       WHERE a IN ('Ag', 'Au', 'At')\G

*************************** 1. row ***************************
           id: 1
  select_type: SIMPLE
        table: elem
   partitions: NULL
         type: range
possible_keys: idx_a_b
          key: idx_a_b
      key_len: 3
          ref: NULL
         rows: 4
     filtered: 100.00
        Extra: Using where; Using index
*************************** 2. row ***************************
           id: 1
  select_type: SIMPLE
        table: elem_names
   partitions: NULL
>         type: eq_ref
possible_keys: PRIMARY
          key: PRIMARY
      key_len: 2
>          ref: test.elem.a
         rows: 1
     filtered: 100.00
        Extra: NULL
```

On a per-table basis, the EXPLAIN plan in Example 2-19 is nothing new, but the join reveals two new details in the second table, elem_names. The first is access type eq_ref: a single-row lookup using the primary key or a unique not-null secondary index. (In this context, *not-null* means all secondary index columns are defined as NOT NULL.) More on the eq_ref access type in the next paragraph. The second is ref: test.elem.a, which you can read as "reference column elem.a". (The database name is test, hence the test. prefix.) To join table elem_names, values from reference column elem.a are used to look up rows by primary key (key: PRIMARY), which covers the join column: symbol. This corresponds to the JOIN condition: ON (elem.a = elem_names.symbol).

On a per-table basis, a join does not change how indexes are used. The main difference is that values for the join condition come from the preceding table.

MySQL can join a table using any access method (see "Table Access Methods" on page 45), but an index lookup using the eq_ref access type is the best and fastest because it matches only one row. The eq_ref access type has two requirements: a primary key or unique not-null secondary index *and* equality conditions on all index columns. Together, these requirements guarantee that an eq_ref lookup matches *at most* one row. If both requirements are not met, then MySQL will probably use a ref index lookup, which is essentially the same but matches any number of rows.

Going back to Figure 2-23, how did I know to rewrite the JOIN...ON clause to a WHERE clause for table elem_names? If you SHOW WARNINGS immediately after EXPLAIN, MySQL prints how it rewrites the query. This is the abridged output of SHOW WARNINGS:

```
/* select#1 */ select
  `test`.`elem_names`.`name` AS `name`
from
       `test`.`elem`
  join `test`.`elem_names`
where
       ((`test`.`elem_names`.`symbol` = `test`.`elem`.`a`)
  and (`test`.`elem`.`a` in ('Ag','Au','At')))
```

Now you can see that /* elem_names */ WHERE symbol = <elem.a> in Figure 2-23 is correct.

Sometimes, running SHOW WARNINGS immediately after EXPLAIN to see how MySQL rewrites a query is necessary to understand the table join order and indexes that MySQL chose.

 Rewritten SQL statements shown by SHOW WARNINGS are not intended to be valid. They're only intended to show how MySQL interprets and rewrites the SQL statement. Do not execute them.

Table join order is critical because MySQL joins tables in the best order possible, *not* the order tables are written in the query. You must use EXPLAIN to see the table join order. EXPLAIN prints tables in the join order from top (first table) to bottom (last table). The default join algorithm, *nested-loop join*, follows the join order. I outline join algorithms at the end of this chapter: "Table Join Algorithms" on page 87.

Never guess or presume the table join order because small changes to a query can yield a significantly different table join order or query execution plan. To demonstrate, the SELECT statement in Figure 2-24 is nearly identically to the SELECT statement in Figure 2-23 with one tiny difference—can you spot it?

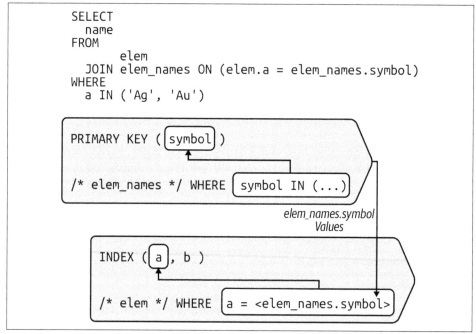

```
SELECT
    name
FROM
        elem
    JOIN elem_names ON (elem.a = elem_names.symbol)
    WHERE
        a IN ('Ag', 'Au')
```

PRIMARY KEY (symbol)

/* elem_names */ WHERE symbol IN (...)

elem_names.symbol
Values

INDEX (a , b)

/* elem */ WHERE a = <elem_names.symbol>

Figure 2-24. Join table on secondary index lookup

Here's a hint: *it's neither gold nor silver.* The tiny difference yields a significantly different query execution plan, as shown in Example 2-20.

Example 2-20. EXPLAIN plan for join table on secondary index lookup

```
EXPLAIN SELECT name
        FROM elem JOIN elem_names ON (elem.a = elem_names.symbol)
        WHERE a IN ('Ag', 'Au')\G

*************************** 1. row ***************************
           id: 1
  select_type: SIMPLE
        table: elem_names
   partitions: NULL
         type: range
possible_keys: PRIMARY
          key: PRIMARY
      key_len: 2
          ref: NULL
```

```
          rows: 2
      filtered: 100.00
         Extra: Using where
*************************** 2. row ***************************
            id: 1
   select_type: SIMPLE
         table: elem
    partitions: NULL
          type: ref
 possible_keys: idx_a_b
           key: idx_a_b
       key_len: 3
           ref: test.elem_names.symbol
          rows: 2
      filtered: 100.00
         Extra: Using index
```

Syntactically, the SELECT statements in Figures 2-23 and 2-24 are identical, but the execution plans (Examples 2-19 and 2-20) are significantly different. What changed? In Figure 2-24, a single value was removed from the IN() list: "At." This is a great example of how a seemingly innocuous change can trigger something in the MySQL query execution planner and voilà: a totally new and different EXPLAIN plan. Let's examine Example 2-20 table by table.

The first table is elem_names, which is different than how the query is written: elem JOIN elem_names. MySQL determines the table join order, not the JOIN clause.[2] The type and key fields indicate a range scan on the primary key, but where are the values coming from? The ref field is NULL, and there are no WHERE conditions on this table. MySQL must have rewritten the query; this is the abridged output of SHOW WARNINGS:

```
/* select#1 */ select
  `test`.`elem_names`.`name` AS `name`
from
  `test`.`elem` join `test`.`elem_names`
where
      ((`test`.`elem`.`a` = `test`.`elem_names`.`symbol`)
  and (`test`.`elem_names`.`symbol` in ('Ag','Au')))
```

Yes, there it is on the last line: MySQL rewrites the query to use the IN() list as the values for elem_names.symbols instead of elem.a as originally written in the query. Now you can see (or imagine) that index usage on table elem_names.symbols is a range scan to look up two values: "Ag" and "Au." Using the primary key, that will be an extremely fast index lookup and match only two rows that MySQL will use to join the second table.

---

2 Unless STRAIGHT_JOIN is used, but don't use this. Let the MySQL query optimizer choose the join order for the best query execution plan.

The second table is elem, and the EXPLAIN plan is familiar: using index idx_a_b to look up index values (not rows, because Extra: Using index) matching the condition on column a. The values for that condition come from matching rows in the preceding table, as indicated by ref: test.elem_names.symbol.

 MySQL joins tables in the best order possible, *not* the order that tables are written in the query.

Although MySQL can change the join order and rewrite the query, index usage for a join is fundamentally the same—on a per-table basis—as everything previously demonstrated and explained in this chapter. Use EXPLAIN and SHOW WARNINGS, and consider the execution plan table by table, from top to bottom.

MySQL can join tables without an index. This is called a *full join* and it's the single worst thing a query can do. A table scan on a single-table query is bad, but a full join is worse because the table scan on the joined table does not happen once, it happens for every matching row from the preceding table. Example 2-21 shows a full join on the second table.

Example 2-21. EXPLAIN plan for full JOIN

```
EXPLAIN SELECT name
        FROM elem STRAIGHT_JOIN elem_names IGNORE INDEX (PRIMARY)
          ON (elem.a = elem_names.symbol)\G

*************************** 1. row ***************************
           id: 1
  select_type: SIMPLE
        table: elem
   partitions: NULL
         type: index
possible_keys: idx_a_b
          key: idx_a_b
      key_len: 6
          ref: NULL
         rows: 10
     filtered: 100.00
        Extra: Using index
*************************** 2. row ***************************
           id: 1
  select_type: SIMPLE
        table: elem_names
   partitions: NULL
         type: ALL
possible_keys: NULL
```

```
         key: NULL
     key_len: NULL
         ref: NULL
        rows: 14
    filtered: 7.14
       Extra: Using where; Using join buffer (hash join)
```

Normally, MySQL would not choose this query execution plan, which is why I had to force it with STRAIGHT_JOIN and IGNORE INDEX (PRIMARY). An index-only scan on the first table (elem) yields all ten rows.[3] For each row, MySQL joins the second table (elem_names) by doing a full table scan (type: ALL) to find matching rows. Since this is a joined table (not the first table in the join order), the table scan counts as a full join. A full join is the single worst thing a query can do because it happens *for each row* from the preceding table: ten full table scans on table elem_names. Whenever you see type: ALL for a joined table, stop everything you're doing and fix it. There's a query metric for full joins: "Select full join" on page 21.

"Using join buffer (hash join)" in the Extra field refers to the hash join algorithm, which is new as of MySQL 8.0.18. I outline it (and other join algorithms) at the end of this chapter: "Table Join Algorithms" on page 87. Looking ahead, the one-line explanation is: hash join builds an in-memory hash table of values and uses that to lookup rows rather than doing repeated table scans. Hash join is a huge performance improvement. Regardless, avoiding full joins remains the best practice.

 Prior to MySQL 8.0, the query in Example 2-21 reports "Using join buffer (Block Nested Loop)" in the Extra field because it uses a different join algorithm: block nested-loop. "Table Join Algorithms" on page 87 outlines this join algorithm.

At first glance, joining tables appears to be a categorically different type of index usage, but it's not. A join involves more tables and indexes, but on a per-table basis, index usage and requirements are the same. Even the leftmost prefix requirement is the same. The main difference is that, for joined tables, values for join conditions come from the preceding table.

It's been a long read since the first example in "WHERE" on page 54. Now you've seen many full-context examples of indexes, queries, and EXPLAIN plans that cover the technical details and mechanics of MySQL indexes. This information is the foundation of direct query optimization on which the next section builds.

---

3 Strictly speaking, the index-only scan on table elem yields ten values, not rows, because full rows are not needed: only column a values are needed.

Indexing: How to Think Like MySQL

Indexes and indexing are different topics. The previous section introduced indexes: standard B-tree indexes on InnoDB tables for WHERE, GROUP BY, ORDER BY, covering indexes, and table joins. This section introduces *indexing*: applying indexes for maximum leverage. You cannot simply index every column to effect amazing performance. If it were that easy, there would be no DBAs. For maximum leverage, you have to index the columns that allow MySQL to access the least number of rows when executing a query. To state it metaphorically: maximum leverage is an index that tells MySQL exactly where to find the needle in the haystack.

In my experience, engineers struggle with indexing because they conflate how they think about a query with how MySQL "thinks" about a query. As engineers, we think about a query in the context of the application: what part of the application executes the query, why (the business logic), and the correct result set. But MySQL does not know or care about any of that. MySQL thinks about a much smaller, simpler context: indexes and table conditions. Under the hood, MySQL is considerably more complex, but part of its indeterminable charm is how well it hides that complexity.

How do we know that MySQL thinks about indexes and table conditions? EXPLAIN. And what is the primary information that EXPLAIN reports? Tables (in join order), table access methods, indexes, and Extra information related to the access of those tables with those indexes.

Thinking like MySQL make indexing easier because it's a deterministic machine—algorithms and heuristics. Human thought is entangled with superfluous details. Clear your mind and get ready to think like a machine. The next four sections walk through a simple, four-step process.

Know the Query

The first step toward thinking like MySQL is to know basic information about the query that you're optimizing. Start by gathering the following metadata for each table:

- SHOW CREATE TABLE
- SHOW TABLE STATUS
- SHOW INDEXES

If the query is already running in production, then get its query report (see "Query report" on page 10) and familiarize yourself with the current values.

Then answer the following questions:

Query
- How many rows should the query access?
- How many rows should the query return?
- Which columns are selected (returned)?
- What are the GROUP BY, ORDER BY, and LIMIT clauses (if any)?
- Are there subqueries? (If yes, repeat the process for each.)

Table access (per-table)
- What are the table conditions?
- Which index should the query use?
- What other indexes could the query use?
- What is the cardinality of each index?
- How large is the table—data size and row count?

Those questions help you mentally parse the query because that's what MySQL does: parse the query. This is especially helpful for seeing complex queries in simpler terms: tables, table conditions, indexes, and SQL clauses.

This information helps you piece together a puzzle that, once complete, reveals query response time. To improve response time, you'll need to change some pieces. But before doing that, the next step is to assemble the current pieces with the help of EXPLAIN.

Understand with EXPLAIN

The second step is to understand the current query execution plan reported by EXPLAIN. Consider each table and its conditions with respect to its indexes, starting with the index that MySQL chose: the key field in the EXPLAIN output. Look at the table conditions to see how they meet the leftmost prefix requirement for this index. If the possible_keys field lists other indexes, think about how MySQL would access rows using those indexes—always with the leftmost prefix requirement in mind. If the Extra field has information (it usually does), then refer to "EXPLAIN Output" (*https://oreil.ly/GDF0g*) in the MySQL manual to learn what it means.

 Always EXPLAIN the query. Make this a habit because direct query optimization is not possible without EXPLAIN.

The query and its response time are a puzzle, but you have all the pieces: execution plan, table conditions, table structures, table sizes, index cardinalities, and query metrics. Keep connecting the pieces until the puzzle is complete—until you can see the query working as MySQL explains it. There is always a reason for the query execution plan.[4] Sometimes MySQL is very clever and uses a nonobvious query optimization, usually mentioned in the Extra field. If you encounter one for a SELECT statement, "Optimizing SELECT Statements" (*https://oreil.ly/Bl4Ja*) in the MySQL manual will elucidate it.

If you get stuck, there are three increasing levels of support:

1. As of MySQL 8.0.16, EXPLAIN FORMAT=TREE prints a more precise and descriptive query execution plan in tree-like output. It's a completely different output than the traditional format, so you'll need to learn how to interpret it, but it's worth the effort.

2. Use optimizer tracing (*https://oreil.ly/Ump3C*) to report an extremely detailed query execution plan with costs, considerations, and reasons. This is a very advanced feature with a high learning curve, so if you're pressed for time, you might prefer the third option.

3. Ask your DBA or hire an expert.

Optimize the Query

The third step is direct query optimization: change the query, its indexes, or both. This is where all the fun happens, and there's no risk yet because these changes are made in development or staging, *not* production. Be certain that your development or staging environment has data that is representative of production because data size and distribution affect how MySQL chooses indexes.

At first, it might seem like the query cannot be modified because it fetches the correct rows, so the query is written correctly. A query "is what it is," right? Not always; the same *result* can be achieved with different *methods*. A query has a result—literally, a result set—and a method of obtaining that result. These two are closely related but independent. Knowing that is tremendously helpful when considering how to modify a query. Start by clarifying the intended result of the query. A clear result allows you to explore new ways of writing the query that achieve the same result.

---

4 Extremely rare query optimizer bugs notwithstanding.

There can be multiple ways to write a query that execute differently but return the same result.

For example, some time ago I was helping an engineer optimize a slow query. His question to me was technical—something about GROUP BY and indexes—but I asked him, "What does the query *do*? What's it supposed to return?" He said, "Oh! It returns the maximum value for a group." After clarifying the intended result of the query, I realized that he didn't need the maximum group value, he simply needed the maximum value. Consequently, the query was completely rewritten to use the ORDER BY col DESC LIMIT 1 optimization.

When a query is extremely simple, like SELECT col FROM tbl WHERE id = 1, there might truly be no way to rewrite it. But the simpler the query, the less likely it needs to be rewritten. If a simple query is slow, the solution is likely a change to indexes rather than the query. (And if index changes don't solve the problem, then the journey continues: *indirect* query optimization, addressed in Chapters 3 and 4.)

Adding or modifying a index is a trade-off between access methods and query-specific optimizations. For example, do you trade an ORDER BY optimization for a range scan? Don't get stuck trying to weigh the trade-offs; MySQL does that for you.[5] Your job is simple: add or alter an index that you think will provide MySQL greater leverage, then use EXPLAIN to see if MySQL agrees by using the new index. Repeat until you and MySQL agree on the most optimized way to write, index, and execute the query.

Do not modify indexes in production until you have thoroughly verified the changes in staging.

Deploy and Verify

The last step is to deploy the changes and verify that they improve response time. But first: know how to roll back the deployment—and be ready to do so—in case the changes have unintended side effects. This happens for many reasons; two examples are: queries running in production that use the index but were not running in

---

5 Try to outsmart MySQL if you're bored, but don't expect to win. It has seen attack ships on fire off the shoulder of Orion. It watched C-beams glitter in the dark near the Tannhäuser Gate.

staging, or production data that is significantly different than staging data. It's most likely going to be fine, but be prepared for *not fine*.

 Always know how to—and be ready to—roll back a deployment to production.

After deploying, verify the changes with query metrics and MySQL server metrics. If the query optimization has significant impact, MySQL server metrics will reflect it. (Chapter 6 elaborates on MySQL server metrics.) It's awesome when this happens, but don't be surprised or discouraged if it doesn't because the most important change is query response time—recall "North Star" on page 3.

Wait five to ten minutes (preferably longer), then check response time in the query profile and query report. (See "Query profile" on page 9 and "Query report" on page 10.) If response time improved, then congratulations: you are doing and accomplishing what MySQL experts do; with this skill, you can achieve remarkable MySQL performance. If response time did not improve, don't worry and don't give up: even MySQL experts encounter queries that require elbow grease. Repeat the process, and consider enlisting another engineer because some queries require heavy lifting. If you're certain the query cannot be further optimized, then it's time for the second part of the journey: indirect query optimization. Chapter 3 addresses changes to data, and Chapter 4 addresses changes to the application.

It Was a Good Index Until...

If *nothing* changes, a good index will stay a good index until the end of time. (But if truly nothing changes, would time ever end?) Realistically, something will change, render a good index bad, and decrease performance. Following are common causes of this regrettable (but avoidable and correctable) decline.

Queries Changed

When queries change—and they often do—the leftmost prefix requirement can be lost. The worst case is when there are no other indexes that MySQL can use, so it reverts to brute force: a full table scan. But tables often have many indexes, and MySQL is determined to use an index, so the more likely case is that query response time becomes noticeably poor because the other indexes aren't as good as the original index. A query analysis and EXPLAIN plan quickly reveal this case. Presuming the query changes were necessary, which is a safe presumption, the solution is to re-index for the new variation of the query.

Excessive, Duplicate, and Unused

Indexes are necessary for performance, but sometimes engineers go overboard with them, which results in too many indexes, duplicate indexes (*dupes*), and unused indexes.

How many indexes is too many? One more than is necessary. An overabundance of indexes creates two problems. The first was mentioned in "Leftmost Prefix Requirement" on page 49: increased index size. More indexes use more RAM which, ironically, decreases the RAM available for each index. The second problem is a decrease in write performance because, when MySQL writes data, it must check, update, and potentially reorganize (the internal B-tree structure of) every index. An inordinate number of indexes can severely degrade write performance.

When you create a duplicate index, the ALTER statement used to create it generates a warning, but you have to SHOW WARNINGS to see it. To find existing duplicate indexes, use pt-duplicate-key-checker (*https://oreil.ly/avm4L*): it safely finds and reports duplicate indexes.

Unused indexes are even trickier to identify because, for example, what if the index is only used once a week by a long-running analytics query? That edge case aside, execute this query to list unused indexes:

```
SELECT * FROM sys.schema_unused_indexes
WHERE object_schema NOT IN ('performance_schema');
```

That query uses the MySQL sys Schema (*https://oreil.ly/xxsL3*), which is a collection of ready-made views that return all sorts of information. The view sys.schema_unused_indexes queries Performance Schema and Information Schema tables to determine which indexes have not been used since MySQL started. (Execute SHOW CREATE VIEW sys.schema_unused_indexes to see how this view works.) The Performance Schema must be enabled; if it is not already enabled, talk with your DBA (or whoever manages MySQL) because enabling it requires restarting MySQL.

Be careful when dropping an index. As of MySQL 8.0, use invisible indexes (*https://oreil.ly/Wx1xT*) to verify that an index is not used or needed before dropping it: make the index invisible, wait and verify that performance is not affected, then drop the index. Invisible indexes are fantastic for this purpose because, when a mistake is made, making an index visible is nearly instantaneous, whereas re-adding an index can take minutes (or hours) on large tables, which feels like an eternity if the mistake causes an application outage. Before MySQL 8.0, caution is the only solution: talk with your team, search the application code, and use your knowledge of the application to carefully and thoroughly verify that the index is not used or needed.

Be careful when dropping (removing) indexes. If a dropped index was used by a query and MySQL cannot use another index, the query will revert to a full table scan. If a dropped index affects several queries, which is not uncommon, it can cause a ripple effect of performance degradation that leads to an application outage.

Extreme Selectivity

Cardinality is the number of unique values in an index. An index on values a, a, b, b has a cardinality of 2: a and b are the two unique values. Use SHOW INDEX (*https://oreil.ly/8hiGi*) to see index cardinality.

Selectivity is cardinality divided by the number of rows in the table. Using the same example, a, a, b, b, where each value is one row, the index selectivity is 2 / 4 = 0.5. Selectivity ranges from 0 to 1, where 1 is a unique index: a value for every row. MySQL doesn't show index selectivity; you have to calculate it manually using SHOW INDEX for cardinality and SHOW TABLE STATUS for the number of rows.

An index with extremely low selectivity provides little leverage because each unique value could match a large number of rows. A classic example is an index on a column with only two possible values: yes or no, true or false, coffee or tea, on so on. If the table has 100,000 rows, then selectivity is practically zero: 2 / 100,000 = 0.00002. It's an index, but not a good one because each value could match many rows. How many? Flip the division: 100,000 rows / 2 unique values = 50,000 rows per value. If MySQL were to use this index (which is unlikely), a single index lookup could match 50,000 rows. That presumes values are evenly distributed, but what if 99,999 rows have value coffee and only 1 row has value tea? Then the index works great for tea but terribly for coffee.

If a query uses an index with extremely low selectivity, see if you can create a better, more selective index; or, consider rewriting the query to use a more selective index; or, think about altering the schema to organize the data better with respect to access patterns—more on this in Chapter 4.

An index with extremely high selectivity might be over-leveraged. As the selectivity of a nonunique secondary index approaches 1, it begins to raise the question of whether or not the index should be unique or—even better—if the query can be rewritten to use the primary key. Such an index doesn't hurt performance, but it's worth exploring alternatives.

If there are many secondary indexes with extremely high selectivity, it likely indicates access patterns that view or search the whole table by different criteria or dimensions (presuming the indexes are used and not duplicates). For example: imagine a table with product inventory that the application searches by many different criteria, each requiring an index to meet the leftmost prefix requirement. In this case, Elasticsearch (*https://www.elastic.co*) might serve the access patterns better than MySQL.

It's a Trap! (When MySQL Chooses Another Index)

In very rare cases, MySQL chooses the wrong index. This is rare enough that it should be your last suspicion if MySQL is using an index but query response time is inexplicably slow. There are several reasons this can occur. A common reason is that, when updating a large number of rows, the number is just shy of triggering an automatic update of the index "stats." Since index statistics are one of many factors that influence which index MySQL chooses, index statistics that have diverged significantly from reality can cause MySQL to choose the wrong index. To be clear: the index itself is never inaccurate; it's only the index *statistics* that are inaccurate.

Index statistics are estimates about how values are distributed in the index. MySQL does random dives into the index to sample pages. (A *page* is a 16 KB unit of logical storage. Almost everything is stored in pages.) If index values are evenly distributed, then a few random dives accurately represent the whole index.

MySQL updates index statistics for a table when:

- The table is first opened
- `ANALYZE TABLE` is run
- 1/16th of the table has been modified since the last update
- `innodb_stats_on_metadata` is enabled and one of the following occurs:
  — `SHOW INDEX` or `SHOW TABLE STATUS` is run
  — `INFORMATION_SCHEMA.TABLES` or `INFORMATION_SCHEMA.STATISTICS` is queried

Running `ANALYZE TABLE` is safe and usually very fast, but be careful on a busy server: it requires a flush lock (except in Percona Server) that can block all queries accessing the table.

Table Join Algorithms

A brief overview of MySQL table join algorithms helps you think about indexes and indexing when analyzing and optimizing `JOIN`. The default table join algorithm is called *nested-loop join* (NLJ), and it operates like nested `foreach` loops in code. For example, suppose that a query joins three tables with a `JOIN` clause like:

```
FROM
    t1 JOIN t2 ON t1.A = t2.B
        JOIN t3 ON t2.B = t3.C
```

And suppose that EXPLAIN reports the join order as t1, t2, and t3. The nested-loop join algorithm works like the pseudocode in Example 2-22.

Example 2-22. NLJ algorithm

```
func find_rows(table, index, conditions) []rows {
    // Return array of rows in table matching conditions,
    // using index for lookup or table scan if NULL
}

foreach find_rows(t1, some_index, "WHERE ...") {
    foreach find_rows(t2, index_on_B, "WHERE B = <t1.A>") {
        return find_rows(t3, NULL, "WHERE C = <t2.B>")
    }
}
```

Using the NLJ algorithm, MySQL begins by using some_index to find matching rows in the outermost table: t1. For each matching row in table t1, MySQL joins table t2 by using an index on the join column, index_on_B, to lookup rows matching t1.A. For each matching row in table t2, MySQL joins table t3 using the same process, but—just for fun—let's say there's no index on the join column, t3.C: the result is a full join. (Recall "Select full join" on page 21 and Example 2-21.)

When no more rows in t3 match the join column value from table t2, the next matching row from t2 is used. When no more rows in t2 match the join column value from table t1, the next matching row from t1 is used. When no more rows in t1 match, the query completes.

The nested-loop join algorithm is simple and effective, but there's one problem: the innermost table is accessed very frequently, and the full join makes that access very slow. In this example, table t3 is accessed for every matching row in t1 multiplied by every matching row in t2. If both t1 and t2 have 10 matching rows, then t3 is accessed 100 times. The *block nested-loop* join algorithm addresses this problem. Join column values from matching rows in t1 and t2 are saved in a *join buffer*. (The join buffer size is set by system variable join_buffer_size (*https://oreil.ly/r1NeH*).) When the join buffer is full, MySQL scans t3 and joins each t3 row that matches join column values in the join buffer. Although the join buffer is accessed many times (for each t3 row), it's fast because it's in memory—significantly faster than 100 table scans required for the NLJ algorithm.

As of MySQL 8.0.20, the hash join algorithm replaces the block nested-loop join algorithm.[6] *Hash join* creates an in-memory hash table of join tables, like table t3 in

---

6 Hash join exists as of MySQL 8.0.18 but replaces block nested-loop as of MySQL 8.0.20.

this example. MySQL uses the hash table to look up rows in the join table, which is extremely fast because a hash table lookup is a constant time operation. For details, read "Hash Join Optimization" (*https://oreil.ly/uS0s3*) in the MySQL manual.

 EXPLAIN indicates a hash join by printing "Using join buffer (hash join)" in the Extra field.

There are more details and nuances to MySQL joins, but this brief overview helps you to think about joins like MySQL: one table at a time and one index per table.

Summary

This chapter taught indexes and indexing with MySQL. The key takeaway points are:

- Indexes provide the most and the best leverage for MySQL performance.
- Do not scale up hardware to improve performance until exhausting other options.
- Tuning MySQL is not necessary to improve performance with a reasonable configuration.
- An InnoDB table is a B-tree index organized by the primary key.
- MySQL accesses a table by index lookup, index scan, or full table scan—index lookup is the best access method.
- To use an index, a query must use a leftmost prefix of the index—the *leftmost prefix requirement*.
- MySQL uses an index to find rows matching WHERE, group rows for GROUP BY, sort rows for ORDER BY, avoid reading rows (covering index), and join tables.
- EXPLAIN prints a *query execution plan* (or *EXPLAIN plan*) that details how MySQL executes a query.
- Indexing requires thinking like MySQL to understand the query execution plan.
- Good indexes can lose effectiveness for a variety of reasons.
- MySQL uses three algorithms to join tables: NLJ, block nested-loop, and hash join.

The next chapter begins to address indirect query optimization with respect to data.

Practice: Find Duplicate Indexes

The goal of this practice is to identify duplicate indexes using pt-duplicate-key-checker (*https://oreil.ly/Oxvjr*): a command-line tool that prints duplicate indexes.

The practice is simple but useful: download and run `pt-duplicate-key-checker`. By default, it checks all tables and prints a report for each duplicate index, such as the following:

```
# #####################################################################
# db_name.table_name
# #####################################################################

# idx_a is a left-prefix of idx_a_b
# Key definitions:
#   KEY `idx_a` (`a`),
#   KEY `idx_a_b` (`a`,`b`)
# Column types:
#         `a` int(11) default null
#         `b` int(11) default null
# To remove this duplicate index, execute:
ALTER TABLE `db_name`.`table_name` DROP INDEX `idx_a`;
```

For each index and its duplicate, the report includes:

- A reason: why one index duplicates the other
- Both index definitions
- Column definitions that the indexes cover
- An `ALTER TABLE` statement to drop the duplicate index

pt-duplicate-key-checker is mature and well tested, but always think carefully before dropping an index—especially in production.

Like "Practice: Identify Slow Queries" on page 33, this practice is simple—but you would be surprised how many engineers never check for duplicate indexes. Checking for and removing duplicate indexes is practicing MySQL performance like an expert.

## CHAPTER 3

Data

This chapter begins the second part of the journey: *indirect query optimization*. As mentioned in "Improving Query Response Time" on page 27, direct query optimization solves a lot of problems, but not all. Even when you surpass the knowledge and skills in Chapter 2, which focuses on direct query optimization, you will encounter queries that are simple and properly indexed but still slow. That's when you begin to optimize *around* the query, starting with the data that it accesses. To understand why, let's think about rocks.

Imagine that your job is to move rocks, and you have three piles of different sized rocks. The first pile contains pebbles: very light, no larger than your thumbnail. The second pile contains cobbles: heavy but light enough to pick up, no larger than your head. The third pile contains boulders: too large and heavy to pick up; you need leverage or a machine to move them. Your job is to move one pile from the bottom of a hill to the top (no matter why; but if it helps, imagine that you're Sisyphus). Which pile do you choose?

I presume that you choose the pebbles because they're light and easy to move. But there's a critical detail that might change your decision: weight. The pile of pebbles weighs two metric tons (the weight of a mid-size SUV). The pile of cobbles weighs one metric ton (the weight of a very small car). And there's only one boulder that weighs half a metric ton (the weight of ten adult humans). Now which pile do you choose?

On the one hand, the pebbles are still a lot easier to move. You can shovel them into a wheelbarrow and roll it up the hill. There's just a lot of them (pebbles, not wheelbarrows). The boulder is a fraction of the weight, but its singular size makes it unwieldy. Special equipment is need to move it up the hill, but it's a one-time task. Tough decision. Chapter 5 provides an answer and an explanation, but we have much more to cover before that chapter.

Data is analogous to a pile of rocks, and executing queries is analogous to moving the rocks uphill. When data size is small, direct query optimization is usually sufficient because the data is trivial to handle—like walking (or running) up a hill with a handful of pebbles. But as data size increases, indirect query optimization becomes increasingly important—like lugging a heavy cobble up a hill and stopping midway to ask, "Can we do something about these rocks?"

Chapter 1 provided a "proof" that data size affects performance: TRUNCATE TABLE dramatically increases performance—but don't use this "optimization." That's a joke, but it also proves a point that is not frequently followed through to its logical consequence: *less data is more performance*. That's the tagline; the full statement is: you can improve performance by reducing data because less data requires fewer system resources (CPU, memory, storage, and so on).

You can tell by now that this chapter is going to argue for *less* data. But isn't *more* data the reality and reason that drives engineers to learn about performance optimization? Yes, and Chapter 5 addresses MySQL at scale, but first it's imperative to learn to reduce and optimize data when it's relatively small and problems are tractable. The most stressful time to learn is when you've ignored data size until it's crushing the application.

This chapter examines data with respect to performance and argues that reducing data access and storage is a technique—an indirect query optimization—for improving performance. There are three major sections. The first reveals three secrets about MySQL performance. The second introduces what I call the *principle of least data* and its numerous implications. The third covers how to quickly *and safely* delete or archive data.

Three Secrets

To keep a secret is to conceal a truth. The following truths are not always revealed in books about MySQL performance for two reasons. First, they complicate matters. It's a lot easier to write about and explain performance without mentioning the caveats and gotchas. Second, they're counterintuitive. That doesn't make them false, but it does make them difficult to clarify. Nevertheless, the following truths are important for MySQL performance, so let's dig into the details with an open mind.

Indexes May Not Help

Ironically, you can expect the majority of slow queries to use an index lookup. That's ironic for two reasons. First, indexes are the key to performance, but a query can be slow even with a good index. Second, after learning about indexes and indexing (as discussed in Chapter 2), engineers become so good at avoiding index scans and table scans that only index lookups remain, which is a good problem but ironic nonetheless.

Performance cannot be achieved without indexes, but that doesn't mean that indexes provide infinite leverage for infinite data size. Don't lose faith in indexes, but be aware of the following cases in which indexes may not help. For each case, presuming the query and its indexes cannot be optimized any further, the next step is indirect query optimization.

Index scan

An index scan provides diminishing leverage as a table grows because the index also grows: more table rows, more index values.[1] (By contrast, the leverage that an index lookup provides almost never diminishes as long as the index fits in memory.) Even an index-only scan tends not to scale because it almost certainly reads a large number of values—a safe presumption because MySQL would have done an index lookup to read fewer rows if possible. An index scan only delays the inevitable: as the number of rows in the table increases, response time for queries that use an index scan also increases.

Finding rows

When I optimize a slow query that uses an index lookup, the first query metric I check is rows examined (see "Rows examined" on page 18). Finding matching rows is the fundamental purpose of a query, but even with a good index, a query can examine too many rows. *Too many* is the point at which response time becomes unacceptable (and the root cause is not something else, like insufficient memory or disk IOPS). This happens because several index lookup access types can match many rows. Only the access types listed in Table 3-1 match *at most* one row.

Table 3-1. Index lookup access types that match at most one row

☐ system

☐ const

☐ eq_ref

☐ unique_subquery

If the type field in an EXPLAIN plan is not one of the access types listed in Table 3-1, then pay close attention to the rows field and the query metric rows examined (see "Rows examined" on page 18). Examining a very large number of rows is slow regardless of the index lookup.

---

1 MySQL does not support sparse or partial indexes.

"EXPLAIN Output Format" (*https://oreil.ly/8dkRy*) in the MySQL manual enumerates access types, which it calls *join types* because MySQL treats every query as a join. In this book, for precision and consistency I use only two terms: *access method* and *access type*, as written throughout Chapter 2.

Very low index selectivity is a likely accomplice. Recall "Extreme Selectivity" on page 86: index selectivity is cardinality divided by the number of rows in the table. MySQL is unlikely to chose an index with very low selectivity because it can match too many rows. Since secondary indexes require a second lookup in the primary key to read rows, it can be faster to eschew an index with extremely low selectivity and do a full table scan instead—presuming there's no better index. You can detect this in an EXPLAIN plan when the access method is a table scan (`type: ALL`) but there are indexes that MySQL could use (`possible_keys`). To see the execution plan that MySQL is not choosing, EXPLAIN the query with FORCE INDEX (*https://oreil.ly/nv1uy*) to use an index listed in the `possible_keys` field. Most likely, the resulting execution plan will be an index scan (`type: index`) with a large number of `rows`, which is why MySQL chooses a table scan instead.

 Recall "It's a Trap! (When MySQL Chooses Another Index)" on page 87: in very rare cases, MySQL chooses the wrong index. If a query examines too many rows but you're certain there's a better index that MySQL should use, there's a small chance that the index statistics are wrong, which causes MySQL to not choose the better index. Run ANALYZE TABLE to update index statistics.

Remember that index selectivity is a function of cardinality and the number of rows in the table. If cardinality remains constant but the number of rows increases, then selectivity decreases. Consequently, an index that helped when the table was small may not help when the table is huge.

Joining tables

When joining tables, a few rows in each table quickly obliterate performance. If you recall from "Table Join Algorithms" on page 87, the nested-loop join (NLJ) algorithm (Example 2-22) entails that the total number of rows accessed for a join is the product of rows accessed for each table. In other words, multiply the values for `rows` in an EXPLAIN plan. A three-table join with only one hundred rows per table can access one *million* rows: $100 \times 100 \times 100 = 1,000,000$. To avoid this, the index lookup on each table joined should match only one row—one of the access types listed in Table 3-1 is best.

MySQL can join tables in almost any order. Use this to your advantage: sometimes the solution to a poor join is a better index on another table that allows MySQL to change the join order.

Without an index lookup, a table join is doomed. The result is a full join, as fore-warned in "Select full join" on page 21. But even with an index, a table join will struggle if the index does not match a single row.

Working set size

Indexes are only useful when they're in memory. If the index values that a query looks up are not in memory, then MySQL reads them from disk. (More accurately, the B-tree nodes that constitute the index are stored in 16 KB pages, and MySQL swaps pages between memory and disk as needed.) Reading from disk is orders of magnitude slower than reading from memory, which is one problem, but the main problem is that indexes compete for memory.

If memory is limited but indexes are numerous and frequently used to look up a large percentage of values (relative to the table size), then index usage can increase storage I/O as MySQL attempts to keep frequently used index values in memory. This is possible but rare for two reasons. First, MySQL is exceptionally good at keeping frequently used index values in memory. Second, frequently used index values and the primary key rows to which they refer are called the *working set*, and it's usually a small percentage of the table size. For example, a database can be 500 GB large, but the application frequently accesses only 1 GB of data. In light of this fact, MySQL DBAs commonly allocate memory for only 10% of total data size, usually rounded to standard memory values (64 GB, 128 GB, and so forth). 10% of 500 GB is 50 GB, so a DBA would probably err on the side of caution and round up to 64 GB of memory. This works surpassingly well and is a good starting point.

As a starting point, allocate memory for 10% of total data size. The working set size is usually a small percentage of total data size.

When the working set size becomes significantly larger than available memory, indexes may not help. Instead, like a fire that burns so hot that water fuels it rather than extinguishing it, index usage puts pressure on storage I/O and everything slows down. More memory is a quick fix, but remember "Better, Faster Hardware!" on page 37: scaling up is not a sustainable approach. The best solution is to address the data size and access patterns responsible for the large working set. If the application truly needs to store and access so much data that the working set size cannot fit within a reasonable amount of memory on a single MySQL instance, then the solution is sharding, which is covered in Chapter 5.

Less Data Is Better

Experienced engineers don't celebrate a huge database, they cope with it. They celebrate when data size is dramatically reduced because less data is better. Better for what? Everything: performance, management, cost, and so on. It's simply a lot faster, easier, and cheaper to deal with 100 GB of data than 100 *TB* on a single MySQL instance. The former is so small that a smartphone can handle it. The latter requires specialized handling: optimizing performance is more challenging, managing the data can be risky (what's the backup and restore time?), and good luck finding affordable hardware for 100 TB. It's easier to keep data size reasonable than to cope with a huge database.

Any amount of data that's legitimately required is worth the time and effort to optimize and manage. The problem is less about data size and more about unbridled data growth. It's not uncommon for engineers to hoard data: storing any and all data. If you're thinking, "Not me. I don't hoard data," then wonderful. But your colleagues may not share your laudable sense of data asceticism. If not, raise the issue of unbridled data growth before data size becomes a problem.

 Don't let an unwieldy database catch you by surprise. Monitor data size (see "Data Size" on page 204) and, based on the current rate of growth, estimate data size for the next four years. If future data size is not feasible with the current hardware and application design, then address the issue now before it becomes a problem.

Less QPS Is Better

You may never find another book or engineer that says *less* QPS is better. Cherish the moment.

I realize that this secret is counterintuitive, perhaps even unpopular. To see its truth and wisdom, consider three less objectionable points about QPS:

QPS is only a number—a measurement of raw throughput
It reveals nothing qualitative about the queries or performance in general. One application can be effectively idle at 10,000 QPS, while another is overloaded and having an outage at half that throughput. Even at the same QPS, there are numerous qualitative differences. Executing SELECT 1 at 1,000 QPS requires almost zero system resources, but a complex query at the same QPS could be very taxing on all system resources. And high QPS—no matter how high—is only as good as query response time.

QPS values have no objective meaning

They're neither good nor bad, high nor low, typical nor atypical. QPS values are only meaningful relative to an application. If one application averages 2,000 QPS, then 100 QPS could be a precipitous drop that indicates a outage. But if another application averages 300 QPS, then 100 QPS could be a normal fluctuation. QPS can also be relative to external events: time of day, day of week, seasons, holidays, and so on.

It is difficult to increase QPS

By contrast, data size can increase with relative ease from 1 GB to 100 GB—a 100x increase. But it's incredibly difficult to increase QPS by 100x (except for extremely low values, like 1 QPS to 100 QPS). Even a 2x increase in QPS can be very challenging to achieve. Maximum QPS—relative to an application—is even more challenging to increase because you cannot purchase more QPS, unlike storage and memory.

In summary of these points: QPS is not qualitative, only relative to an application, and difficult to increase. To put a point on it: *QPS does not help you*. It's more of a liability than an asset. Therefore, less QPS is better.

Experienced engineers celebrate when QPS is reduced (intentionally) because less QPS is more capacity for growth.

Principle of Least Data

I define the principle of least data as: *store and access only needed data*. That sounds obvious in theory, but it's far from the norm in practice. It's also deceptively simple, which is why the next two sections have many fine details.

> Common sense is not so common.
>
>   —Voltaire

Data Access

Do not access more data than needed. *Access* refers to all the work that MySQL does to execute a query: find matching rows, process matching rows, and return the result set—for both reads (`SELECT`) and writes. Efficient data access is especially important for writes because it's more difficult to scale writes.

Table 3-2 is a checklist that you can apply to a query—hopefully every query—to verify its data access efficiency.

Table 3-2. Efficient data access checklist

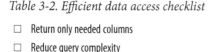

☐   Return only needed columns
☐   Reduce query complexity
☐   Limit row access
☐   Limit the result set
☐   Avoid sorting rows

To be fair and balanced, ignoring a single checklist item is unlikely to affect performance. For example, the fifth item—avoid sorting rows—is commonly ignored without affecting performance. These items are best practices. If you practice them until they become habit, you will have greater success and performance with MySQL than engineers who ignore them completely.

Before I explain each item in Table 3-2, let's take one paragraph to revisit an example in Chapter 1 that I deferred to this chapter.

Perhaps you recall this example from "Query profile" on page 9: "As I write this, I'm looking at a query with load 5,962. How is that possible?" That query load is possible thanks to *incredibly* efficient data access and an extremely busy application. The query is like `SELECT col1, col2 WHERE pk_col = 5`: a primary key look up that returns only two columns from a single row. When data access is that efficient, MySQL functions *almost* like an in-memory cache, and it executes the query at incredible QPS and query load. *Almost*, but not entirely, because every query is a transaction that entails overhead. (Chapter 8 focuses on transactions.) To optimize a query like this, you must change access patterns because the query cannot be optimized any further and the data size cannot be reduced. I revisit this query one more time in Chapter 4.

Return only needed columns

Queries should return only needed columns.

Do not `SELECT *`. This is especially important if the table has any `BLOB`, `TEXT`, or `JSON` columns.

You've probably heard this best practice before because the database industry (not just MySQL) has been harping on it for decades. I can't recall the last time I saw `SELECT *` in production, but it's important enough to keep repeating.

Reduce query complexity

Queries should be as simple as possible.

Query complexity refers to all tables, conditions, and SQL clauses that constitute a query. In this context, complexity is relative only to a query, not to engineers. Query `SELECT col FROM tbl WHERE id = 1` is less complex than a query that joins five tables with many `WHERE` conditions.

Complex queries are a problem for engineers, not MySQL. The more complex a query, the more difficult it is to analyze and optimize. If you're lucky, a complex query works well and never shows up as a slow query (see "Query profile" on page 9). But luck is not a best practice. Keep queries simple from the start (when first written), and reduce query complexity when possible.

With respect to data access, simple queries tend to access less data because they have fewer tables, conditions, and SQL clauses—less work for MySQL. But be careful: the wrong simplification can yield a worse EXPLAIN plan. For example, Figure 2-21 in Chapter 2 demonstrates how removing a condition negates an `ORDER BY` optimization, resulting in a (slightly) worse EXPLAIN plan. Always confirm that a simpler query has an equivalent or better EXPLAIN plan—and the same result set.

Limit row access

Queries should access as few rows as possible.

Accessing too many rows usually comes as a surprise; it's not something engineers do intentionally. Data growth over time is a common cause: a fast query starts by accessing a few rows, but years and gigabytes later, it becomes a slow query because it accesses too many rows. Simple mistakes are another cause: an engineer writes a query that they think will access a few rows, but they're wrong. At the intersection of data growth and simple mistakes is the most important cause: *not limiting ranges and lists.* An open-ended range like `col > 75` can access countless rows if MySQL does a range scan on `col`. Even if this is intended because the table is presumed to be small, be aware that row access is virtually unbounded as the table grows, especially if the index on `col` is nonunique.

A `LIMIT` clause does not limit row access because `LIMIT` applies to the result set *after* matching rows. The exception is the `ORDER BY...LIMIT` optimization: if MySQL can access rows in index order, then it stops reading rows when the `LIMIT` number of matching rows are found. But here's the fun part: EXPLAIN does not report when this optimization is used. You must infer the optimization from what an EXPLAIN does and does not report. Let's take a moment to see this optimization in action and prove that it limits row access.

Using table `elem` (Example 2-1) from Chapter 2, let's first execute a query that does not have a `LIMIT` clause. Example 3-1 shows that the query returns eight rows.

Example 3-1. Rows for query without LIMIT

```
SELECT * FROM elem WHERE a > 'Ag' ORDER BY a;

+----+----+----+----+
| id | a  | b  | c  |
+----+----+----+----+
|  8 | Al | B  | Cd |
|  9 | Al | B  | Cd |
|  3 | Al | Br | Cr |
| 10 | Ar | B  | Cd |
|  4 | Ar | Br | Cd |
|  5 | Ar | Br | C  |
|  7 | At | Bi | Ce |
|  2 | Au | Be | Co |
+----+----+----+----+
8 rows in set (0.00 sec)
```

Without a LIMIT clause, the query accesses (and returns) eight rows. Accordingly, EXPLAIN reports rows: 8 even with a LIMIT 2 clause—as shown in Example 3-2— because MySQL cannot know how many rows in the range will *not* match until it executes the query. Worst case: MySQL reads all rows because none match. But for this simple example, we can see that the first two rows (id values 8 and 9) will match the only table condition. If we're right, query metrics will report two rows examined, not eight. But first, let's see how to infer the optimization from the EXPLAIN plan in Example 3-2.

Example 3-2. EXPLAIN plan for ORDER BY...LIMIT optimization

```
EXPLAIN SELECT * FROM elem WHERE a > 'Ag' ORDER BY a LIMIT 2\G

*************************** 1. row ***************************
           id: 1
  select_type: SIMPLE
        table: elem
   partitions: NULL
         type: range
possible_keys: a
          key: a
      key_len: 8
          ref: NULL
         rows: 8
     filtered: 100.00
        Extra: Using index condition
```

You can infer that MySQL uses the ORDER BY...LIMIT optimization to access only two rows (LIMIT 2) because:

- The query uses an index (type: range)
- The ORDER BY column is a leftmost prefix of that index (key: a)
- The Extra field does *not* report "Using filesort"

The proof is shown in Example 3-3: a snippet of the slow query log after MySQL executed the query.

Example 3-3. Query metrics for ORDER BY...LIMIT optimization

```
# Query_time: 0.000273  Lock_time: 0.000114  Rows_sent: 2  Rows_examined: 2
SELECT * FROM elem WHERE a > 'Ag' ORDER BY a LIMIT 2;
```

Rows_examined: 2 at the end of the first line in Example 3-3 proves that MySQL used the ORDER BY...LIMIT optimization to access only two rows instead of all eight rows. To learn more about this query optimization, read "LIMIT Query Optimization" (*https://oreil.ly/AnurD*) in the MySQL manual.

With respect to limiting ranges and lists, there's an important factor to verify: *does the application limit the input used in a query?* Way back in "Average, Percentile, and Maximum" on page 25, I related a story: "Long story short, the query was used to look up data for fraud detection, and occasionally a big case would look up several thousand rows at once, which caused MySQL to switch query execution plans." In that case, the solution was simple: limit application input to one thousand values per request. That case also highlights the fact that a human can input a flood of values. Normally, engineers are careful to limit input when the user is another computer, but their caution relaxes when the user is another human because they think a human wouldn't or couldn't input too many values. But they're wrong: with copy-paste and a looming deadline, the average human can overload any computer.

For writes, limiting row access is critical because, generally speaking, InnoDB locks every row that it accesses before it updates matching rows. Consequently, InnoDB can lock more rows than you might expect. "Row Locking" on page 260 goes into detail.

For table joins, limiting row access is also critical: recall from "Joining tables" on page 94 that, on join, a few rows in each table quickly obliterates performance. In that section, I was pointing out that a table join is doomed without an index lookup. In this section, I'm pointing out that a table join is double-doomed unless it also accesses *very* few rows. Remember: an index lookup on a nonunique index can access any number of duplicate rows.

Know your access patterns: for each query, what limits row access? Use EXPLAIN to see estimated row access (the rows field), and monitor rows examined (see "Rows examined" on page 18) to avoid the surprise of accessing too many rows.

Limit the result set

Queries should return as few rows as possible.

This is more involved than putting a `LIMIT` clause on a query, although that certainly helps. It refers to the application not using the entire *result set*: the rows returned by a query. This problem has three variations.

The first variation occurs when the application uses some rows, but not all. This can be done intentionally or unintentionally. Unintentionally, it indicates that the `WHERE` clause needs better (or more) conditions to match only needed rows. You can spot this in application code that filters rows instead of using `WHERE` conditions. If you spot this, talk with your team to make sure it's not intentional. Intentionally, an application might select more rows to avoid a complex query by shifting row matching from MySQL to the application. This technique is useful only when it reduces response time—akin to MySQL choosing a table scan in rare cases.

The second variation occurs when a query has an `ORDER BY` clause and the application uses an ordered subset of rows. Row order doesn't matter for the first variation, but it's the defining characteristic of the second variation. For example, a query returns 1,000 rows but the application only uses the first 20 rows in order. In this case, the solution might be as simple as adding a `LIMIT 20` clause to the query.

What does the application do with the remaining 980 rows? If those rows are never used, then definitely the query should not return them—add the `LIMIT 20` clause. But if those rows are used, then the application is most likely paginating: using 20 rows at a time (for example, showing 20 results per page). In that case, it might be faster and more efficient to use `LIMIT 20 OFFSET N` to fetch pages on demand—where N = 20 × (page number − 1)—only if the `ORDER BY...LIMIT` optimization can be used (see the previous section, "Limit row access" on page 99). The optimization is required because, without it, MySQL must find and sort all matching rows before it can apply the `OFFSET` part of the `LIMIT` clause—a lot of wasted work to return only 20 rows. But even without the optimization, there's another solution: a large but reasonable `LIMIT` clause. If, for example, you measure application usage and find that most requests only use the first five pages, then use a `LIMIT 100` clause to fetch the first five pages and reduce the result set size by 90% for most requests.

The third variation occurs when the application *only* aggregates the result set. If the application aggregates the result set *and* uses the individual rows, that's acceptable. The antipattern is *only* aggregating the result set instead of using a SQL aggregate function, which limits the result set. Table 3-3 lists four antipatterns and corresponding SQL solutions.

Table 3-3. Four result set antipatterns in an application

Antipattern in Application	Solution in SQL
Adding a column value	`SUM(column)`
Counting the number of rows	`COUNT(*)`
Counting the number of values	`COUNT(column)...GROUP BY column`
Counting the number of distinct values	`COUNT(DISTINCT column)`
Extracting distinct values	`DISTINCT`

Adding a column value applies to other statistical functions: `AVG()`, `MAX()`, `MIN()`, and so on. Let MySQL do the calculation rather than returning the rows.

Counting the number of rows is an extreme antipattern, but I've seen it, so I'm sure there are other applications quietly wasting network bandwidth on needless rows. Never use the application only to count rows; use `COUNT(*)` in the query.

 As of MySQL 8.0.14, `SELECT COUNT(*) FROM table` (without a `WHERE` clause) uses multiple threads to read the primary key in parallel. This is not parallel query execution; the MySQL manual calls it "parallel clustered index reads."

Counting the number of values is, perhaps, easier for programmers to express in code than a SQL `GROUP BY` clause, but the latter should be used to limit the result set. Using table `elem` (Example 2-1) again, Example 3-4 demonstrates how to count the number of values for a column using `COUNT(column)...GROUP BY column`.

Example 3-4. Counting the number of values

```
SELECT a, COUNT(a) FROM elem GROUP BY a;
```

```
+----+----------+
| a  | COUNT(a) |
+----+----------+
| Ag |        2 |
| Al |        3 |
| Ar |        3 |
| At |        1 |
| Au |        1 |
+----+----------+
```

For column `a` in table `elem`, two rows have value "Ag," three rows have value "Al," and so forth. The SQL solution returns five rows, whereas the antipattern would return all ten rows. These aren't dramatic numbers—five versus ten rows—but they make the point: a query can limit its result set by aggregating in SQL, not application code.

COUNT(*) Versus COUNT(column)

COUNT(*) counts the number of matching rows—the result set size. COUNT(column) counts the number of non-NULL values in the column of the matching rows. When COUNT(column) is used with other columns (including itself), you need a GROUP BY clause for proper aggregation, as shown in Example 3-4.

Extracting distinct values—deduplicating column values—is trivial in the application with an associative array; but MySQL can do it, too, with DISTINCT, which limits the result set. (DISTINCT qualifies as an aggregate function because it's a special case of GROUP BY.) DISTINCT is especially clear and useful with a single column. For example, SELECT DISTINCT a FROM elem returns a list of unique values from column a. (If you're curious, column a has five unique values: "Ag," "Al," "Ar," "At," and "Au.") The gotcha with DISTINCT is that it applies to all columns. SELECT DISTINCT a, b FROM elem returns a list of unique *rows* with values from columns a and b. To learn more, check out "DISTINCT Optimization" (*https://oreil.ly/j3IjK*) in the MySQL manual.

Avoid sorting rows

Queries should avoid sorting rows.

Sorting rows in the application instead of MySQL reduces query complexity by removing the ORDER BY clause, and it scales better by distributing work to application instances, which are much easier to scale out than MySQL.

An ORDER BY clause without a LIMIT clause is a telltale sign that the ORDER BY clause can be dropped and the application can sort the rows. (It might also be the second variation of the problem discussed in the preceding section.) Look for queries with an ORDER BY clause but no LIMIT clause, then determine whether the application can sort the rows instead of MySQL—the answer should be yes.

Data Storage

Do not store more data than needed.

Although data is valuable to you, it's dead weight to MySQL. Table 3-4 is a checklist for efficient data storage.

I highly encourage you to audit your data storage because surprises are easy to discover. I mentioned one such surprise at the beginning of Chapter 2: the application I created that accidentally stored one *billion* rows.

Table 3-4. Efficient data storage checklist

☐ Only needed rows are stored
☐ Every column is used
☐ Every column is compact and practical
☐ Every value is compact and practical
☐ Every secondary index is used and not a duplicate
☐ Only needed rows are kept

If you can check off all six items, then you will be very well positioned to scale data to any size. But it's not easy: some items are easier to ignore than to implement, especially when the database is small. But don't delay: the very best time to find and correct storage inefficiencies is when the database is small. At scale, a byte or two can make a big difference when multiplied by high throughput and all 86,400 seconds in a typical Earth day. Design for scale and plan for success.

Only needed rows are stored

As an application changes and grows, engineers can lose track of what it stores. And when data storage is not an issue, engineers have no reason to look at or ask about what it stores. If it's been a long time since you or anyone else reviewed what the application is storing, or if you're new to the team or application, then take a look. I have seen, for example, forgotten services writing data (for years, no less) that no one was using.

Every column is used

One level deeper than storing only needed rows is having only needed columns. Again, as the application changes and grows, engineers can lose track of columns, especially when using object-relational mapping (ORM).

Unfortunately, there's no tool or automated way to find unused columns in MySQL. MySQL tracks which databases, tables, and indexes are used, but it does not track column usage. Nothing is more furtive than an unused column. The only solution is a manual review: compare columns used by application queries to columns that exist in the tables.

Every column is compact and practical

Two levels deeper than storing only needed rows is having every column be compact and practical. *Compact* means using the smallest data type to store values. *Practical* means not using a data type so small that it's onerous or error-prone for you or the application. For example, using an unsigned INT as a bit field is compact (nothing smaller than a bit) but usually not practical.

Familiarize yourself with all the MySQL data types (*https://oreil.ly/x7fTF*).

The classic antipattern is data type VARCHAR(255). This specific data type and size are a common but inefficient default for many programs and engineers, who likely copied the practice from another program or engineer. You will see it used to store anything and everything, which is why it's inefficient.

For example, let's reuse table elem (Example 2-1). Atomic symbols are one or two characters. Column definition atomic_symbol VARCHAR(255) is technically compact —a VARCHAR is variable length, so it would use only one or two characters—but it allows *garbage in, garbage out*: invalid values like "Carbon" instead of "C," which could have unknown consequences for the application. A better column definition is atomic_symbol CHAR(2), which is compact and practical.

Is column definition atomic_symbol ENUM(...) even better for table elem? ENUM is more compact than CHAR(2), but is it more practical with over one hundred atomic symbols? That's a trade-off you could decide; either choice is patently better than VARCHAR(255).

ENUM (*https://oreil.ly/WMXfA*) is one of the great unsung heroes of efficient data storage.

Beware the column character set. If not explicitly defined, it defaults to the table character set which, if also not explicitly defined, defaults to the server character set. As of MySQL 8.0, the default server character set is utf8mb4. For MySQL 5.7 and older, the default server character set is latin1. Depending on the character set, a single character like é might be stored as multiple bytes. For example, using the latin1 character set, MySQL stores é as a single byte: 0xE9. But using the utf8mb4 character set, MySQL stores é as two bytes: 0xC3A9. (Emoji use four bytes per character.) Character sets are a special and erudite world beyond the scope of most books. For now, all you need to know is this: *one character* can require *several bytes* of storage, depending on the character and character set. Bytes add up quickly in large tables.

Be very conservative with BLOB, TEXT, and JSON data types. Do not use them as a dumping ground, a catch-all, or generic buckets. For example, do not store images in a BLOB—you can, it works, but don't. There are far better solutions, like Amazon S3 (*https://aws.amazon.com/s3*).

Compact and practical extend all the way down to the bit level. Another surprisingly common yet easily avoidable column storage inefficiency is wasting the high-order bit of integer data types (*https://oreil.ly/6CdwC*). For example, using INT instead of INT UNSIGNED: the maximum value is roughly two billion versus four billion, respectively. If the value cannot be negative, then use an unsigned data type.

 As of MySQL 8.0.17, UNSIGNED is deprecated for data types FLOAT, DOUBLE, and DECIMAL.

In the world of software engineering, details like these might be considered micro-optimizations or premature optimization, which are frowned upon, but in the world of schema design and database performance, they're best practices.

Every value is compact and practical

Three levels deeper than storing only needed rows is having every value be compact and practical. *Practical* has the same meaning as defined in the previous section, but *compact* means the smallest representation of the value. Compact values are highly dependent on how the application uses them. For example, consider a string with one leading and one trailing space: " and ". Table 3-5 lists six ways that an application could compact this string.

Table 3-5. Six ways to compact the string " and "

Compact value	Possible use
"and"	Strip all whitespace. This is common for strings.
" and"	Strip trailing whitespace. In many syntaxes (like YAML and Markdown), leading whitespace is syntactically significant.
"and "	Strip leading whitespace. Perhaps less common but still possible. Sometimes used by programs to join space-separated arguments (like command-line arguments).
""	Delete the value (empty string). Maybe the value is optional, like *AS* in FROM table AS table_alias, which can be written as FROM table table_alias.
"&"	Replace string with equivalent symbol. In written language, the ampersand character is semantically equivalent to the word "and".
NULL	No value. Maybe the value is completely superfluous and can be removed, resulting in no value (not even an empty string, which is still technically a value).

The transformations in Table 3-5 represent three ways to compact a value: minimize, encode, and deduplicate.

Minimize. To minimize a value, remove superfluous and extraneous data: white space, comments, headers, and so on. Let's consider a more difficult yet familiar value in Example 3-5.

Example 3-5. Formatted SQL statement (not minimized)

```
SELECT
  /*!40001 SQL_NO_CACHE */
  col1,
  col2
FROM
  tbl1
WHERE
  /* comment 1 */
  foo = ' bar '
ORDER BY col1
LIMIT 1; - comment 2
```

If an application stores only the the functional parts of the SQL statement in Example 3-5, then it can minimize the value by collapsing white space between keywords (not within values) and removing the last two comments (not the first). Example 3-6 is the minimized (compact) value.

Example 3-6. Minimized SQL statement

```
SELECT /*!40001 SQL_NO_CACHE */ col1, col2 FROM tbl1 WHERE foo=' bar ' LIMIT 1
```

Examples 3-5 and 3-6 are functionally equivalent (same EXPLAIN plan), but the data size of the minimized value is almost *50% smaller* (48.9%): 137 bytes to 70 bytes, respectively. For long-term data growth, a 50% reduction—or even just 25%—is significant and impactful.

Minimizing a SQL statement illustrates an important point: minimizing a value is not always trivial. A SQL statement isn't a meaningless string: it's a syntax that requires syntactical awareness to minimize correctly. The first comment cannot be removed because it's functional. (See "Comments" (*https://oreil.ly/3l8zy*) in the MySQL manual.) Likewise, the white space in the quoted value ' bar ' is functional: ' bar ' is not equal to 'bar'. And you might have noticed a tiny detail: the trailing semicolon was removed because it's not functional in this context, but it is functional in other contexts.

When considering how to minimize a value, begin with its data format. The syntax and semantics of the data format dictate which data is superfluous and extraneous. In YAML, for example, comments # like this are pure comments (unlike certain SQL comments) and can be removed if the application doesn't need them. Even if your data format is custom-built, it must have some syntax and semantics, else the application could not programmatically read and write it. It's necessary to know the data format to minimize a value correctly.

The most minimal value is no value at all: NULL. I know that dealing with NULL can be a challenge, but there's an elegant solution that I highly encourage you to use: COALESCE() (*https://oreil.ly/muYZW*). For example, if column middle_name is nullable (not all people have middle names), then use COALESCE(middle_name, '') to return the value if set, else return an empty string. This way, you get the benefits of NULL storage—which requires only one bit—without the hassle of handling null strings (or pointers) in the application. Use NULL instead of empty strings, zero values, and magical values when practical. It requires a little extra work, but it's the best practice.

> NULL and NULL are unique; that is, two null values are unique. Avoid unique indexes on nullable columns, or be certain that the application properly handles duplicate rows with NULL values.

If you really want to avoid using NULL, the previous warning is your technical reason. These two sets of values are *unique*: (1, NULL) and (1, NULL). That is not a typo. To humans, those values look identical, but to MySQL they are unique because the comparison of NULL to NULL is undefined. Check out "Working with NULL Values" (*https://oreil.ly/oyTPZ*) in the MySQL manual. It begins with a humble admission: "The NULL value can be surprising until you get used to it."

Encode. To encode a value, convert it from human-readable to machine-encoded. Data can be encoded and stored one way for computers, and decoded and displayed another way for humans. The most efficient way to store data on a computer is to encode it for the computer.

> Store for the machine, display for the human.

The quintessential example and antipattern is storing an IP address as a string. For example, storing 127.0.0.1 as a string in a CHAR(15) column. IP addresses are four-byte unsigned integers—that's the true machine encoding. (If you're curious, 127.0.0.1 is decimal value 2130706433.) To encode and store IP addresses, use data type INT UNSIGNED and functions INET_ATON() and INET_NTOA() to convert to and from a string, respectively. If encoding IP addresses is impractical, then data type CHAR(15) is an acceptable alternative.

Another similar example and antipattern is storing a UUID as a string. A UUID is a multibyte integer represented as a string. Since UUID byte lengths vary, you need to use data type BINARY(N), where N is the byte length, and functions HEX() and UNHEX() to convert the value. Or, if you're using MySQL 8.0 (or newer) and RFC 4122 UUIDs (which MySQL UUID() generates), you can use functions UUID_TO_BIN() and BIN_TO_UUID(). If encoding UUIDs is impractical, at least store the string representation using data type CHAR(N), where N is the string length in characters.

There is a more compact, computer-encoded method to store data: compression. But this is an extreme method that creeps into the gray zone of space-speed trade-offs, which are beyond the scope of this book. I have not seen a case where compression was required for performance or scale. A rigorous application of the efficient data storage checklist (Table 3-4) scales data to sizes so large that other problems become blockers: backup and restore time, online schema changes, and so forth. If you think you need compression to scale performance, consult with an expert to verify.

While we're on the topic of encoding, there's an important best practice that I'll shoehorn into this section: store and access dates and times only as UTC. Convert dates and times to local time (or whatever time zone is appropriate) only on display (or on print). Also be aware that the MySQL TIMESTAMP data type ends on January 19, 2038. If you received this book as a holiday gift in December 2037 and your databases have TIMESTAMP columns, you might want to go back to work a little earlier.

Deduplicate. To deduplicate a value, normalize the column into another table with a one-to-one relationship. This method is entirely application-specific, so let's consider a concrete example. Imagine an overly simple catalogue of books stored in a table with only two columns: title and genre. (Let's focus on the data and ignore the details like data types and indexes.) Example 3-7 shows a table with five books and three unique genres.

Example 3-7. Book catalogue with duplicate genre values

```
+--------------------------------+-----------+
| title                          | genre     |
+--------------------------------+-----------+
| Efficient MySQL Performance    | computers |
| TCP/IP Illustrated             | computers |
| The C Programming Language     | computers |
| Illuminations                  | poetry    |
| A Little History of the World  | history   |
+--------------------------------+-----------+
```

Column genre has duplicate values: three instances of value computers. To deduplicate, normalize the column into another table with a one-to-one-relationship. Example 3-8 shows the new table at top and the modified original table at bottom. The two tables have a one-to-one relationship on column genre_id.

Example 3-8. Normalized book catalogue

```
+----------+-----------+
| genre_id | genre     |
+----------+-----------+
|        1 | computers |
|        2 | poetry    |
|        3 | history   |
+----------+-----------+


+------------------------------+-----------+
| title                        | genre_id  |
+------------------------------+-----------+
| Efficient MySQL Performance  | 1         |
| TCP/IP Illustrated           | 1         |
| The C Programming Language    | 1         |
| Illuminations                | 2         |
| A Little History of the World | 3        |
+------------------------------+-----------+
```

The original table (at bottom) still has duplicate values for column genre_id, but the reduction in data size at scale is huge. For example, it takes 9 bytes to store the string "computers" but only 2 bytes to store the integer 1 as data type SMALLINT UNSIGNED, which allows for 65,536 unique genres (probably enough). That's a 77.7% reduction in data size: 9 bytes to 2 bytes.

Deduplicating values in this way is accomplished by *database normalization*: separating data into tables based on logical relationships (one to one, one to many, and so forth). However, deduplicating values data is *not* the goal or purpose of database normalization.

 Database normalization is beyond the scope of this book, so I won't explain it further. There are many books on the subject, so you won't have any trouble finding a great one to learn about database normalization.

From this example, it looks like database normalization *causes* deduplication of values, but that's not strictly true. The single table in Example 3-7 is technically valid first, second, and third normal forms (presuming there's a primary key)—fully normalized, just poorly designed. It's more accurate to say that deduplication of values is a common (and desired) side effect of database normalization. And since you should normalize your databases in any case, you're likely to avoid duplicate values.

There's an interesting flip side: *denormalization*. Denormalization is the opposite of normalization: combining related data into one table. The single table in Example 3-7 could be a denormalized table, if that was the intention behind its design. Denormalization is a technique to increase performance by eliminating table joins and attendant complexities. But don't rush to denormalize your schemas because there are details and trade-offs to consider that are beyond the scope of this book. In fact, denormalization is the opposite of *less data* because it intentionally duplicates data to trade space for speed.

 The safe bet and best practice is database normalization and less data. Incredible scale and performance are possible with both.

Every secondary index is used and not a duplicate

Second to last on the efficient data storage checklist (Table 3-4): every secondary index is used and not a duplicate. Avoiding unused indexes and duplicate indexes is always a great idea, but it's especially important for data size because indexes are copies of data. Granted, secondary indexes are much smaller than the full table (the primary key) because they only contain index column values and corresponding primary key column values, but these add up as the table grows.

Dropping unused and duplicate secondary indexes is an easy way to reduce data size, but be careful. As mentioned in "Excessive, Duplicate, and Unused" on page 85, finding unused indexes is tricky because an index might not be used frequently, so be sure to check index usage over a sufficiently long period. By contrast, duplicate indexes are easier to find: use pt-duplicate-key-checker (*https://oreil.ly/qSStI*). Again: be careful when dropping indexes.

Dropping an index only recovers a data size equal to the index size. There are three methods to see index sizes. Let's use the employees sample database (*https://oreil.ly/lwWxR*) because it has a few megabytes of index data. The first and preferred method to see index sizes is querying table INFORMATION_SCHEMA.TABLES, as shown in Example 3-9.

Example 3-9. Index sizes of employees sample database (INFORMATION_SCHEMA)

```
SELECT
  TABLE_NAME, DATA_LENGTH, INDEX_LENGTH
FROM
  INFORMATION_SCHEMA.TABLES
```

```
WHERE
  TABLE_TYPE = 'BASE TABLE' AND TABLE_SCHEMA = 'employees';

+--------------+-------------+--------------+
| TABLE_NAME   | DATA_LENGTH | INDEX_LENGTH |
+--------------+-------------+--------------+
| departments  |       16384 |        16384 |
| dept_emp     |    12075008 |      5783552 |
| dept_manager |       16384 |        16384 |
| employees    |    15220736 |            0 |
| salaries     |   100270080 |            0 |
| titles       |    20512768 |            0 |
+--------------+-------------+--------------+
```

TABLE_NAME is the table name in the employees sample database—only six tables. (The database has some views that are filtered out by condition TABLE_TYPE = 'BASE TABLE'.) DATA_LENGTH is the size of the primary key (in bytes). INDEX_LENGTH is the size of all secondary indexes (in bytes). The last four tables have no secondary indexes, only a primary key.

The second and historical (but still widely used) method to see index sizes is SHOW TABLES STATUS. You can add a LIKE clause to show only one table, as demonstrated in Example 3-10.

Example 3-10. Index sizes of table employees.dept_emp (SHOW TABLE STATUS)

```
SHOW TABLE STATUS LIKE 'dept_emp'\G

*************************** 1. row ***************************
          Name: dept_emp
        Engine: InnoDB
       Version: 10
    Row_format: Dynamic
          Rows: 331143
Avg_row_length: 36
   Data_length: 12075008
Max_data_length: 0
  Index_length: 5783552
     Data_free: 4194304
Auto_increment: NULL
   Create_time: 2021-03-28 11:15:15
   Update_time: 2021-03-28 11:15:24
    Check_time: NULL
     Collation: utf8mb4_0900_ai_ci
      Checksum: NULL
 Create_options:
       Comment:
```

The fields Data_length and Index_length in the SHOW TABLE STATUS output are the same columns and values from INFORMATION_SCHEMA.TABLES. It's better to query INFORMATION_SCHEMA.TABLES because you can use functions in the SELECT clause like ROUND(DATA_LENGTH / 1024 / 1024) to convert and round the values from bytes to other units.

The third method to see index sizes is currently the only method to see the size of each index: query table mysql.innodb_index_stats, as shown in Example 3-11 for table employees.dept_emp.

Example 3-11. Size of each index on table employees.dept_emp (mysql.innodb_index_stats)

```
SELECT
  index_name, SUM(stat_value) * @@innodb_page_size size
FROM
  mysql.innodb_index_stats
WHERE
    stat_name = 'size'
  AND database_name = 'employees'
  AND table_name = 'dept_emp'
GROUP BY index_name;

+------------+----------+
| index_name | size     |
+------------+----------+
| PRIMARY    | 12075008 |
| dept_no    |  5783552 |
+------------+----------+
```

Table employees.dept_emp has two indexes: a primary key and a secondary index named dept_no. Column size contains the size of each index in bytes, which is actually the number of index pages multiplied by the InnoDB page size (16 KB by default).

The employees sample database is not a spectacular display of secondary index size, but real-world databases can be overflowing with secondary indexes that account for a significant amount of total data size. Regularly check index usage and index sizes, and reduce total data size by carefully dropping unused and duplicate indexes.

Only needed rows are kept

Last item on the efficient data storage checklist (Table 3-4): only needed rows are kept. This item brings us full circle, closing the loop with the first item: "Only needed rows are stored" on page 105. A row might be needed when stored, but that need changes over time. Delete (or archive) rows that are no longer needed. That sounds obvious, but it's common to find tables with forgotten or abandoned data. I've lost count of how many times I've seen teams drop entire tables that were forgotten.

Deleting (or archiving) data is a lot easier said than done, and the next section takes on the challenge.

Delete or Archive Data

I hope this chapter instills in you a desire to delete or archive data. Too much data has woken me from too many pleasant dreams: it's as if MySQL has a mind of its own and waits until 3 a.m. to fill up the disk. I once had an application page me in the middle of the night in three different time zones (my time zone changed due to meetings in different parts of the world). But enough about me; let's talk about how to delete or archive data without negatively impacting the application.

For brevity, I refer only to deleting data, not deleting *or archiving* data, because the challenge lies almost entirely in the former: deleting data. Archiving data requires copying the data first, then deleting it. Copying data should use nonlocking SELECT statements to avoid impacting the application, then write the copied rows to another table or data store that the application doesn't access. Even with nonlocking SELECT statements, you must rate-limit the copy process to avoid increasing QPS beyond what MySQL and the application can handle. (Recall from "Less QPS Is Better" on page 96 that QPS is relative to the application and difficult to increase.)

Tools

You will have to write your own tools to delete or archive data. Sorry to lead with bad news, but it's the truth. The good news is that deleting and archiving data is not difficult—it's probably trivial compared to your application. The *critically important* part is throttling the loop that executes SQL statements. Never do this:

```
for {
    rowsDeleted = execute("DELETE FROM table LIMIT 1000000")
    if rowsDeleted == 0 {
        break
    }
}
```

The LIMIT 1000000 clause is probably too large, and the for loop has no delay between statements. That pseudocode is likely to cause an application outage. *Batch size* is the key to a safe and effective data archiving tool.

Batch Size

First, a shortcut that might allow you to skip reading this section until needed: it's safe to *manually* delete 1,000 rows or less in a single DELETE statement if the rows are small (no BLOB, TEXT, or JSON columns) and MySQL is not heavily loaded. *Manually* means that you execute each DELETE statement in series (one after the other), not in parallel. Do not write a program to execute the DELETE statements. Most humans are too slow for MySQL to notice, so no matter how fast you are, you cannot manually execute DELETE...LIMIT 1000 statements fast enough to overload MySQL. Use this shortcut judiciously, and have another engineer review any manual deletes.

 The method described in this section focuses on DELETE but applies in general to INSERT and UPDATE. For INSERT, batch size is controlled by the number of rows inserted, not a LIMIT clause.

The rate at which you can quickly *and safely* delete rows is determined by the batch size that MySQL and the application can sustain without impacting query response time or replication lag. (Chapter 7 covers replication lag.) *Batch size* is the number of rows deleted per DELETE statement, which is controlled by a LIMIT clause and throttled by a simple delay, if necessary.

Batch size is calibrated to an execution time; 500 milliseconds is a good starting point. This means that each DELETE statement should take no longer than 500 ms to execute. This is critically important for two reasons:

Replication lag
Execution time on a source MySQL instance creates replication lag on replica MySQL instances. If a DELETE statement takes 500 ms to execute on the source, then it also takes 500 ms to execute on a replica, which creates 500 ms of replication lag. You cannot avoid replication lag, but you must minimize it because replication lag is data loss. (For now, I gloss over many details about replication that I clarify in Chapter 7.)

Throttling
In some cases, it's safe to execute DELETE statements with no delay—no throttling—because the calibrated batch size limits query execution time, which limits QPS. A query that takes 500 ms to execute can only execute at 2 QPS in series. But these are no ordinary queries: they're purpose-built to access and write (delete) as many rows as possible. Without throttling, bulk writes can disrupt other queries and impact the application.

Throttling is paramount when deleting data: always begin with a delay between DELETE statements, and monitor replication lag.[2]

---

2 Check out freno (*https://oreil.ly/vSmUb*) by GitHub Engineering: an open source throttle for MySQL.

Always build a throttle into bulk operations.

To calibrate the batch size to a 500 ms execution time (or whatever execution time you chose), start with batch size 1,000 (`LIMIT 1000`) and a 200 ms delay between `DELETE` statements: 200 ms is a long delay, but you decrease it after calibrating the batch size. Let that run for at least 10 minutes while monitoring replication lag and MySQL stability—don't let MySQL lag or destabilize. (Replication lag and MySQL stability are covered in Chapters 7 and 6, respectively.) Use query reporting (see "Reporting" on page 8) to inspect the maximum execution time of the `DELETE` statement, or measure it directly in your data archiving tool. If the maximum execution time is well below the target—500 ms—then double the batch size and re-run for another 10 minutes. Keep doubling the batch size—or making smaller adjustments—until the maximum execution time is consistently on target—preferably just a little below target. When you're done, record the calibrated batch size and execution time because deleting old data should be a recurring event.

To set the throttle using the calibrated batch size, repeat the process by slowly reducing the delay on each 10-minute rerun. Depending on MySQL and the application, you might reach zero (no throttling). Stop at the first sign of replication lag or MySQL destabilizing, then increase the delay to the previous value that didn't cause either problem. When you're done, record the delay for the same reason as before: deleting old data should be a recurring event.

With the batch size calibrated and the throttle set, you can finally calculate the rate: how many rows per second you can delete without impacting query response time: `batch size * DELETE QPS`. (Use query reporting to inspect the QPS of the `DELETE` statement, or measure it directly in your data archiving tool.) Expect the rate to change throughout the day. If the application is extremely busy during business hours, the only sustainable rate might be zero. If you're an ambitious go-getter who's on a rocket ride to the top of your career, your industry, and the world, then wake up in the middle of the night and try a higher rate when the database is quiet: larger batch size, lower delay, or both. Just remember to reset the batch size and delay before the sun rises and database load increases.

 MySQL backups almost always run in the middle of the night. Even if the application is quiet in the dead of night, the database might be busy.

Row Lock Contention

For write-heavy workloads, bulk operations can cause elevated *row lock contention*: queries waiting to acquire row locks on the same (or nearby) rows. This problem mainly affects INSERT and UPDATE statements, but DELETE statements could be affected, too, if deleted rows are interspersed with kept rows. The problem is that the batch size is too large even though it executes within the calibrated time. For example, MySQL might be able to delete 100,000 rows in 500 ms, but if the locks for those rows overlap with rows that the application is updating, then it causes row lock contention.

The solution is to reduce the batch size by calibrating for a much smaller execution time—100 ms, for example. In extreme cases, you might need to increase the delay, too: small batch size, long delay. This reduces row lock contention, which is good for the application, but it makes data archiving slower. There's no magical solution for this extreme case; it's best to avoid with *less data* and *fewer QPS*.

Space and Time

Deleting data does not free disk space. Row deletes are logical, not physical, which is a common performance optimization in many databases. When you delete 500 GB of data, you don't get 500 GB of disk space, you get 500 GB of free pages. Internal details are more complex and beyond the scope of this book, but the general idea is correct: deleting data yields free pages, not free disk space.

Free pages do not affect performance, and InnoDB reuses free pages when new rows are inserted. If deleted rows will soon be replaced by new rows, and disk space isn't limited, then free pages and unclaimed disk space are not a concern. But please be mindful of your colleagues: if your company runs its own hardware and MySQL for your application shares disk space with MySQL for other applications, then don't waste disk space that can be used by other applications. In the cloud, storage costs money, so don't waste money: reclaim the disk space.

The best way to reclaim disk space from InnoDB is to rebuild the table by executing a no-op ALTER TABLE...ENGINE=INNODB statement. This is a solved problem with three great solutions:

- pt-online-schema-change (*https://oreil.ly/8EJph*)
- gh-ost (*https://oreil.ly/IsV83*)
- ALTER TABLE...ENGINE=INNODB (*https://oreil.ly/JhWdg*)

Each solution works differently, but they have one thing in common: all of them can rebuild huge InnoDB tables *online*: in production without impacting the application. Read the documentation for each to decide which one works best for you.

To rebuild a table with `ALTER TABLE...ENGINE=INNODB`, replace ...
with the table name. Do not make any other changes.

Deleting large amounts of data takes time. You might read or hear about how fast MySQL can write data, but that's usually for benchmarks (see "MySQL Tuning" on page 39). In the glamorous world of laboratory research, sure: MySQL will consume every clock cycle and disk IOP you can give it. But in the quotidian world that you and I slog through, data must be deleted with significant restraint to avoid impacting the application. To put it bluntly: it's going to take a lot longer than you think. The good news is: if done correctly—as detailed in "Batch Size" on page 115—then time is on your side. A well-calibrated, sustainable bulk operation can run for days and weeks. This includes the solution that you use to reclaim disk space from InnoDB because rebuilding the table is just another type of bulk operation. It takes time to delete rows, and it takes additional time to reclaim the disk space.

The Binary Log Paradox

Deleting data creates data. This paradox happens because data changes are written to the binary logs. Binary logging can be disabled, but it never is in production because the binary logs are required for replication, and no sane production system runs without replicas.

If the table contains large `BLOB`, `TEXT`, or `JSON` columns, then binary log size could increase dramatically because the MySQL system variable `binlog_row_image` (*https:// oreil.ly/0bNcG*) defaults to `full`. That variable determines how row images are written to the binary logs; it has three settings:

full
    Write the value of every column (the full row).

minimal
    Write the value of columns that changed and columns required to identify the row.

noblob
    Write the value of every column *except* `BLOB` and `TEXT` columns that aren't required.

It's both safe and recommended to use `minimal` (or `noblob`) if there are no external services that rely on full row images in the binary logs—for example, a data pipeline service that stream changes to a data lake or big data store.

If you use pt-online-schema-change (*https://oreil.ly/2EB4l*) or gh-ost (*https://oreil.ly/ nUuvv*) to rebuild the table, these tools copy the table (safely and automatically), and that copy process writes even more data changes to the binary logs. However, ALTER TABLE...ENGINE=INNODB defaults to an in-place alter—no table copy.

 When deleting a lot of data, disk usage will *increase* because of binary logging and the fact that deleting data does not free disk space.

Paradoxically, you must ensure that the server has enough free disk space to delete data and rebuild the table.

Summary

This chapter examined data with respect to performance and argued that reducing data access and storage is a technique—an indirect query optimization—for improving performance. The primary takeaway points are:

- Less data yields better performance.
- Less QPS is better because it's a liability, not an asset.
- Indexes are necessary for maximum MySQL performance, but there are cases when indexes may not help.
- The principle of least data means: store and access only needed data.
- Ensure that queries access as few rows as possible.
- Do not store more data than needed: data is valuable to you, but it's dead weight to MySQL.
- Deleting or archiving data is important and improves performance.

The next chapter centers on access patterns that determine how you can change the application to use MySQL efficiently.

Practice: Audit Query Data Access

The goal of this practice is to audit queries for inefficient data access. This is the efficient data access checklist (Table 3-2):

- ☐ Return only needed columns
- ☐ Reduce query complexity
- ☐ Limit row access
- ☐ Limit the result set
- ☐ Avoid sorting rows

Apply the checklist to the top 10 slow queries. (To get slow queries, refer back to "Query profile" on page 9 and "Practice: Identify Slow Queries" on page 33.) An easy fix is any `SELECT *`: explicitly select only the columns needed. Also pay close attention to any query with an `ORDER BY` clause: is it using an index? Does it have a `LIMIT`? Can the application sort rows instead?

Unlike "Practice: Identify Slow Queries" on page 33 and "Practice: Find Duplicate Indexes" on page 90, there is no tool to audit query data access. But the checklist is only five items, so it doesn't take long to audit queries manually. Carefully and methodically auditing queries for optimal data access is expert-level MySQL performance practice.

## CHAPTER 4

Access Patterns

Access patterns describe how an application uses MySQL to access data. Changing access patterns has a powerful effect on MySQL performance, but it usually requires a greater level of effort than other optimizations. That's why it's the last leg of the journey mapped out in "Improving Query Response Time" on page 27: first optimize queries, indexes, and data—then optimize access patterns. Before we begin, let's think again about the rocks from Chapter 3.

Suppose you have a truck, which is analogous to MySQL. If used efficiently, the truck makes moving any pile of rocks uphill easy. But if used inefficiently, the truck provides little value, and it might even make the job take longer than necessary. For example, you could use the truck to haul the cobbles *one by one* up the hill. That's easy for you (and the truck), but it's terribly inefficient and time-consuming. A truck is only as useful as the person who uses it. Likewise, MySQL is only as useful as the application that uses it.

Sometimes, an engineer puzzles over why MySQL isn't running faster. For example, when MySQL is executing 5,000 QPS and the engineer wonders why it's not executing 9,000 QPS instead. Or when MySQL is using 50% CPU and the engineer wonders why it's not using 90% CPU instead. The engineer is unlikely to find an answer because they're focused on the effect (MySQL) rather than the cause: the application. Metrics like QPS and CPU usage say very little—almost nothing—about MySQL; they only reflect how the application uses MySQL.

 MySQL is only as fast and efficient as the application that uses it.

An application can outgrow the capacity of a *single* MySQL instance, but again: that says more about the application than MySQL because there are innumerable large, high-performance applications using a single MySQL instance. Without a doubt, MySQL is fast enough for the application. The real question is: does the application use MySQL efficiently? After many years with MySQL, hundreds of different applications, and thousands of different MySQL instances, I assure you: MySQL performance is limited by the application, not the other way around.

This chapter centers on data access patterns that determine how you can change the application to use MySQL efficiently. There are six major sections. The first clarifies what MySQL does apart from the application and why it's important. The second proves that database performance does not scale linearly; instead, there is a limit past which performance destabilizes. The third contemplates why a Ferrari is faster than a Toyota even though both car brands work roughly the same. The answer explains why some applications excel with MySQL while others can't get out of first gear. The fourth enumerates data access patterns. The fifth presents several application changes to improve or modify data access patterns. The sixth revisits an old friend: better, faster hardware.

MySQL Does Nothing

When the application is idle, MySQL is idle. When the application is busy executing queries, MySQL is busy executing those queries. MySQL has several background tasks (like "Page flushing" on page 212), but they are only busy reading and writing data for those queries. In fact, background tasks increase performance by allowing foreground tasks—executing queries—to defer or avoid slow operations. Therefore, if MySQL is running slowly and there are no external issues, the cause can only be what drives MySQL: the application.

QPS is directly and only attributable to the application. Without the application, QPS is zero.

Some data stores have *ghosts in the machine*: internal processes that can run at any time and degrade performance if they run at the worst time: when the data store is busy executing queries. (Compaction and vacuuming are two examples—MySQL has neither.) MySQL has no ghosts in the machine—unless the application is executing queries that you don't know about. Knowing this helps you avoid looking for non-existent causes and, more importantly, focus on what MySQL is busy doing: executing queries. From Chapter 1, you know how to see that: "Query profile" on page 9. A query profile shows more than just slow queries, it shows what MySQL is busy doing.

Queries affect other queries. The general term for this is *query contention*: when queries compete and wait for shared resources. There are specific types of contention: row lock contention, CPU contention, and so forth. Query contention can make it seem like MySQL is busy doing other things, but don't be misled: MySQL is only busy executing application queries.

It's nearly impossible to see or prove query contention because MySQL reports only one type of contention: row lock contention. (Even row lock contention is difficult to see precisely because row locking is complex.) Moreover, contention is fleeting—almost imperceptible—because the problem is intrinsic to high QPS (where *high* is relative to the application). Query contention is like a traffic jam: it requires a lot of cars on the road. Although it's nearly impossible to see or prove, you need to be aware of it because it might explain inexplicably slow queries.

Query contention plays a major role when performance is pushed to the limit.

Performance Destabilizes at the Limit

At the end of "MySQL: Go Faster" on page 30, I said that MySQL can easily push most modern hardware to its limits. That's true, but the limit might surprise you. Figure 4-1 illustrates what engineers expect: as load increases, database performance increases until it utilizes 100% of *system capacity*—throughput of the hardware and operating system—then performance remains steady. This is called *linear scaling* (or *linear scalability*), and it's a myth.

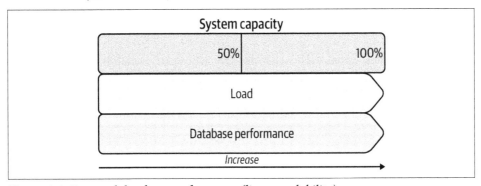

Figure 4-1. Expected database performance (linear scalability)

Linear scaling is the dream of every DBA and engineer, but it cannot happen. Instead, Figure 4-2 illustrates the reality of database performance with respect to load and system capacity.

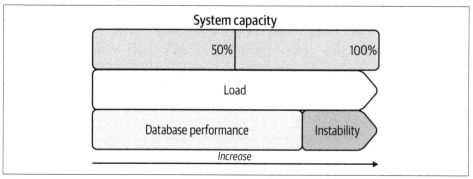

Figure 4-2. Real database performance

Database performance increases with load only to a limit that is less than 100% of system capacity. Realistically, the limit of database performance is 80% to 95% of system capacity. When load increases past the limit, database performance *destabilizes*: throughput, response time, and other metrics fluctuate markedly—sometimes wildly —from their normal value. At best, the result is decreased performance for some (or most) queries; at worst, it causes an outage.

Equation 4-1 shows the *Universal Scalability Law* articulated by Neil Gunther: an equation that models the scalability of hardware and software systems.

Equation 4-1. Equation 4-1. Universal Scalability Law

$$X(N) = \frac{\gamma N}{1 + \alpha(N-1) + \beta N(N-1)}$$

Table 4-1 outlines what each term in the Universal Scalability Law equation represents.

Table 4-1. Universal Scalability Law terms

Term	Represents
X	Throughput
N	Load: concurrent requests, running processes, CPU cores, nodes in a distributed system, and so on
γ	Concurrency (ideal parallelism)
α	Contention: waiting for shared resources
β	Coherency: coordinating shared resources

A deep dive into the Universal Scalability Law is beyond the scope of this book, so I limit the explanation to the current topic: the limit of database performance. To learn more, read *Guerrilla Capacity Planning* (*https://oreil.ly/WZEd8*) by Neil Gunther.

Throughput is a function of load: $X(N)$. Concurrency (γ) helps throughput increase as load (N) increases. But contention (α) and coherency (β) reduce throughput as load increases. This precludes linear scalability and limits database performance.

Worse than limiting performance, coherency causes *retrograde performance*: decreasing performance at high load. The term *retrograde* is an understatement. It suggests that MySQL simply reverts to less throughput when it cannot handle the load, but the reality is worse than that. I prefer the terms *instability* and *destabilize* because they convey the reality: the system is breaking down, not just running more slowly.

The Universal Scalability Law models real-world MySQL performance surprisingly well.[1] But as a model, it only describes and predicts the scalability of a workload; it does not say anything about how or why the workload scales (or fails to scale). The USL is primarily used by experts who measure and fit data to the model to determine the parameters (γ, α, and β), then toil heroically to reduce them. Everyone else just watches graphs (Chapter 6 covers MySQL metrics) and waits until MySQL performance destabilizes—that's the limit.

Figure 4-3 shows three charts from a real outage when the application pushed MySQL past the limit.

The outage had three periods:

The Rise (6 a.m. to 9 a.m.)
> The application was stable at the beginning of the rise, but its developers were beginning to worry because the metrics shown were rising slowly but steadily. In the past, the application had outages that began with steadily rising metrics. In response, the application developers increased transaction throughput to cope with the rising demand. (The application is able to throttle transaction throughput; this isn't a feature of MySQL.) The rise and the response repeated until it no longer worked: MySQL had reached the limit.

---

1 Watch the video Universal Scalability Law Modeling Workbook (*https://oreil.ly/hzXnb*) by renowned MySQL expert Baron Schwartz to see the USL in action with values from real MySQL servers.

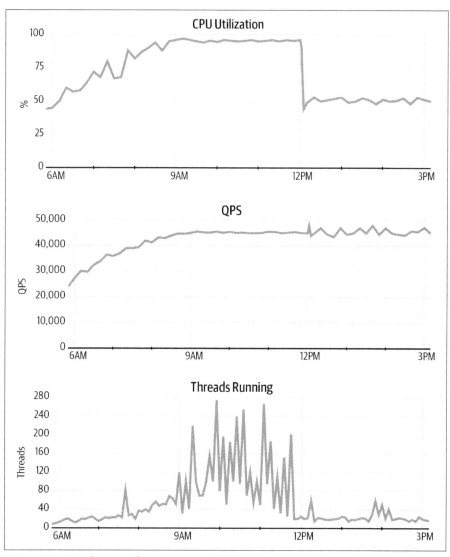

Figure 4-3. Database performance past the limit

The Limit (9 a.m. to noon)

The application was completely unstable and effectively offline during the limit. Although CPU usage and QPS were high and steady, threads running told a different story. The whipsaw pattern of threads running shown in Figure 4-3 was a telltale sign that MySQL had destabilized. Since one query requires one thread to run, the big swings in threads running indicated that queries were not flowing smoothly through the system. Instead, queries were hammering MySQL in uneven, disconcerted strikes.

High and steady CPU usage and QPS were misleading: steady is only good with a little variation, as seen before and after the limit. Steady with no variation, as seen during the limit, is flatline. To understand why, here's a strange but effective analogy. Imagine an orchestra. When the orchestra is playing correctly, there are variations in all aspects of the music. In fact, those variations *are* the music: rhythm, tempo, pitch, tone, melody, dynamics, and so forth. A flatline metric is analogous to a deranged clarinetist playing a single, continuous note *fortissimo*: steady, but not music.

During the limit, application developers kept trying to increase transaction throughput, but it didn't work. MySQL would not use the last 5% of CPU, QPS would not increase, and threads running would not stabilize. From the USL (Equation 4-1), you know why: contention and coherency. As load increased (N), transaction throughput (X) increased, but so did the limiting effects of contention (α) and coherency (β) until MySQL reached the limit.

The Fix (noon to 3 p.m.)

Since increasing transaction throughput was its own demise, the fix was to *reduce* transaction throughput. That seems counterintuitive, but the math doesn't lie. At noon, application developers reduced transaction throughput, and the results are clear in the charts: CPU usage dropped to 50%, QPS returned to a steady variation (and even increased a little), and threads running also returned to a steady variation (with a few spikes, which MySQL had spare capacity to absorb).

To imagine how this works, consider another analogy. Imagine a highway. When there are many cars on the road, they all slow down (hopefully) because humans need time to think and react to others cars, especially at highway speeds. When there are too many cars on the road, they cause a traffic jam. The only solution (apart from adding more lanes) is to reduce the number of cars on the highway: fewer cars can drive faster. Reducing transaction throughput is analogous to reducing the number of cars on the highway, which lets the remaining cars go faster and traffic flow smoothly.

This example nicely models the limit of database performance according to the Universal Scalability Law (Equation 4-1), but it's also an exceptional case because the application was able to push MySQL and the hardware to the limit. More typically, high load destabilizes the application, and that prevents it from increasing load on MySQL. In other words: the application fails before it can push MySQL to the limit. But in this example, the application didn't fail, it kept scaling up until it pushed MySQL to the limit.

Two more points about MySQL performance at the limit before we turn our attention to the application:

- The limit is difficult to reach unless the hardware is blatantly insufficient. As mentioned in "Better, Faster Hardware!" on page 37, this is one of two exceptions for which you should scale up to reasonable hardware. It's also difficult for an application to fully and *simultaneously* utilize all hardware—CPU, memory, and storage. An application is most likely to incur a bottleneck in one piece of hardware long before it can fully and simultaneously utilize all hardware. When this happens, the application has not reached the limit of database performance, only the limit of that one piece of hardware.

- When high load causes MySQL to respond slowly, this does *not* mean the limit has been reached. The reason is simple: γ. Gamma (γ) represents concurrency or ideal parallelism. Recall from the Universal Scalability Law equation (Equation 4-1) that gamma is in the numerator.[2] Slow database performance does *not* mean the limit has been reached because increasing concurrency (γ) raises the limit. Decreasing contention (α) also raises the limit. (Coherency [β] is out of our control: it's inherent to MySQL and the operating system, but it's usually not a problem.)

The second point leads to the question: how do we increase concurrency, or decrease contention, or both? That seems like a critically important question, but it's not: it's misleading because the North Star of MySQL performance is query response time. The values of concurrency (γ) and contention (α) are not directly measurable. They are determined by fitting throughput and load measurements to the model. Experts use the Universal Scalability Law to understand system capacity, not to improve performance. And this section has used it to prove that performance destabilizes at the limit.

Toyota and Ferrari

Some applications achieve incredible MySQL performance while others struggle with low throughput. Some applications can fully utilize the hardware—up to the limit—while others barely warm the CPUs. Some applications don't have any performance problems while others continually struggle with slow queries. It's a sweeping generalization, but I'm going to claim that every engineer wants their application be on the left side of *while*: incredible performance, fully utilizing the hardware, and no

---

2 In fact, renowned MySQL expert Baron Schwartz put it there. Neil Gunther wrote in a blog post, "USL Scalability Modeling with Three Parameters" (*https://oreil.ly/s2BL8*), that Baron added the third parameter because it allowed the USL to fit data from real databases.

problems. The difference between applications on the left of *while* versus those on the right is understood by contemplating why a Ferrari is faster than a Toyota.

Both car brands use roughly the same parts and design, but the top speed of a Toyota is generally 130 MPH, whereas the top speed of a Ferrari is 200 MPH.[3] A Ferrari does not have special parts that make it 70 MPH faster than a Toyota. So why is a Ferrari so much faster than a Toyota? The answer is the difference in engineering *design* and *details*.

A Toyota is not designed for high speed. Achieving high speed (like high performance) requires careful attention to many details. For a car, those details include:

- Engine size, configuration, and timing
- Transmission gear ratios, shift points, and timing
- Tire size, traction, and rotational force
- Steering, suspension, and braking
- Aerodynamics

Both car brands design and engineer for those details, but the exacting level of detail in a Ferrari explains why it achieves greater performance. You can see this in one of those details: aerodynamics. The unique exterior design of a Ferrari is flamboyant but also functional: it lowers the drag coefficient, which increases efficiency.

High performance, like high speed, is not accomplished accidentally or by brute force. It is the result of meticulous engineering with the goal of high performance. A Ferrari is faster than a Toyota because it's designed and engineered in every detail to be faster.

Is your application designed and engineered in every detail for maximum MySQL performance? If yes, then I suppose you can skip the rest of this chapter. If not, which is the usual answer, then the next section addresses the fundamental technical differences that separate Toyota-like applications from Ferrari-like applications: data access patterns.

Data Access Patterns

Data access patterns describe how an application uses MySQL to access data.

The term *data access patterns* (or *access patterns* for short) is commonly used but rarely explained. Let's change that by clarifying three details about access patterns:

---

3 Toyota: 210 Km/h; Ferrari: 320 Km/h.

- It's so common to discuss access patterns in the plural that they begin to blur together. But it's important to realize that they are not an undifferentiated blob. An application has many access patterns. For convenience, they're discussed in the plural. But in practice, you modify access patterns individually.

- An access pattern ultimately refers to a query, and you change queries (and the application) to change access patterns, but queries are *not* the focus. In Go programming language terms (*https://golang.org*), an access pattern is an interface and a query is an implementation. Focus on the interface, not the implementation. This makes it possible to envision (and possibly apply) access patterns to different data stores. For example, certain access patterns executed on MySQL are better suited for a key-value data store, but that's difficult to see by focusing on SQL queries that bear no resemblance to key-value queries. In this book, I discuss modifying access patterns, but in practice you modify queries (and the application).

- An access pattern comprises a name and a list of technical traits. The name is used to identify and communicate the access pattern with other engineers. (Access patterns do not have intrinsic names.) Choose a name that's succinct and meaningful. The list of technical traits depends on and varies by data store. MySQL data access, for example, is quite different than Redis data access. This section enumerates and explains nine traits for MySQL data access.

In theory, application developers should identify every individual access pattern, but let's be honest: that is very tedious. (I've never seen it done, and it might not even be feasible if the application changes quickly.) Nevertheless, that is the goal. Here are three reasonable and achievable approaches toward that goal:

- Brainstorm with your team to identify the most obvious and common access patterns.

- Use the query profile (see "Query profile" on page 9) to identify the top, slowest access patterns.

- Peruse the code for lesser-known (or forgotten) access patterns.

At the very least, you need to follow the first or second approach one time to accomplish the goal of this chapter: indirect query optimization by changing access patterns.

Once you have identified (and named) an access pattern, ascertain the value or answer to each of the following nine traits. Not knowing the value or answer to a trait is a great opportunity to learn and possibly improve part of the application. Don't leave a trait unknown; find or figure out the value or answer.

Before explaining each of the nine traits, there's one more question to settle: how do you use access patterns? Access patterns are pure knowledge, and that knowledge forms a bridge between the previous section and the next section. The previous section, "Toyota and Ferrari" on page 130, makes the point that high-performance MySQL requires a high-performance application. The next section, "Application Changes" on page 140, presents common application changes that help re-engineer the application for high performance with respect to the database. Access patterns help decide (and sometimes dictate) how to re-engineer the application from a Toyota to a Ferrari.

Without further ado, let's examine nine traits of data access patterns for MySQL.

Read/Write

Does the access read or write data?

Read access is clear: SELECT. Write is less clear when you consider the fine details. For example, INSERT is write access, but INSERT...SELECT is read and write access. Likewise, UPDATE and DELETE should use a WHERE clause, which makes them read and write access, too. For simplicity: INSERT, UPDATE, and DELETE are always considered write access.

Internally, reads and writes are not equal: they have different technical impacts and invoke different internal parts of MySQL. An INSERT and a DELETE, for example, are different writes under the hood—not simply because the former adds and the latter removes. For simplicity again: all reads are equal and all writes are equal.

The *read/write* trait is one of the most fundamental and ubiquitous because scaling reads and writes requires different application changes. Scaling reads is usually accomplished by offloading reads, which I cover later in "Offload Reads" on page 141. Scaling write is more difficult, but enqueuing writes is one technique (see "Enqueue Writes" on page 145), and Chapter 5 covers the ultimate solution: sharding.

Although this trait is quite simple, it's important because knowing if an application is read-heavy or write-heavy quickly focuses your attention on relevant application changes. Using a cache, for example, is not relevant for a write-heavy application. Furthermore, other data stores are optimized for reads or writes, and there is a write-optimized storage engine for MySQL: MyRocks (*https://myrocks.io*).

Throughput

What is the throughput (in QPS) and variation of the data access?

First of all, throughput is *not* performance. Low throughput access—even just 1 QPS—can wreak havoc. You can probably imagine how; in case not, here's an example: a SELECT...FOR UPDATE statement that does a table scan and locks every row. It's rare to find access that terrible, but it proves the point: throughput is not performance.

Terrible access notwithstanding, very high QPS (where *high* is relative to the application) is usually an issue to abate for all the reasons eloquently stated in "Less QPS Is Better" on page 96. For example, if the application executes stock trades, it probably has a huge burst of read and write access at 9:30 a.m. Eastern Time when the American stock exchanges open. That level of throughput conjures entirely different considerations than a steady 500 QPS.

Variation—how QPS increases and decreases—is equally important. The previous paragraph mentioned *burst* and *steady*; another type of variation is *cyclical*: QPS increases and decreases over a period of time. A common cyclical pattern is higher QPS during business hours—9 a.m. to 5 p.m. Eastern Time, for example—and lower QPS in the middle of the night. A common problem is that high QPS during business hours prevents developers from making schema changes (ALTER TABLE) or backfilling data.

Data Age

What is the age of the data accessed?

Age is relative to access order, not time. If an application inserts one million rows in 10 minutes, the first row is the oldest because it was the last row accessed, not because it's 10 minutes old. If the application updates the first row, then it becomes the newest because it was the most recent row accessed. And if the application never accesses the first row again, but it continues to access other rows, then the first row becomes older and older.

This trait is important because it affects the working set. Recall from "Working set size" on page 95 that the working set is frequently used index values and the primary key rows to which they refer—which is a long way of saying *frequently accessed data*—and it's usually a small percentage of the table size. MySQL keeps as much data in memory as possible, and data age affects whether or not the data in memory is part of the working set. It usually is because MySQL is exceptionally good at keeping the working set in memory thanks to a mélange of algorithms and data structures. Figure 4-4 is a highly simplified illustration of the process.

The rectangle in Figure 4-4 represents all data. The working set is a small amount of data: from the dashed line to the top. And memory is smaller than both: from the solid line to the top. In MySQL lingo, data is *made young* when accessed. And when data is not accessed, it becomes old and is eventually evicted from memory.

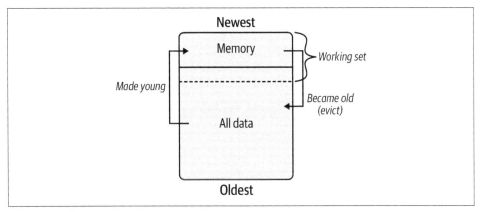

Figure 4-4. Data aging

Since accessing data keeps it young and in memory, the working set stays in memory because it's frequently accessed. This is how MySQL is very fast with a little memory and a lot of data.

Frequently accessing old data is problematic in more than one way. To explain why, I must delve into technical details beyond the scope of this section, but I clarify later in "InnoDB" on page 205. Data is loaded into *free pages* (in memory): pages that don't already contain data. (A *page* is a 16 KB unit of logical storage inside InnoDB.) MySQL uses all available memory, but it also keeps a certain number of free pages. When there are free pages, which is normal, the problem is only that reading data from storage is slow. When there are zero free pages, which is abnormal, the problem worsens threefold. First, MySQL must evict old pages, which it tracks in a least recently used (LRU) list. Second, if an old page is dirty (has data changes not persisted to disk) MySQL must flush (persist) it before it can evict it, and flushing is slow. Third, the original problem remains: reading data from storage is slow. Long story short: frequently dredging up old data is problematic for performance.

Occasionally accessing old data is not a problem because MySQL is clever: the algorithms driving the process in Figure 4-4 prevent occasional access of old data from interfering with new (young) data. Therefore, take data age and throughput into consideration together: old and slow access is probably harmless, but old and fast is bound to cause trouble.

Data age is nearly impossible to measure.[4] Fortunately, you only need to estimate the age of the data accessed, which you can do with your understanding of the application, the data, and the access pattern. If, for example, the application stores

---

4 It's technically possible by inspecting the LSN of data pages in the InnoDB buffer pool, but that's disruptive, so it's practically never done.

financial transactions, you know that access is mostly limited to new data: the last 90 days of transactions. Accessing data older than 90 days should be infrequent because transactions have settled and become immutable. By contrast, another part of the same application that manages user profiles might frequently access old data if the percentage of active users is high. Remember: old data is relative to access, not time. The profile of a user who last logged in a week ago isn't necessarily old by time, but their profile data is relatively old because millions of other profile data have since been accessed, which means their profile data was evicted from memory.

Knowing this trait is a prerequisite for understanding "Partition Data" on page 146 and sharding in Chapter 5.

Data Model

What data model does the access exhibit?

Although MySQL is a relational data store, it's commonly used with other data models: key-value, document, complex analytics, graph, and so forth. You should be keenly aware of nonrelational access because it's not the best fit for MySQL; therefore, it cannot yield the best performance. MySQL excels with other data models but only to a point. For example, MySQL works well as a key-value data store, but RocksDB (*https://rocksdb.org*) is incomparably better because it's a purpose-built key-value data store.

The data model trait cannot be programmatically measured like other traits. Instead, you need to determine which data model the access exhibits. The verb *exhibits* is meaningful: the access might be relational only because MySQL was the only available data store when the access was created, but it *exhibits* another data model when you consider all data stores. Access is often jammed into the data model of the available data stores. But the best practice is the reverse: determine the ideal data model for the access, then use a data store built for that data model.

Transaction Isolation

What transaction isolation does the access require?

Isolation is one of four ACID properties: atomicity, consistency, isolation, and durability. Since the default MySQL storage engine, InnoDB, is transactional, every query executes in a transaction by default—even a single SELECT statement. (Chapter 8 examines transactions.) Consequently, the access has isolation whether it needs it or not. This trait clarifies whether isolation is required and if so, what level.

When I ask engineers this question, the answer falls into one of three categories:

None

No, the access does not require any isolation. It would execute correctly on a nontransactional storage engine. Isolation is just useless overhead, but it doesn't cause any problems or noticeably impact performance.

Default

Presumably, the access requires isolation, but it's unknown or unclear which level is required. The application works correctly with the default transaction isolation level for MySQL: REPEATABLE READ. Careful thought would be required to determine if another isolation level—or no isolation—would work correctly.

Specific

Yes, the access requires a specific isolation level because it's part of a transaction that executes concurrently with other transactions that access the same data. Without the specific isolation level, the access could see incorrect versions of the data, which would be a serious problem for the application.

In my experience, *Default* is the most common category, and that makes sense because the default transaction isolation level for MySQL, REPEATABLE READ, is correct for most cases. But the answer to this trait should lead to *None* or *Specific*. If the access does not require any isolation, then it might not require a transactional data store. Else, if the access requires isolation, now you specifically know which isolation level and why.

Other data stores have transactions—even data stores that are not fundamentally transactional. For example, the document store MongoDB (*https://www.mongodb.com*) introduced multidocument ACID transactions in version 4.0. Knowing which isolation level is required and why allows you to translate and move access from MySQL to another data store.

Transactions in other data stores can be very different than MySQL transactions, and transactions affect other aspects, like locking.

Read Consistency

Does the read access require strong or eventual consistency?

Strong consistency (or *strongly consistent reads*) means that a read returns the most current value. Reads on the source MySQL instance (not replicas) are strongly consistent, but the transaction isolation level determines the *current* value. A long-running transaction can read an old value, but it's technically the current value with respect to the transaction isolation level. Chapter 8 delves into these details. For now, remember that strong consistency is the default (and only option) on the source MySQL instance. This is not true for all data stores. Amazon DynamoDB (*https://oreil.ly/EDCme*), for example, defaults to eventually consistent reads, and strongly consistent reads are optional, slower, and more expensive.

Eventual consistency (or *eventually consistent reads*) means that a read might return an old value, but eventually it will return the current value. Reads on MySQL replicas are eventually consistent because of *replication lag*: the delay between when data is written on the source and when it's written (applied) on the replica. The duration of *eventually* is roughly equal to replication lag, which should be less than a second. Replicas used to serve read access are called *read replicas*. (Not all replicas serve reads; some are only for high availability, or other purposes.)

In the world of MySQL, it's common for all access to use the source instance, which makes all reads strongly consistent by default. But it's also common for reads *not* to require strong consistency, especially when replication lag is subsecond. When eventual consistency is acceptable, offloading reads (see "Offload Reads" on page 141) becomes possible.

Concurrency

Is the data accessed concurrently?

Zero concurrency means that the access does not read (or write) the same data at the same time. If it reads (or writes) the same data at *different* times, that's also zero concurrency. For example, an access pattern that inserts unique rows has zero concurrency.

High concurrency means that the access frequently reads (or writes) the same data at the same time.

Concurrency indicates how important (or troublesome) row locking will be for write access. Unsurprisingly, the higher the write concurrency on the same data, the greater the row lock contention. Row lock contention is acceptable as long as the increased response time that it causes is also acceptable. It becomes unacceptable when it causes lock wait timeouts, which is a query error that the application must handle and retry. When this begins to happen, there are only two solutions: decrease concurrency (change the access pattern), or shard (see Chapter 5) to scale out writes.

Concurrency also indicates how applicable a cache might be for read access. If the same data is read with high concurrency but infrequently changed, then it's a good fit for a cache. I discuss this in "Offload Reads" on page 141.

As addressed in "Data Age" on page 134, concurrency is nearly impossible to measure, but you only need to estimate concurrency, which you can do with your understanding of the application, the data, and the access pattern.

Row Access

How are rows accessed? There are three types of row access:

Point access
    A single row

Range access
    Ordered rows between two values

Random access
    Several rows in any order

Using the English alphabet (*A* to *Z*), point access is any single character (*A*, for example); range access is any number of characters in order (*ABC*, or *AC* if *B* doesn't exist); and random access is any number of random characters (*ASMR*).

This trait seems simplistic, but it's important for write access for two reasons:

- Gap locking: range and random access writes that use nonunique indexes exacerbate row lock contention due to gap locks. "Row Locking" on page 260 goes into detail.

- Deadlocks: random access writes are a setup for *deadlocks*, which is when two transactions hold row locks that the other transaction needs. MySQL detects and breaks deadlocks, but they kill performance (MySQL kills one transaction to break the deadlock) and they're annoying.

Row access is also important when planning how to shard. Effective sharding requires that access patterns use a single shard. Point access works best with sharding: one row, one shard. Range and random access work with sharding but require careful planning to avoid negating the benefits of sharding by accessing too many shards. Chapter 5 covers sharding.

Result Set

Does the access group, sort, or limit the result set?

This trait is easy to answer: does the access have a `GROUP BY`, `ORDER BY`, or `LIMIT` clause? Each of these clauses affects if and how the access might be changed or run on another data store. "Data Access" on page 97 covers several changes. At the very least, optimize access that groups or sorts rows. Limiting rows is not a problem—it's a benefit—but it works differently on other data stores. Likewise, other data stores may or may not support grouping or sorting rows.

Application Changes

You must change the application to change its data access patterns. The changes presented in this section are common, not exhaustive. They are highly effective but also highly dependent on the application: some could work, others might not. (Except the first change, "Audit the Code" on page 140: that always works.) Consequently, each change is an idea that needs further discussion and planning with your team.

All changes except the first have a subtle commonality: they require additional infrastructure. I point that out to mentally prepare you for the fact that, in addition to code changes, you will need infrastructure changes, too. As foretold from the beginning, "Improving Query Response Time" on page 27, indirect query optimization requires a greater level of effort. Whereas changing data (Chapter 3) is potentially work, changing access patterns is certainly work. But it's worth the effort because these changes are, by definition, *transformative*: how the application changes from a Toyota to a Ferrari.

You might wonder: if these changes are so powerful, why not make them first—before optimizing queries and data? Since the focus of this book is *efficient* MySQL performance, I planned the journey to end with application changes because they require the most effort. By contrast, direct query optimization (Chapter 2) and changes to data (Chapter 3) require far less effort, and the former solves a lot of—if not most—performance problems. But if you have the time and energy to jump straight into re-engineering the application, you have my support. Just remember the lesson from Chapter 2: indexes provide the most *and the best* leverage. Bad queries ruin wonderful access patterns; or, to quote renowned MySQL expert Bill Karwin:

> Your unoptimized queries are killing the database server.

Audit the Code

You might be surprised by how long code can exist and run without any human looking at it. In a certain sense, that's a sign of good code: it just works and doesn't cause problems. But "doesn't cause problems" does not necessarily mean that the code is efficient or even required.

You don't have to audit all the code (although that's not a bad idea), just the code that accesses the database. Look at the actual queries, of course, but also consider the context: the business logic that the queries accomplish. You might realize a different and better way to accomplish the same business logic.

With respect to queries, look for the following:

- Queries that are no longer needed
- Queries that execute too frequently

- Queries that retry too fast or too often
- Large or complex queries—can they be simplified?

If the code uses ORM—or any kind of database abstraction—double check its defaults and configuration. One consideration is that some database libraries execute SHOW WARNINGS after every query to check for warnings. That's usually not a problem, but it's also quite wasteful. Also double-check the driver defaults, configuration, and release notes. For example, the MySQL driver for the Go programming language has had very useful developments over the years, so Go code should be using the latest version.

Indirectly audit the code by using the query profile to see what queries the application executes—no query analysis required; just use the query profile as an auditing tool. It's quite common to see unknown queries in the profile. Given "MySQL Does Nothing" on page 124, unknown queries likely originate from the application—either your application code or any kind of database abstraction, like ORM—but there is another possibility: ops. *Ops* refers to whoever runs and maintains the data store: DBAs, cloud providers, and so on. If you find unknown queries and you're certain that the application isn't executing them, check with whoever operates the data store.

 To make query auditing easier, add application metadata to queries in /* SQL comments */. For example, SELECT.../* file:app.go line:75 */ reveals where the query originates in the application source code. SQL comments are removed from digest texts, so your query metric tool must include samples (see Example 1-1) or parse metadata from SQL comments.

Lastly and most overlooked: review the MySQL error log (*https://oreil.ly/hmLlY*). It should be quiet: no errors, warnings, and so forth. If it's noisy, look into the errors because they signify a wide array of issues: network, authentication, replication, MySQL configuration, nondeterministic queries, and so forth. These types of problems should be incredibly rare, so don't ignore them.

Offload Reads

By default, a single MySQL instance called *the source* serves all reads and writes. In production, the source should have at least one *replica*: another MySQL instance that replicates all writes from the source. Chapter 7 addresses replication, but I mention it here to set the stage for a discussion about offloading reads.

Performance can be improved by offloading reads from the source. This technique uses MySQL replicas or cache servers to serve reads. (More on these two in a moment.) It improves performance in two ways. First, it reduces load on the source, which frees time and system resources to run the remaining queries faster. Second, it improves response time for the offloaded reads because the replicas or caches serving those reads are not loaded with writes. It's a win-win technique that's commonly used to achieve high-throughput, low-latency reads.

Data read from a replica or cache is *not* guaranteed to be current (the latest value) because there is inherent and unavoidable delay in MySQL replication and writing to a cache. Consequently, data from replicas and caches is *eventually consistent*: it becomes current after a (hopefully very) short delay. Only data on the source is current (transaction isolation levels notwithstanding). Therefore, before serving reads from a replica or cache, the following must be true: *reading data that is out-of-date (eventually consistent) is acceptable, and it will not cause problems for the application or its users.*

Give that statement some thought because more than once I've seen developers think about it and realize, "Yeah, it's fine if the application returns slightly out-of-date values." A commonly cited example is the number of "likes" or up-votes on a post or video: if the current value is 100 but the cache returns 98, that's close enough —especially if the cache returns the current value a few milliseconds later. If that statement is *not* true for your application, do not use this technique.

In addition to the requirement that eventual consistency is acceptable, offloaded reads must not be part of a multi-statement transaction. Multi-statement transactions must be executed on the source.

Always ensure that offload reads are acceptable with eventual consistency and not part of a multi-statement transaction.

Before serving reads from replicas or caches, thoroughly address this question: *how will the application run degraded when the replicas or caches are offline?*

The only wrong answer to that question is not knowing. Once an application offloads reads, it tends to depend heavily on the replicas or caches to serve those reads. It's imperative to design, implement, and test the application to run degraded when the replicas or caches are offline. *Degraded* means that the application is running but noticeably slower, limiting client requests, or not fully functional because some parts are offline or throttled. As long as the application is not *hard down*—completely offline and unresponsive with no human-friendly error message—then you've done a good job making the application run degraded.

Last point before we discuss using MySQL replicas versus cache servers: do not offload all reads. Offloading reads improves performance by not wasting time on the source for work that a replica or cache can accomplish. Therefore, start by offloading slow (time-consuming) reads: reads that show up as slow queries in the query profile.

This technique is potent, so offload reads one by one because you might only need to offload a few to significantly improve performance.

MySQL replica

Using MySQL replicas to serve reads is common because every production MySQL setup should already have at least one replica, and more than two replicas is common. With the infrastructure (the replicas) already in place, you only have to modify the code to use the replicas for offloaded reads instead of the source.

Before stating why replicas are preferable to cache servers, there's one important issue to settle: can the application use the replicas? Since replicas are used for high availability, whoever manages MySQL might not intend for replicas to serve reads. Be sure to find out because, if not, replicas might be taken offline without notice for maintenance.

Presuming your replicas can be used to serve reads, they are preferable to cache servers for three reasons:

Availability
    Since replicas are the foundation of high availability, they should have the same availability as the source—99.95% or 99.99% availability, for example. That makes replicas nearly worry-free: whoever manages MySQL is also managing the replicas.

Flexibility
    In the previous section, I said that you should start by offloading slow (time-consuming) reads. For caches, this is especially true because the cache server most likely has limited CPU and memory—resources not to be wasted on trivial reads. By contrast, replicas used for high availability should have the same hardware as the source, so they have resources to spare. Offloading trivial reads to a replica doesn't matter as much, hence the flexibility when choosing what to offload. On the off chance that you have pure *read replicas*—replicas *not* used for high availability—with less powerful hardware, then don't waste resources on trivial reads. This is more common in the cloud because it's easy to provision read replicas with large storage but small CPU and memory (to save money).

Simplicity
    The application doesn't have to do anything to keep replicas in sync with the source—that's intrinsic to being a replica. With a cache, the application must manage updates, invalidation, and (possibly) eviction. But the real simplicity is that replicas don't require any query changes: the application can execute the exact same SQL statements on a replica.

Those are three compelling reasons to prefer MySQL replicas to cache servers, but the latter has one important point in its favor: a cache server can be incredibly faster than MySQL.

Cache server

A cache server is not encumbered with SQL, transactions, or durable storage. That makes it incredibly faster than MySQL, but it also takes more work in the application to use properly. As mentioned in the previous section, the application must manage cache updates, invalidation, and (possibly) eviction. Moreover, the application needs a data model that works with the cache, which is usually a key-value model. The extra work is worth the effort because practically nothing is faster than a cache. Memcached (*https://memcached.org*) and Redis (*https://redis.io*) are two popular and widely-used cache servers.

 If you hear that MySQL has a built-in query cache: forget it and never use it. It was deprecated as of MySQL 5.7.20 and removed as of MySQL 8.0.

Caching is ideal for data that's frequently accessed but infrequently changed. This is not a consideration for MySQL replicas because all changes replicate, but a cache stores only what the application puts in it. A bad example is the current Unix timestamp in seconds: it's always changing. The exception in a bad case like this: if the frequency of access is significantly *greater than* the frequency of change. For example, if the current Unix timestamp in seconds is requested one million times per second, then caching the current timestamp might be appropriate. A good example is the current year: it changes infrequently. However, the exception in a good case like this: if the frequency of access is significantly *less than* the frequency of change. For example, if the current year is requested only once per second, then a cache provides almost no value because 1 QPS doesn't make any difference for this data access.

A word of caution when using a cache: *decide whether the cache is ephemeral or durable*. This, too, is not a consideration for MySQL replicas because they are always durable, but some cache servers can be either. If the cache is truly ephemeral, then you should be able to do the equivalent of TRUNCATE TABLE on the cache data without affecting the application. You also need to decide how the ephemeral cache is rebuilt. Some applications rebuild the cache on *cache miss*: when the requested data is not in the cache. Other applications have an external process to rebuild the cache from another data source (for example, loading the cache with images stored in Amazon S3 (*https://oreil.ly/XMQxR*)). And some applications rely so heavily on the cache, or the cache is so large, that rebuilding it is not feasible. For such applications, a durable cache is required. Either way—ephemeral or durable—test your decision to verify that the application functions as expected when the cache fails and recovers.

Enqueue Writes

Use a queue to stabilize write throughput. Figure 4-5 illustrates unstable—erratic—write throughput that spikes above 30,000 QPS and dips below 10,000 QPS.

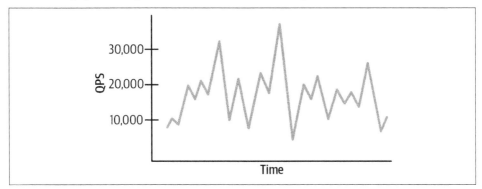

Figure 4-5. Erratic write throughput

Even if performance is currently acceptable with unstable write throughput, it's not a recipe for success because unstable throughput worsens at scale—it never spontaneously stabilizes. (And if you recall Figure 4-3 from "Performance Destabilizes at the Limit" on page 125, a flatline value is not stable.) Using a queue allows the application to process changes (writes) at a stable rate, as shown in Figure 4-6.

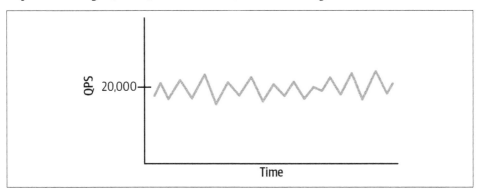

Figure 4-6. Stable write throughput

The real power of enqueueing writes and stable write throughput is that they allow the application to respond gracefully and predictably to a *thundering herd*: a flood of requests that overwhelms the application, or the database, or both. For example, imagine that the application normally processes 20,000 changes per second. But it goes offline for five seconds, which results in 100,000 pending changes. The moment the application comes back online, it's hit with the 100,000 pending changes—a thundering herd—plus the normal 20,000 changes for the current second. How will the application and MySQL handle the thundering herd?

With a queue, the thundering herd does not affect MySQL: it goes into the queue, and MySQL processes the changes as usual. The only difference is that some changes happen later than usual. As long as write throughput is stable, you can increase the number of queue consumers to process the queue more quickly.

Without a queue, experience teaches that one of two things will happen. Either you'll be super lucky and MySQL will handle the thundering herd, or it won't. Don't count on luck. MySQL does not throttle query execution, so it will try to execute all queries when the thundering herd hits. (However, MySQL Enterprise Edition, Percona Server, and MariaDB Server have a *thread pool* that limits the number of concurrently executing queries, which acts as a throttle.) This never works because CPU, memory, and disk I/O are inherently limited—not to mention the Universal Scalability Law (Equation 4-1). Regardless, MySQL always tries because it's incredibly ambitious and a little foolhardy.

This technique bestows other advantages that make it worth the effort to implement. One advantage is that it decouples the application from MySQL availability: the application can accept changes when MySQL is offline. Another advantage is that it can be used to recover lost or abandoned changes. Suppose a change requires various steps, some of which might be long-running or unreliable. If a step fails or times out, the application can re-enqueue the change to try again. A third advantage is the ability to replay changes if the queue is an event stream, like Kafka (*https://oreil.ly/ fRZpa*).

 For write-heavy applications, enqueueing writes is the best practice and practically a requirement. Invest the time to learn and implement a queue.

Partition Data

After Chapter 3, it should be no surprise that it's easier to improve performance with *less data*. Data is valuable to you, but it's dead weight to MySQL. If you cannot delete or archive data (see "Delete or Archive Data" on page 115), then you should at least partition (physically separate) the data.

First, let's briefly address then put aside MySQL partitioning (*https://oreil.ly/BNopd*). MySQL supports partitioning, but it requires special handling. It's not trivial to implement or maintain, and some third-party MySQL tools don't support it. Consequently, I don't recommend using MySQL partitioning.

The type of data partitioning that is most useful, more common, and easier for application developers to implement is separating *hot* and *cold* data: frequently and infrequently accessed data, respectively. Separating hot and cold data is a combination of partitioning and archiving. It partitions by access, and it archives by moving the infrequently accessed (cold) data out of the access path of the frequently accessed (hot) data.

Let's use an example: a database that stores payments. The hot data is the last 90 days of payments for two reasons. First, payments usually do not change after settling, but there are exceptions like refunds that can be applied later. After some period, however, payments are finalized and cannot be changed. Second, the application shows only the last 90 days of payments. To see older payments, users have to look up past statements. The cold data is payments after 90 days. For a year, that's 275 days, which is roughly 75% of data. Why have 75% of data sit idly in a transactional data store like MySQL? That's a rhetorical question: there's no good reason.

Separating hot and cold data is primarily an optimization for the former. Storing cold data elsewhere yields three immediate advantages: more hot data fits in memory, queries don't waste time examining cold data, and operations (like schema changes) are faster. Separating hot and cold data is also an optimization for the latter when it has completely different access patterns. In the preceding example, old payments might be grouped by month into a single data object that no longer requires a row for each payment. In that case, a document store or key-value store might be better suited for storing and accessing the cold data.

At the very least, you can archive cold data in another table in the same database. That's relatively easy with a controlled `INSERT...SELECT` statement to select from the hot table and insert into the cold table. Then `DELETE` the archived cold data from the hot table. Wrap it all up in a transaction for consistency. See "Delete or Archive Data" on page 115.

This technique can be implemented many different ways, especially with respect to how and where the cold data is stored and accessed. But fundamentally it's very simple and highly effective: move infrequently accessed (cold) data out of the access path of frequently accessed (hot) data to improve performance for the latter.

Don't Use MySQL

I want to put a figurative capstone on the current discussion about application changes: the most significant change is not using MySQL when it's clearly not the best data store for the access patterns. Sometimes it's very easy to see when MySQL is not the best choice. For example, in previous chapters I made reference to a query with load 5,962. That query is used to select vertices in a graph. Clearly, a relational database is not the best choice for graph data; the best choice is a graph data store. Even a key-value store would be better because graph data has nothing to do with relational database concepts like normalization and transactions. Another easy and common example is time series data: a row-oriented transactional database is not the best choice; the best choice is a time series database, or perhaps a columnar store.

MySQL scales surprising well for a wide range of data and access patterns even when it's not the best choice. But never take that for granted: be the first engineer on your team to say, "Maybe MySQL isn't the best choice." It's okay: if I can say that, then you can too. If anyone gives you grief, tell them I support your decision to use the best tool for the job.

That said, MySQL is amazing. Please at least finish this chapter and the next, Chapter 5, before you swipe left on MySQL.

Better, Faster Hardware?

"Better, Faster Hardware!" on page 37 cautions against scaling up hardware to increase performance. But the first sentence of that section is carefully worded: "When MySQL performance isn't acceptable, do *not* begin by scaling up…" The key word in that sentence is *begin*, and the pivotal question that it leads to is: *when is the correct time to scale up hardware?*

That question is difficult to answer because it depends on a combination of factors: queries, indexes, data, access patterns, and how those utilize the current hardware. For example, let's say that the application has a super inefficient access pattern: it uses MySQL as a queue and polls it very quickly from many application instances. I would not scale up hardware until fixing the access pattern first. But sometimes, engineers don't have the luxury of time necessary to make such application changes.

Table 4-2 is a checklist to help determine if it's time to scale up the hardware. When you can check all items in column 1 and at least two items in column 2, then it's a strong indication that it's time to scale up the hardware.

Table 4-2. Hardware upgrade checklist

1. Check all	2. Check at least two
☐ Response time is too high	☐ CPU utilization is greater than 80%
☐ Slow queries have been optimized	☐ Threads running greater than number of CPU cores
☐ Data has been deleted or archived	☐ Memory is less than 10% of total data size
☐ Access patterns have been reviewed and optimized	☐ Storage IOPS utilization is greater than 80%

Column 1 is an unapologetic reiteration of everything since Chapter 1, but it's also an unequivocal justification for spending money to upgrade the hardware. Column 2 requires at least two checks because hardware works together. Heavily utilizing only one piece of hardware doesn't guarantee a problem or slow performance. Instead, it's probably a good sign: you're fully utilizing that piece of hardware. But when one piece of hardware is overloaded, it usually begins to affect other pieces of hardware. For example, when slow storage causes a backlog of queries which causes a backlog of clients which causes high CPU utilization because MySQL is trying to execute too many threads. That's why column 2 requires two checks.

Values in column 2 should be consistently greater or less than the suggested thresholds. Occasional spikes and dips are normal.

The maximum number of storage IOPS is determined by the storage device, if running your own hardware. If you're not sure, check the device specifications, or ask the engineers who manage the hardware. In the cloud, storage IOPS are allocated or provisioned, so it's usually easier to tell the maximum because you purchase the IOPS. But if you're not sure, check the MySQL storage settings, or ask the cloud provider. "IOPS" on page 208 shows which metrics report storage IOPS.

Storage IOPS utilization has an additional consideration based on whether the application is read-heavy or write-heavy (see "Read/Write" on page 133):

Read-heavy

For read-heavy access patterns, consistently high IOPS is probably due to insufficient memory, not insufficient IOPS. MySQL reads data from disk when it's not in memory, and it's exceptionally good at keeping the working set in memory (see "Working set size" on page 95). But a combination of two factors can cause high IOPS for reads: the working set size is significantly larger than memory, and read throughput is exceptionally high (see "Throughput" on page 133). That combination causes MySQL to swap so much data between disk and memory that the problem shows up as high IOPS. This is rare, but possible.

Write-heavy

For write-heavy access patterns, consistently high IOPS is probably due to insufficient IOPS. Simply put: the storage can't write data fast enough. Normally, storage achieves high throughput (IOPS) with write caches, but caches are not durable. MySQL requires *durable storage*: data physically on disk, not in caches. (The phrase "on disk" is still used even for flash-based storage that doesn't have disks.) Consequently, MySQL must *flush* data—force it to be written to disk. Flushing severely limits storage throughput, but MySQL has sophisticated techniques and algorithms to achieve performance with durability—"Page flushing" on page 212 goes into detail. The only solution at this point—because you've already optimized queries, data, and access patterns—is more storage IOPS.

With a cautious nod to scaling up hardware, it might seem that we've reached the end. No matter how many pebbles, or cobbles, or boulders we have to move, we can always use a bigger truck to move them. But what if you have to move a mountain? Then you need the next chapter: sharding.

Summary

This chapter centered on data access patterns that determine how you can change the application to use MySQL efficiently. The important takeaway points are:

- MySQL does nothing but execute application queries.
- Database performance destabilizes at a limit that is less than 100% of hardware capacity.
- Some applications have far greater MySQL performance because every detail is engineered for high performance.
- Access patterns describe how an application uses MySQL to access data.
- You must change the application to change its data access patterns.
- Scale up hardware to improve performance after exhausting other solutions.

The next chapter introduces the basic mechanics of sharding MySQL to achieve MySQL at scale.

Practice: Describe an Access Pattern

The goal of this practice is to describe the access pattern of the slowest query. (To get slow queries, refer back to "Query profile" on page 9 and "Practice: Identify Slow Queries" on page 33.) For the slowest query, describe all nine access pattern traits from "Data Access Patterns" on page 131. As mentioned in that section, access patterns are pure knowledge. Use that knowledge to consider what "Application Changes" on page 140 could be made to indirectly optimize the query by changing its access pattern. Even if no application changes are possible, knowing access patterns is an expert practice because MySQL performance depends on queries, data, and access patterns.

## CHAPTER 5

Sharding

On a single instance of MySQL, performance depends on queries, data, access patterns, and hardware. When direct and indirect query optimization—assiduously applied—no longer deliver acceptable performance, you have reached the relative limit of single-instance MySQL performance for the application workload. To surpass that relative limit, you must divide the application workload across multiple instances of MySQL to achieve MySQL at scale.

Sharding a database is the common and widely used technique of *scaling out* (or, *horizontal scaling*): increasing performance by distributing the workload across multiple databases. (By contrast, *scaling up*, or *vertical scaling*, increases performance by increasing hardware capacity.) Sharding divides one database into many databases. Each database is a shard, and each shard is typically stored on a separate MySQL instance running on separate hardware. Shards are physically separate but logically the same (very large) database.

MySQL at scale requires sharding. I'm going to repeat that sentence several times in this chapter because it's a fact that engineers hesitate to accept. Why? Because sharding is not an intrinsic feature or capability of MySQL. Consequently, sharding is complex and entirely application-specific, which means there's no easy solution. But don't be discouraged: sharding is a solved problem. Engineers have been scaling out MySQL for decades.

This chapter introduces the basic mechanics of sharding to achieve MySQL at scale. There are four major sections. The first explains why a single database does not scale—why sharding is necessary. The second completes the analogy from Chapters 3 and 4: why pebbles (database shards) are better than boulders (huge databases). The third is a brief introduction to the complex topic of relational database sharding. The fourth presents alternatives to sharding.

Why a Single Database Does Not Scale

Nobody questions that a single application can overload a single server—that's why scaling out is necessary for all types of servers and applications, not just MySQL. Sharding is therefore necessary because it's how MySQL scales out: more databases. But it's reasonable to wonder why a single MySQL database does not scale given that very powerful hardware is available and some benchmarks demonstrate incredible performance on that hardware. Five reasons follow, beginning with the most fundamental: the application workload can significantly outpace the speed and capacity of single-server hardware.

Application Workload

Figure 5-1 is a simple illustration of hardware capacity on a single server with zero load.

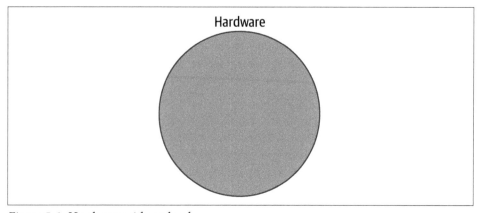

Figure 5-1. Hardware without load

Figure 5-1 is intentionally simple—but not simplistic—because it subtly conveys a critically important point: *hardware capacity is finite and limited*. The circle represents the limits of the hardware. Let's presume the hardware is dedicated to running a single MySQL instance for one application—no virtualization, crypto coin mining, or other load. Everything that runs on the hardware must fit inside the circle. Since this is dedicated hardware, the only thing running on it is the application workload shown in Figure 5-2: queries, data, and access patterns.

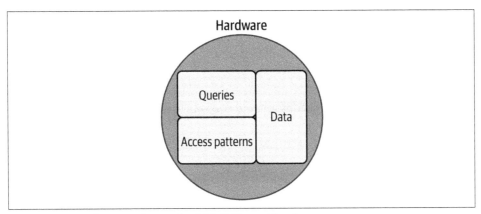

Figure 5-2. Hardware with standard MySQL workload

It's no coincidence that *Queries* refer to Chapter 2, *Data* to Chapter 3, and *Access Patterns* to Chapter 4. These constitute the application workload: everything that causes load on MySQL which, in turn, causes load on the hardware (CPU utilization, disk I/O, and so forth). The box sizes are important: the bigger the box, the bigger the load. In Figure 5-2, the workload is within the capacity of the hardware, with a little room to spare because the operating system needs hardware resources, too.

Queries, data, and access patterns are inextricable with respect to performance. (I proved this with `TRUNCATE TABLE` in "Indirect Query Optimization" on page 28.) Data size is a common reason for scaling out because, as shown in Figure 5-3, it causes the workload to exceed the capacity of a single server.

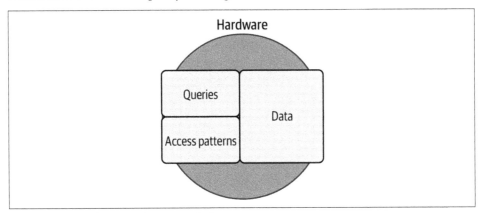

Figure 5-3. Hardware with too much data

Data size cannot increase without eventually affecting queries and access patterns. Buying a bigger hard drive won't solve the problem because, as Figure 5-3 shows, there's plenty of capacity for the data, but the data is not the only part of the workload.

Figure 5-4 illustrates a common misconception that leads engineers to think that a single database can scale to maximum data size, which is currently 64 TB for a single InnoDB table.

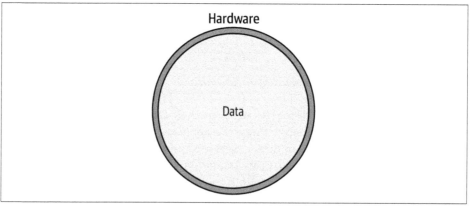

Figure 5-4. Hardware with only data (scaling misconception)

Data is only one part of the workload, and the other two parts (queries and access patterns) cannot be ignored. Realistically, for acceptable performance with a lot of data on a single sever, the workload must look like Figure 5-5.

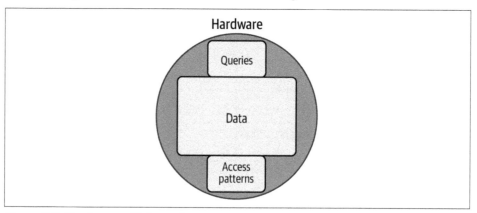

Figure 5-5. Hardware with large data

If the queries are simple and have exceptionally good indexes, and the access patterns are trivial (for example, very low-throughput reads), then a single server can store a lot of data. This isn't just a clever illustration; real applications have workloads like Figure 5-5.

These five illustrations reveal that a single database cannot scale because the application workload—which comprises queries, data, and access patterns—must fit within the capacity of the hardware. After "Better, Faster Hardware!" on page 37 and "Better, Faster Hardware?" on page 148, you already know that hardware won't solve this problem.

MySQL at scale requires sharding because application workloads can significantly outpace the speed and capacity of single-server hardware.

Benchmarks Are Synthetic

Benchmarks use synthetic (fake) queries, data, and access patterns. These are necessarily fake because they're not real applications and certainly not your application. Therefore, benchmarks cannot tell you—or even suggest—how your application will perform and scale—even on the same hardware. Moreover, benchmarks largely focus on one or more access pattern (see "Data Access Patterns" on page 131), which produces a workload like the one pictured in Figure 5-6.

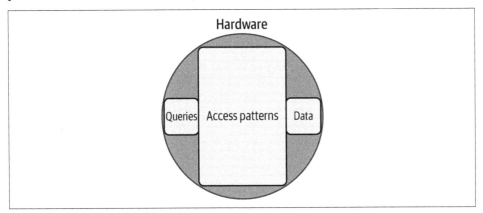

Figure 5-6. Hardware with benchmark workload

Most applications don't have a workload where performance is dominated by one or more access pattern. But it's common for benchmarks because it allows MySQL experts to stress and measure a particular aspect of MySQL. For example, if a MySQL expert wants to measure the effectiveness of a new page flushing algorithm, they might use a 100% write-only workload with a few perfectly optimized queries and very little data.

But let me be perfectly clear: benchmarks are important and necessary for MySQL experts and the MySQL industry. (As mentioned in "MySQL Tuning" on page 39, benchmarking is laboratory work.) Benchmarks are used to do the following:

- Compare hardware (one storage device against another)
- Compare server optimizations (one flushing algorithm against another)
- Compare different data stores (MySQL versus PostgreSQL—the classic rivalry)
- Test MySQL at the limit (see "Performance Destabilizes at the Limit" on page 125)

That work is incredibly important for MySQL, and it's why MySQL is capable of amazing performance. But conspicuously absent from that list is anything related to your application and its particular workload. Consequently, whatever amazing MySQL performance you read or hear about in benchmarks will not translate to your application, and the very same experts producing those benchmarks will tell you: MySQL at scale requires sharding.

Writes

Writes are difficult to scale on a single MySQL instance for several reasons:

Single writable (source) instance
> For high availability, MySQL in production employs several instances connected in a replication topology. But writes are effectively limited to a single MySQL instance to avoid *write conflicts*: multiple writes to the same row at the same time. MySQL supports multiple writable instances, but you will have a difficult time finding anyone who uses this feature because write conflicts are too troublesome.

Transactions and locking
> Transactions use locking to guarantee consistency—the C in an ACID-compliant database. Writes must acquire row locks, and sometimes they lock significantly more rows than you might expect—"Row Locking" on page 260 explains why. Locks lead to lock contention, which makes access pattern trait "Concurrency" on page 138 a critical factor in how well writes scale. If the workload is write-heavy on the same data, even the best hardware in the world won't help.

Page flushing (durability)
> *Page flushing* is the delayed process by which MySQL persists changes (from writes) to disk. The entire process is too complex to explain in this section, but the salient point is: page flushing is the bottleneck of write performance. Although MySQL is very efficient, the process is inherently slow because it must ensure that data is *durable*: persisted to disk. Without durability, writes

are incredibly fast due to caching, but durability is a requirement because all hardware crashes eventually.

Write amplification

Write amplification refers to writes requiring more writes. Secondary indexes are the simplest example. If a table has 10 secondary indexes, a single write could write 10 additional writes to update those indexes. Page flushing (durability) incurs additional writes, and replication incurs even more writes. This is not unique to MySQL; it affects other data stores, too.

Replication

Replication is required for high availability, so all writes must replicate to other MySQL instances—replicas. Chapter 7 addresses replication, but here are a few salient points with respect to scaling writes. MySQL supports asynchronous replication, semisynchronous replication, and Group Replication (*https:// oreil.ly/oeJtD*). Asynchronous replication has a small effect on write performance because data changes are written and flushed to binary logs on transaction commit—but after that, there's no effect. Semisynchronous replication has a greater effect on write performance: it attenuates transaction throughput to network latency because every commit must be acknowledged by at least one replica. Since network latency measures in milliseconds, the effect on write performance is noticeable, but it's a worthwhile trade-off because it guarantees that no committed transactions are lost, which is not true for asynchronous replication. Group Replication is more complex and it's more difficult to scale writes. For various reasons explained in Chapter 7, I do not cover Group Replication in this book.

These five reasons are formidable challenges to scaling writes on a single MySQL instance—even for MySQL experts. MySQL at scale requires sharding to overcome these challenges and scale write performance.

Schema Changes

Schema changes are more than routine; they're practically required. Furthermore, it's not uncommon for the largest tables to change frequently because their size reflects their usage, and usage leads to development, which leads to changes. Even if you manage to overcome all other obstacles and scale a single table to an enormous size, the time required to change that table will be untenable. How long? It can take days or weeks to alter a large table.

The long wait is not a problem for MySQL or the application because online schema change (OSC) tools like pt-online-schema-change (*https://oreil.ly/tSrrr*) and gh-ost (*https://oreil.ly/nUuvv*) and certain built-in online DDL operations (*https:// oreil.ly/5KiA7*) can run for days or weeks while allowing the application to function normally—which is why they're called *online*. But it is a problem for engineers developing the application because waiting that long does not go unnoticed; rather, it tends to become an increasingly annoying blocker to you, other engineers, and possibly other teams.

For example, just a few weeks ago I helped a team alter several tables, each with one *billion* rows, that had failed to complete after nearly two weeks of trying (for various technical reasons not related to MySQL). The blocker went far beyond the table or the team: long story short, it blocked an organization-level goal—months of work by several other teams. Luckily, the needed schema change happened to be an instant online DDL operation (*https://oreil.ly/5KiA7*). But instant schema changes are exceedingly rare, so don't count on them. Instead, don't let a table become so large that you cannot alter it in a reasonable amount of time—whatever you, your team, and your company deem *reasonable*.

MySQL at scale requires sharding because engineers cannot wait days or weeks to change a schema.

Operations

If you directly and indirectly optimize queries with exacting precision and unmitigated meticulousness, you can scale up a single database to a size that people won't believe until you show them. But the illustrations of hardware and workload in "Application Workload" on page 152 do not depict the following *operations* (or *ops* as they're more commonly called):

- Backup and restore
- Rebuilding failed instances
- Upgrading MySQL
- MySQL shutdown, startup, and crash recovery

The larger the database, the longer those operations take. As an application developer, you might not manage any of those operations, but they will affect you unless the engineers managing the database are exceptionally adept at—and deeply committed to—zero-downtime operations. Cloud providers, for example, are neither adept nor committed; they only attempt to minimize downtime, which can mean anything from 20 seconds to hours of the database being offline.

MySQL at scale requires sharding to efficiently manage the data, which leads us to the next section: pebbles, not boulders.

Pebbles, Not Boulders

It's significantly easier to move pebbles than boulders. I belabor this analogy because it's apt: MySQL at scale is achieved by using many small instances. (To refresh your memory on the analogy, read the introductory sections of Chapters 3 and 4.)

Small, in this context, means two things:

- The application workload runs with acceptable performance on the hardware.
- Standard operations (including OSC) take an acceptable amount of time.

At first glance, that makes *small* seem so relative that it's useless, but in practice the limited range of hardware capacity significantly narrows the scope to an almost objective measure. For example, at the time of this writing, I advise engineers to limit the total data size of a single MySQL instance to 2 or 4 TB:

2 TB

For average queries and access patterns, commodity hardware is sufficient for acceptable performance, and operations complete in reasonable time.

4 TB

For exceptionally optimized queries and access patterns, mid- to high-end hardware is sufficient for acceptable performance, but operations might take slightly longer than acceptable.

These limits only reflect the hardware capacity that you can readily purchase today (December 2021). Years ago, the limits were significantly lower. (Remember when disks would physically spin and make crackling sounds? Weird.) Years from now, the limits will be significantly greater.

Once a database is sharded, the number of shards is trivial to the application because it accesses them programmatically. But to operations—especially the engineers operating the MySQL instances—the *size* of shards is critically important: it's significantly easier to manage a 500 GB database than a 7 TB database. And since operations are automated, it's easy to mange any number of small databases.

MySQL performance is truly unlimited when sharded and operated as many small databases—pebbles, not boulders.

Sharding: A Brief Introduction

The solution and implementation of sharding are necessarily coupled to the application workload. This is true even for the alternative solutions presented in the next section, "Alternatives" on page 170. Consequently, no one can tell you how to shard, and there are no fully-automated solutions. Prepare for a long but worthwhile journey.

Sharding has two paths from idea to implementation:

Designing a new application for sharding

> The first and rarest path is when an application is designed from the beginning for sharding. If you're developing a new application, I highly encourage you to take this path *if needed* because it's incomparably easier to shard from the start than to migrate later.
>
> To determine whether sharding is needed, estimate data size and growth for the next four years. If the estimated data size in four years fits within the capacity of your hardware *today*, then sharding might not be needed. I call this the *four-year fit*. Also try to estimate the four-year fit for the other two aspects of the application workload: queries and access patterns. These are difficult to estimate (and likely to change) for a new application, but you should have some ideas and expectations because they're a necessary part of designing and implementing an application.
>
> Also consider whether the data set is bounded or unbounded. A *bounded data set* has an intrinsic maximum size or intrinsically slow growth. For example, the number of new smart phones released every year is very small, and its growth is intrinsically slow because there's no reason to believe that manufacturers will ever release thousands of new phones per year. An *unbounded data set* has no intrinsic limits. For example, pictures are unbounded: people can post unlimited pictures. Since hardware capacity is bounded, applications should always define and impose extrinsic limits on unbounded data sets. Never let data grow unbounded. An unbounded data set strongly indicates the need for sharding, unless old data is frequently deleted or archived (see "Delete or Archive Data" on page 115).

Migrating an existing application to sharding

> The second and more common path is migrating an existing database and application to sharding. This path is significantly more difficult, time-consuming, and risky because, by the time it's required, the database is large—MySQL is hauling a boulder uphill. With a team of experienced developers, plan for the migration to take a year or longer.

In this book, I cannot cover how to migrate a single database to a sharded database because it's a bespoke process: it depends on the sharding solution and application workload. But one thing is certain: you will copy data from the original (single) database to the new shards—probably many times—because the initial migration is essentially the first resharding, which is a challenge addressed in "Resharding" on page 168.

Four-Year Fit

Why estimate data size and growth for the next four years? One or two years is too soon: it takes at least a year to implement a big project like sharding. Three years is reasonable, and four years is safe: better hardware is a safe bet in four years. Also, stock grants commonly vest after four years, which causes turnover. Read "Tours of Duty: The New Employer-Employee Compact" (*https://oreil.ly/goj9j*) by Reid Hoffman, Ben Casnocha, and Chris Yeh. A responsible engineer improves the system for future engineers. If the database won't scale past one's four-year tenure, they should fix it now to ensure that future engineers inherit a scalable system.

Sharding is a complex process for either path. To begin, choose a shard key and strategy, and understand the challenges that you will face. This knowledge gives the journey a destination: a sharded database that you can operate with relative ease. Then chart a path from one database to that destination.

Shard Key

To shard MySQL, the application must programmatically map data to shards. Therefore, the most fundamental decision is the *shard key*: the column (or columns) by which the data is sharded. The shard key is used with a sharding strategy (discussed in the next section) to map data to shards. The application, not MySQL, is responsible for mapping and accessing data by shard key because MySQL has no built-in concept of sharding—MySQL is oblivious to sharding.

The term *shard* is used interchangeably for the database or the MySQL instance where the database is stored.

An ideal shard key has three properties:

High cardinality
An ideal shard key has high cardinality (see "Extreme Selectivity" on page 86) so that data is evenly distributed across shards. A great example is a website that lets

you watch videos: it could assign each video a unique identifier like dQw4w9WgXcQ. The column that stores that identifier is an ideal shard key because every value is unique, therefore cardinality is maximal.

Reference application entities

An ideal shard key references application entities so that access patterns do *not* cross shards. A great example is an application that stores payments: although each payment is unique (maximal cardinality), the customer is the application entity. Therefore, the primary access pattern for the application is by customer, not by payment. Sharding by customer is ideal because all payments for a single customer should be located on the same shard.

Small

An ideal shard key is as small as possible because it's heavily used: most—if not all—queries include the shard key to avoid scatter queries—one of several "Challenges" on page 167.

It should go without saying, but to ensure that it has been said: an ideal shard key, in combination with the sharding strategy, avoids or mitigates the "Challenges" on page 167, especially transactions and joins.

Spend ample time to identify or create the ideal shard key for your application. This decision is half of the foundation: the other half is the sharding strategy that uses the shard key.

Strategies

A sharding strategy maps data to shards by shard key value. The application implements the sharding strategy to route queries to the shard with the data corresponding to the shard key value. This decision is the other half of the foundation. Once the shard key and strategy are implemented, it's exceedingly difficult to change, so choose very carefully.

There are three common strategies: hash, range, and lookup (or directory). All three are widely used. The best choice depends on the application access patterns—especially row access (see "Row Access" on page 139), as mentioned in the next three sections.

Hash

Hash sharding maps hash key values to shards using a hashing algorithm (to produce an integer hash value), the modulo operator (mod), and the number of shards (N). Figure 5-7 depicts the strategy starting with the hash key value at top and following the solid arrows to a shard at bottom.

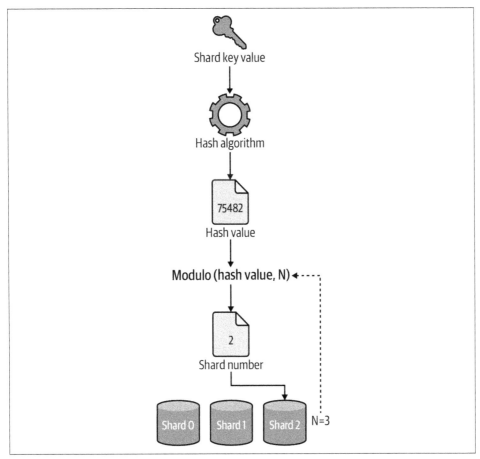

Figure 5-7. Hash sharding

A hashing algorithm outputs a hash value using the shard key value as input. The hash value (which is an integer) mod the number of shards (N) returns the shard number: an integer between zero and N – 1, inclusive. In Figure 5-7, the hash value 75482 mod 3 = 2, so the data for the shard key value is located on shard 2.

> How to map shard numbers to MySQL instances is your choice. For example, you could deploy a map of shard numbers to MySQL hostnames with each application instance. Or, applications could query a service like etcd (*https://etcd.io*) to discover how shard numbers map to MySQL instances.

If you're thinking, "Won't changing the number of shards (N) affect the mapping of data to shards?" you are correct. For example, 75483 mod 3 = 0, but increase the number of shards to five and the same shard key value maps to a new shard number: 75483 mod 5 = 3. Luckily, this is a solved problem: a *consistent hashing algorithm* outputs a consistent hash value independent of N. The key word is *consistent*: it's still possible, but far less likely, that hash values will change when shards change. Since shards are likely to change, you should choose a consistent hashing algorithm.

Hash sharding works for all shard keys because it abstracts the value to an integer. That doesn't mean it's better or faster, only that it's easier because the hashing algorithm automatically maps all shard key values. However, *automatically* is also its downside because, as "Rebalancing" on page 169 discusses, it's virtually impossible to manually relocate data.

Point access (see "Row Access" on page 139) works well with hash sharding because one row can map to only one shard. By contrast, range access is probably infeasible with hash sharding—unless the ranges are *very* small—because of "Cross-shard queries" on page 167 (one of the common challenges). Random access is probably infeasible, too, for the same reason.

Range

Range sharding defines contiguous key value ranges and maps a shard to each, as depicted in Figure 5-8.

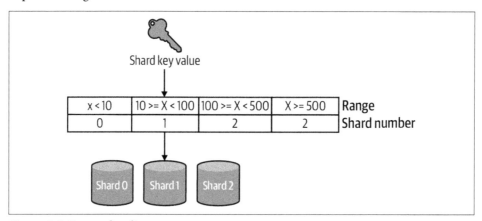

Figure 5-8. Range sharding

You must define the key value ranges in advance. This gives you flexibility when mapping data to shards, but it requires a thorough knowledge of data distribution to ensure that the data is evenly distributed across shards. Since data distribution changes, expect to deal with resharding (see "Resharding" on page 168). A benefit to range sharding is that, unlike hash sharding, you can change (redefine) the ranges, which helps to manually relocate data.

All data can be sorted and divided into ranges, but this doesn't make sense for some data, like random identifiers. And some data appears random but, upon closer inspection, is actually closely ordered. For example, here are three UUIDs generated by MySQL:

```
f15e7e66-b972-11ab-bc5a-62c7db17db19
f1e382fa-b972-11ab-bc5a-62c7db17db19
f25f1dfc-b972-11ab-bc5a-62c7db17db19
```

Can you spot the differences? Those three UUIDs appear random but would most likely sort into the same range, depending on the range size. At scale, this would map most data to the same shard, thereby defeating the purpose of sharding. (UUID algorithms vary: some intentionally generate closely ordered values, while others intentionally generate randomly ordered values.)

Range sharding works best when:

- The range of shard key values is bounded
- You can determine the range (minimum and maximum values)
- You know the distribution of values, and it's mostly even
- The range and distribution are unlikely to change

For example, stock data could be sharded by stock symbols ranging from AAAA to ZZZZ. Although the distribution is probably less in the Z range, overall it will be even enough to ensure that one shard is not significantly larger or accessed more frequently than the other shards.

Point access (see "Row Access" on page 139) works well with range sharding as long as row access distributes evenly over the ranges, avoiding hot shards—a common challenge discussed in "Rebalancing" on page 169. Range access works well with range sharding as long as the row ranges are within the shard ranges; if not, "Cross-shard queries" on page 167 become a problem. Random access is probably infeasible for the same reason: cross-shard queries.

Lookup

Lookup (or directory) sharding is custom mapping of shard key values to shards. Figure 5-9 depicts a lookup table that maps country code top-level domains to shards.

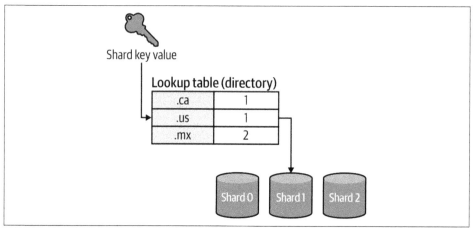

Figure 5-9. Lookup (directory) sharding

Lookup sharding is the most flexible, but it requires maintaining a lookup table. A *lookup table* functions as a key-value map: shard key values are the keys, and database shards are the values. You can implement a lookup table as a database table, a data structure in a durable cache, a configuration file deployed with the application, and so forth.

The keys in the lookup table can be singular values (as shown in Figure 5-9) or ranges. If the keys are ranges, then it's essentially range sharding, but the lookup table gives you more control of the ranges. But that control has a cost: changing ranges means resharding—one of the common challenges. If the keys are singular values, then lookup sharding is sensible when the number of unique shard key values is manageable. For example, a website that stores public health statistics in the United States could shard by state and county name because there are fewer than 3,500 counties total, and they almost never change.[1] Lookup sharding has an advantage that makes it a good choice for this example: it's trivial to map all the counties with very low population to one shard, whereas this custom mapping isn't possible with hash or range sharding.

All three row access patterns (see "Row Access" on page 139) work with lookup sharding, but how well they work depends on the size and complexity of the lookup table you need to create and maintain to map shard key values to database shards. The notable mention is random access: lookup sharding allows you to map (or remap) shard key values to alleviate cross-shard queries caused by random access, which is nearly impossible with hash and range sharding.

---

1 County names are unique only within a state, which is why the state name is required.

Challenges

If sharding were perfect, you would shard only once, and every shard would have equal data size and access. That might be the case when you first shard, but it won't remain the case. The following challenges will affect your application and sharded database, so plan ahead: know how you will avoid or mitigate them.

Transactions

Transactions do not work across shards. This is more of a blocker than a challenge because there is essentially no workaround short of implementing a two-phase commit in the application, which is perilous and far beyond the scope of this book.

I strongly recommend that you avoid this blocker. Review your application transactions (see "Reporting" on page 286) and the data they access. Then choose a shard key and strategy that work given how the transactions access data.

Joins

A SQL statement cannot join tables across shards. The solution is a *cross-shard join*: the application join results from multiple queries executed on multiple shards. It's not a trivial solution—it might even be complex depending on the join—but it's feasible. Apart from complexity, the main concern is consistency: since transactions do not work across shards, the results from each shard are not a consistent view of all data.

A cross-shard join is a special-purpose cross-shard query (joining the results is the special purpose); therefore, it's susceptible to the same challenges.

Cross-shard queries

A *cross-shard query* requires the application to access more than one shard. The term refers to application access, not literal queries, because a single query cannot execute on more than one MySQL instance. (A more accurate term would be *cross-shard application access*.)

Cross-shard queries incur latency: delay inherent to accessing multiple MySQL instances. Sharding is most effective when cross-shard queries are the exception, not the norm.

If sharding were perfect, every application request would access *only one* shard. That's the goal, but don't drive yourself crazy trying to achieve it because some applications, even when efficiently sharded, must access multiple shards to accomplish certain requests. A peer-to-peer payment application is a good example. Each customer is a well delineated application entity: all data related to a customer should be located on the same shard, which entails that the data is sharded by customer. But customers interact by sending and receiving money. Inevitably, the application will access at least two shards: one for the customer sending money, and another for the customer receiving the money. Cross-shard queries should be minimized, but again: don't drive yourself crazy trying to eliminate them, especially if the application logic necessitates them for certain requests.

A related challenge is *scatter queries* (or *scatter-gather queries*): queries that require the application to access many (or all) shards. (Again, the term refers to application access, not literal queries.) A moderate number of cross-shard queries is inevitable and acceptable, but scatter queries are antithetical to the purpose and benefits of sharding. Therefore, you should both prevent and eliminate scatter queries. If you cannot—if the application requires scatter queries—then sharding is probably not the correct solution, or the access pattern needs to be changed (see "Data Access Patterns" on page 131).

Resharding

Resharding (or a *shard split*) divides one shard into two or more new shards. Resharding is necessary to accommodate data growth, and it can also be used to redistribute data across shards. If and when resharding is necessary depends on capacity planning: the estimated rate of data growth and how many shards are created initially. For example, I've seen a team split a database into four shards then reshard less than two years later because data size increased much faster than estimated. By contrast, I've seen a team split a database into 64 shards to accommodate more than five years of estimated data growth. If you can afford extra shards at the beginning (when you first shard), then create enough shards for at least four years of data growth—don't wildly overestimate, but estimate generously.

This is the dark secret of sharding: sharding begets more sharding. If you're wondering, "Can I shard once and be done?" the answer is "probably not." Since your database grew to the point of needing to shard, it's likely to keep growing and keep needing more shards—unless you become fervent about the idea that less data is better (see "Less Data Is Better" on page 96).

Resharding is a challenge because it requires a data migration process from the old shard to the new shards. Describing how to migrate data is beyond the scope of this book, but I will point out three high-level requirements:

- An initial bulk data copy from old to new shards
- Sync changes on old shard to new shards (during and after data copy)
- Cutover process to switch to new shards

Deep MySQL expertise is required to migrate data safely and correctly. Since data migrations are specific to the application and infrastructure, you won't find any books or other resources that detail the process. If necessary, hire a MySQL consultant to help design a process. Also check out Ghostferry (*https://oreil.ly/7aM3I*) by the engineers at Shopify who are experts in MySQL sharding.

Rebalancing

Rebalancing relocates data in order to distribute access more evenly. Rebalancing is necessary to handle *hot shards*: shards with significantly more access than other shards. Although the shard key and sharding strategy determine how data is distributed, the application and its users determine how data is accessed. If one shard (a hot shard) contains all the most frequently accessed data, then performance is not evenly distributed, which defeats the purpose of scaling out. The goal is equal access—and equal performance—on all shards.

Rebalancing depends on the sharding strategy:

Hash
It's virtually impossible to relocate data with hash sharding because the hashing algorithm automatically maps data to shards. One solution (or workaround) is to use a lookup table that contains relocated shard keys. The application checks the lookup table first: if the shard key is present, it uses the shard indicated by the lookup table; otherwise, it uses the hashing algorithm.

Range
Relocating data with range sharding is possible (but nontrivial) by redefining the ranges to divide the hot shard into smaller, separate shards. This is the same process as resharding.

Lookup
Relocating data with lookup sharding is relatively easy because you control the mapping of data to shards. Therefore, you update the lookup table to remap the shard key value corresponding to the hot data.

Physically relocating the hot data requires the same (or similar) data migration process used for resharding.

Online schema changes

Altering a table on one database is easy, but how do you alter it on every shard? You run the OSC on each shard, but that's not the challenge. The challenge is automating the OSC process to run on multiple shards, and keeping track of which shards have been altered. For MySQL, there are no open source solutions at the time of this writing; you must develop a solution. (However, a couple of the alternatives to MySQL in the next section have a solution.) This is the least complex challenge of sharding, but it's a challenge nevertheless. It cannot be overlooked because schema changes are routine.

Alternatives

Sharding is complex, and it's not directly valuable to users or customers. It's valuable to the application to keep scaling, but it's exacting work for engineers. Unsurprisingly, alternative solutions are increasingly popular and robust. However, don't be too quick to trust your data to new technology. MySQL is eminently reliable and deeply understood—a very mature technology—which makes it a safe and reasonable choice.

NewSQL

NewSQL refers to a relational, ACID-compliant data store with built-in support for scaling out. In other words, it's a SQL database that you don't have to shard. If you're thinking, "Wow! Then why use MySQL at all?" the following five points explain why MySQL—sharded or not—is still the most popular open source database in the world:

Maturity
   SQL hails from the 1970s and MySQL from the 1990s. Database maturity means two things: you can trust the data store not to lose or corrupt your data, and there is deep knowledge about every aspect of the data store. Pay close attention to the maturity of NewSQL data stores: when was the first truly stable GA (generally available) release? What has the cadence and quality of releases been since then? What deep and authoritative knowledge is publicly available?

SQL compatibility
   NewSQL data stores use SQL (it's in the name, after all) but compatibility varies significantly. Do not expect any NewSQL data store to be a drop-in replacement for MySQL.

Complex operations
   Built-in support for scaling out is achieved with a distributed system. That usually entails multiple different yet coordinated components. (If MySQL is as a solo saxophonist, then NewSQL is as a five-piece band.) If the NewSQL data store is fully managed, then perhaps its complexity doesn't matter. But if you have to manage it, then read its documentation to understand how it's operated.

Distributed system performance
   Recall the Universal Scalability Law (Equation 4-1):

$$X(N) = \frac{\gamma N}{1 + \alpha(N-1) + \beta N(N-1)}$$

   N represents software load (concurrent requests, running processes, and forth), or hardware processors, *or nodes in a distributed system*. If the application has queries that require a response time less than 10 milliseconds, a NewSQL data store might not work because of the latency inherent in distributed systems. But that level of response time is not the bigger, more common problem that NewSQL solves: built-in scale out to large data size (relative to a single instance) with reasonable response time (75 ms, for example).

Performance characteristics

What accounts for the response time (performance) of a query? For MySQL, the high-level constituents are indexes, data, access patterns, and hardware—everything in the previous four chapters. Add to those some lower-level details—like "Leftmost Prefix Requirement" on page 49, "Working set size" on page 95, and "MySQL Does Nothing" on page 124—and you understand MySQL performance and how to improve it. A NewSQL data store will have new and different performance characteristics. For example, indexes always provide the most and the best leverage, but they can work differently for a NewSQL data store because of how the data is stored and accessed in the distributed system. Likewise, some access patterns that are good on MySQL are bad on NewSQL, and vice versa.

Those five points are a disclaimer: NewSQL is a promising technology that you should investigate as an alternative to sharding MySQL, but NewSQL is not an effortless drop-in replacement for MySQL.

At the time of this writing, there are only two viable open source NewSQL solutions that are MySQL-compatible: TiDB (*https://oreil.ly/GSCc0*) and CockroachDB (*https://oreil.ly/wKZ2Z*). Both of these solutions are exceptionally new for a data store: CockroachDB v1.0 GA released May 10, 2017; and TiDB v1.0 GA released October 16, 2017. Therefore, be cautious and diligent using TiDB and CockroachDB until at least 2027—even MySQL was 10 years old by the time it was mainstream in the early 2000s. If you use TiDB or CockroachDB, please write about what you learn and, if possible, contribute to these open source projects.

Middleware

A middleware solution works between the application and the MySQL shards. It attempts to hide or abstract the details of sharding, or at least make sharding easier. When direct, manual sharding is too difficult, and NewSQL is infeasible, a middleware solution could help bridge the gap. The two leading open source solutions are Vitess (*https://oreil.ly/6AvRY*) and ProxySQL (*https://oreil.ly/5iTkH*), and they are entirely different. ProxySQL *can* shard and Vitess *is* sharding.

ProxySQL, as its name suggests, is a proxy that supports sharding by several mechanisms. To get an idea how it works, read "Sharding in ProxySQL" (*https://oreil.ly/N0eYa*) and "MySQL Sharding with ProxySQL" (*https://oreil.ly/KDvjE*). Using a proxy in front of MySQL is similar to the classic Vim versus Emacs rift minus all the vitriol: engineers do a lot of great work with both editors; it's just a matter of personal preference. Likewise, companies are successful with and without a proxy; it's just a matter of personal preference.

Vitess is a purpose-built MySQL sharding solution. Since sharding is complex, Vitess is not without its own complexity, but its greatest advantage is that it addresses all challenges, especially resharding and rebalancing. Moreover, Vitess was created by MySQL experts at YouTube who deeply understand MySQL at massive scale.

Before you shard, be sure to evaluate ProxySQL and Vitess. Any middleware solution entails additional infrastructure to learn and maintain, but the benefits can outweigh the costs because manually sharding MySQL also costs significant engineering time, effort, and serenity.

Microservices

Sharding focuses on one application (or service) and its data, especially data size and access. But sometimes the real problem is the application: it has too much data or access because it serves too many purposes or business functions. Avoiding monolithic applications is standard engineering design and practice, but that doesn't mean it's always achieved. Before you shard, review the application design and its data to ensure that parts cannot be factored out into a separate microservice. This is a lot easier than sharding because the new microservice and its database are completely independent—no shard key or strategy required. It might also be the case that the new microservice has completely different access patterns (see "Data Access Patterns" on page 131) that allow it to use less hardware while storing more data—or perhaps the new microservice doesn't need a relational data store.

Don't Use MySQL

Similar to "Don't Use MySQL" on page 147, a completely honest assessment of the alternatives to sharding MySQL must conclude with: don't use MySQL if another data store or technology works better. If your path is designing a new application for sharding, then definitely evaluate other solutions. Sharding MySQL is a solved problem, but it's never a quick or easy solution. If your path is migrating an existing application to sharding, then you should still consider the trade-offs of sharding MySQL against migrating to another solution. That sounds burdensome at scale—and it is—but companies do it all the time, and so can you.

Summary

This chapter introduced the basic mechanics of sharding MySQL to achieve MySQL at scale. The essential takeaway points are:

- MySQL scales out by sharding.
- Sharding divides one database into many databases.
- A single database does not scale primarily because the combination of queries, data, and access patterns—the application workload—significantly outpace the speed and capacity of single-server hardware.
- It's significantly easier to manage many small databases (shards) than one huge database—pebbles, not boulders.
- Data is sharded (divided) by a shard key, which you must choose carefully.
- The shard key is used with a sharding strategy to map data (by shard key) to shards.
- The most common sharding strategies are hash (a hashing algorithm), range, and lookup (directory).
- Sharding has several challenges that must be addressed.
- There are alternatives to sharding that you should evaluate.

The next chapter looks into MySQL server metrics.

Practice: Four-Year Fit

The goal of this practice is to determine the four-year fit of the data size. From "Sharding: A Brief Introduction" on page 160, the four-year fit is an estimate of data size or access in four years applied to the capacity of your hardware *today*. Sharding might not be required if the estimated data size or access fits (figuratively) within your hardware capacity today. (Refer back to "Application Workload" on page 152 for the discussion of hardware fit.)

You will need historical data sizes to complete this practice. If you're not already measuring and recording data sizes, then jump ahead to "Data Size" on page 204 to learn how.

The simplest possible calculation is sufficient. If, for example, a database has historically increased by 10 GB every month, then the database will be 12 months × 4 years × 10 GB/month = 480 GB *larger* in four years—if no data is deleted or archived (see "Delete or Archive Data" on page 115). If the database is 100 GB today, then 580 GB in four years fits: you don't need to shard any time soon (four-year fit for access load notwithstanding) because MySQL on hardware *today* can easily handle 580 GB of data.

If your four-year fit for data size indicates that you might need to shard, take it seriously and dive deeper to determine for sure: is the database on a steady path to becoming too large for a single MySQL instance? If yes, then *shard early* because sharding is essentially a complex data migration process; therefore, the less data, the easier the process. If not, then congratulations: ensuring that the system will continue to scale for years to come is an expert practice in all fields of engineering.

## CHAPTER 6

Server Metrics

MySQL metrics are closely related to MySQL performance—that's obvious. After all, the purpose of metrics in any system is to measure and report how the system is operating. What's not obvious is how they are related. It's not unreasonable if you currently see MySQL metrics as depicted in Figure 6-1: MySQL is a black box with metrics inside that, in some way, indicate something about MySQL.

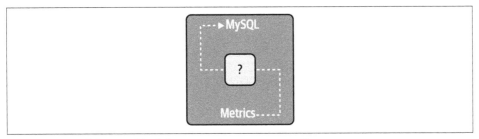

Figure 6-1. MySQL as a black box: metrics are not revealing

That view is not unreasonable (or uncommon) because MySQL metrics are often discussed but never taught. Even in my career with MySQL, I have never read or heard an exposition of MySQL metrics—and I have worked with people who created them. The lack of pedagogy for MySQL metrics is due to a false presumption that metrics do not require understanding or interpretation because their meaning is self-evident. That presumption has a semblance of truth when considering a single metric in isolation, such as `Threads_running`; it's the number of threads running—what more is there to know? But isolation is the fallacy: MySQL performance is revealed through a spectrum of MySQL metrics.

Think of MySQL as a prism. The application figuratively shines a workload into MySQL. That workload physically interacts with MySQL and the hardware on which it runs. Metrics are the spectrum revealed by the figurative refraction of the workload through MySQL, as depicted in Figure 6-2.

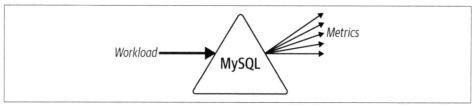

Figure 6-2. MySQL as a prism: metrics reveal workload performance

In the physical sciences, this technique is called *spectrometry*: understanding matter through its interaction with light. For MySQL, this is more than a clever analogy, it's the actual relationship between MySQL metrics and MySQL server performance, and there are two proofs:

- When you shine a light through a real prism, the resulting color spectrum reveals properties of the light, not the prism. Likewise, when you run a workload on MySQL, the resulting metrics reveal properties of the workload, not MySQL.

- Given previous chapters—especially "MySQL Does Nothing" on page 124—performance is directly attributable to workload: queries, data, and access patterns. Without a workload, all metric values are zero (generally speaking).

Viewed this way, MySQL metrics can be taught in a new light, and that is the focus of this chapter.

This analogy has another pedagogical utility: it separates MySQL metrics into *spectra* (the plural of *spectrum*). This is very useful because MySQL metrics are vast and unorganized (several hundred metrics strewn throughout MySQL), but effective teaching requires focus and organization. As a result, the "Spectra" section, which illuminates over 70 metrics divided into 11 spectra, makes up the bulk of this chapter.

A final note before we shine a light on MySQL: only a fraction of metrics are essential for understanding and analyzing MySQL server performance. The relevance and importance of the remaining metrics varies widely:

- Some are noise
- Some are historical
- Some are disabled by default

- Some are very technically specific
- Some are only useful in specific cases
- Some are informational, not proper metrics
- Some are inscrutable by feeble mortal creatures

This chapter analyzes the spectra of MySQL metrics that are essential for understanding how the workload interacts with and affects MySQL server performance. There are six major sections. The first draws a distinction between query performance and server performance. Previous chapters focus on the former, but this chapter focuses on the latter. The second is boring—you'll see why. The third lists key performance indicators (KPIs) that quickly gauge MySQL performance. The fourth explores the field of metrics: a model to more deeply understand how metrics describe and relate to MySQL server performance. The fifth presents the spectra of MySQL metrics: over 70 MySQL metrics organized into 11 spectra—an epic and exciting journey that tours the inner workings of MySQL, after which you will see MySQL in a new light. The sixth addresses important topics related to monitoring and alerting.

Query Performance Versus Server Performance

MySQL performance has two sides: query performance and server performance. Previous chapters address *query performance*: improving response time by optimizing the workload. This chapter addresses *server performance*: analyzing the performance of MySQL as a function of executing the workload.

 In this chapter, *MySQL performance* means *server performance*.

In simplest terms, the workload is input and server performance is output, as shown in Figure 6-3.

If you put an optimized workload into MySQL, you get high performance out of MySQL. Server performance is almost always an issue with the workload, not MySQL. Why? Because MySQL is incredibly good at executing a variety of workloads. MySQL is a mature, highly optimized data store—*decades* of tuning by world-class database experts. That's why the first five chapters of this book extol query performance, and only one chapter (this one) analyzes server performance.

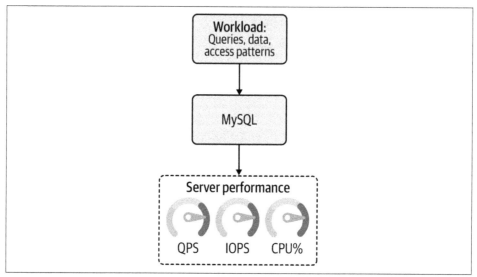

Figure 6-3. Query and server performance

There are three reasons to analyze server performance:

Concurrency and contention

Concurrency leads to contention that reduces query performance. A query executed in isolation exhibits different performance when executed with other queries. Recall the Universal Scalability Law in Equation 4-1: contention (σ) is in the divisor of the equation, which means it reduces throughput as load increases. Unless you're living in a different universe than the rest of us, concurrency and contention are unavoidable.

Analyzing server performance is most useful and most commonly undertaken to see how MySQL handles the workload when all queries (concurrency) are competing for shared and limited system resources (contention). Certain workloads have very little—if any—contention, while other workloads kill performance—both query and server performance—despite the best efforts of MySQL. The access pattern trait "Concurrency" on page 138 is, unsurprisingly, a major factor in contention, but all the access pattern traits are important, too. Analyzing server performance reveals how well the queries in the workload play together. As engineers responsible for those queries, we need to ensure that they play well.

Tuning

Server performance is directly *but not entirely* attributable to workload. There are three additional factors in server performance: MySQL, operating system, and hardware. In query performance, it's presumed that MySQL, operating system, and hardware are properly configured and adequate for the workload. Problems (like faulty hardware) and bugs notwithstanding, these three affect performance far less than the workload because we're living in an age of abundance: MySQL is very mature and highly optimized, operating systems are advanced and sophisticated, and hardware is fast and affordable.

Matters discussed in "MySQL Tuning" on page 39 still hold true: tuning MySQL is akin to squeezing blood from a turnip. You most likely never need to tune MySQL. But if you do, it requires analyzing server performance with a known and stable workload; otherwise, you cannot be certain that any performance gains are the result of tuning—it's basic science: controls, variables, reproducibility, and falsifiability.

Performance regressions

I praise MySQL throughout this book, but I would be remiss if I did not, at least once, clearly state: sometimes, MySQL is wrong. But MySQL did not become the most popular open source relational database in the world by being wrong. It is usually correct, and suspecting a performance regression (or bug) is the last resort of experts after ensuring that query performance, MySQL tuning, and faulty hardware are not the problem.

The blog posts "Checkpointing in MySQL and MariaDB" (*https://oreil.ly/MuRIt*) and "More on Checkpoints in InnoDB MySQL 8" (*https://oreil.ly/NDQkP*) by renowned MySQL expert Vadim Tkachenko contain perfect examples of analyzing server performance to reveal a performance regression. It's normal for Vadim to be doing this type of work; the rest of us plod through much simpler problems, like indexing and whether or not to have a third cup of coffee before lunch.

Flawed Optics

Tuning and performance regressions are an exception to the analogy of MySQL as a prism (Figure 6-2) that only reveals properties of the workload, not MySQL. A known and stable workload is analogous to shining a pure blue light through a prism: presuming the input is correct, an incorrect output reveals something about the prism.

Concurrency and contention are the implicit focus of this chapter because they are the responsibility of the engineers who maintain the application that executes the queries. Tuning and performance regressions are the responsibility of MySQL DBAs and experts. Learning to analyze server performance for the former (concurrency and contention) is excellent training for the latter because the difference is primarily a matter of focus. I hope the former sparks an interests in the latter because the MySQL industry needs more DBAs and experts.

Normal and Stable: The Best Database Is a Boring Database

For the most part, *normal* and *stable* are intuitively understood by engineers once they become familiar with the application and how its workload runs on MySQL. Humans are good at pattern recognition, so it's easy to see when the charts for any metric are unusual. Therefore, I won't belabor terminology that is generally well understood, but I need to make two clarifying points to ensure that we're on the same page, and to address the rare times when engineers ask "What is normal?" with respect to MySQL performance:

Normal

Every application, workload, MySQL configuration, and environment are different. Therefore, normal is whatever performance MySQL exhibits for your application on a typical day when everything is working properly. That normal—your normal—is the baseline for determining if some aspect of performance is higher or lower, faster or slower, better or worse than normal. It's as simple as that.

When I state a presumptive norm like "It's normal for Threads_running to be less than 50," it's only an abbreviation of language, short for "A stable value for Threads_running is less than 50 given my experience, and given that current hardware typically has less than 48 CPU cores, and given that benchmarks show that MySQL performance does not currently scale well past 64 running threads." But if 60 threads running is normal and stable for your application, then great: you have achieved extraordinary performance.

Stable

Don't lose sight of stable performance in your quest for greater performance. "Performance Destabilizes at the Limit" on page 125 illustrates and explains why squeezing maximum performance from MySQL is not the goal: at the limit, performance destabilizes, and then you have bigger problems than performance. Stability does not limit performance; it ensures that performance—at any level— is sustainable, because that's what we really want: MySQL fast all the time, not sometimes.

At times, MySQL performance is glamorous—the highs, the lows, the screaming fans and packed stadiums—but the real art is optimizing the database into pristine boredom: all queries respond quickly, all metrics are stable and normal, and all users are happy.

Key Performance Indicators

Four metrics quickly gauge MySQL performance:

Response time
> Response time is no surprise: as noted in "North Star" on page 3, it's the only metric anyone truly cares about. Even if response time is great, you must factor in other KPIs. For example, if every query fails with an error, response time might be amazing (near zero), but that's not normal. The goal is normal and stable response time, and lower is better.

Errors
> Errors is the rate of errors. Which errors? At least query errors, but ideally all errors: query, connection, client, and server. Don't expect a zero error rate because, for example, there's nothing you, the application, or MySQL can do if a client aborts a connection. The goal is a normal and stable error rate, and lower (near zero) is better.

QPS
> Queries per second is also no surprise: executing queries is the main purpose and work of MySQL. QPS indicates performance, but it does not equal performance. Abnormally high QPS, for example, can signal problems. The goal is normal and stable QPS, and the value is arbitrary.

Threads running
> Threads running gauges how hard MySQL is working to achieve QPS. One thread executes one query, so you must consider both metrics because they're closely related. The goal is normal and stable threads running; lower is better.

I expound these metrics in "Spectra" on page 187. Here, the point is that these four metrics are the KPIs for MySQL: when the values for all four are normal, MySQL performance is practically guaranteed also to be normal. Always monitor response time, errors, QPS, and threads running. Whether or not to alert on them is discussed later in "Alert on User Experience and Objective Limits" on page 226.

Simplifying the performance of a complex system to a handful of metrics is not unique to MySQL or computers. For example, you have vital signs (I hope): height, weight, age, blood pressure, and heart rate. Five biological metrics succinctly and accurately gauge your health. Likewise, four MySQL metrics succinctly and accurately gauge server performance. That's nifty, but what's really insightful is the field of metrics in which all metrics are situated.

Field of Metrics

Every MySQL metric belongs to one of six classes shown as boxes in Figure 6-4. Collectively, I call it the *field of metrics*.

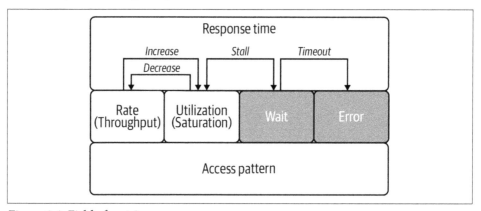

Figure 6-4. Field of metrics

MySQL performance cannot be fully understood by analyzing metrics in isolation because performance is not an isolated property. Performance is the result of many factors for which there are many related metrics. The field of metrics is a model to understand how metrics are related. The relationships connect the proverbial dots (the metrics) to complete the intricate picture that is MySQL performance.

Response Time

Response time metrics indicate *how long* MySQL takes to respond. They are top level in the field because they encompass (or hide) details from lower levels.

Query response time is, of course, the most important one and the only one commonly monitored. MySQL executes statements in stages, and stages can be timed.

These are response time metrics, too, but they measure around query execution, not within it. Actual query execution is just one stage of many. If you recall Example 1-3 in Chapter 1, executing the actual UPDATE of an UPDATE statement was only 1 of 15 stages. Consequently, stage response times are mostly used by MySQL experts to investigate deep server performance issues.

Response time metrics are important but also completely opaque: what was MySQL doing that accounts for the time? To answer that, we must dig deeper into the field.

Rate

Rate metrics indicate *how fast* MySQL completes a discrete task. Queries per second (QPS) is the ubiquitous and universally known database rate metric. Most MySQL metrics are rates because—no surprise—MySQL does many discrete tasks.

When a rate increases, it can increase related utilizations. Some rates are innocuous and don't increase utilization, but the important and commonly monitored rates do increase utilization.

The rate-utilization relationship presumes no other changes. That means you can increase a rate without increasing utilization only if you change something about the rate or the utilization that it affects. It's usually easier to change the rate rather than the utilization because the rate is the cause in the relationship. For example, when QPS increases across the board, CPU utilization could increase because more queries require more CPU time. (Increasing QPS could increase other utilizations; CPU is just one example.) To avoid or reduce the increase in CPU utilization, you should optimize the queries so they require less CPU time to execute. Or, you could increase the number of CPU cores by scaling up the hardware, but "Better, Faster Hardware!" on page 37 and "Better, Faster Hardware?" on page 148 address the shortcomings of this approach.

The rate-utilization relationship is not a novel insight—you probably already knew it—but it's important to highlight because it's the beginning of a series of relationships that unify the field. Don't feel sorry for utilization: it pushes back.

Utilization

Utilization metrics indicate *how much* MySQL uses a finite resource. Utilization metrics are everywhere in computers: CPU usage, memory usage, disk usage, and so on. Since computers are finite machines, almost everything can be expressed as a utilization because nothing has infinite capacity—not even the cloud.

Bounded rates can be expressed as a utilization. A rate is bounded if there is a maximum rate. Disk I/O, for example, is usually expressed as a rate (IOPS), but every storage device has a maximum rate. Therefore, disk I/O utilization is the current rate over the maximum rate. By contrast, *unbounded rates* cannot be expressed as a utilization because there's no maximum rate: QPS, bytes sent and received, and so forth.

When a utilization increases, it can decrease related rates. I bet you've seen or experienced something like this before: a rogue query causes 100% disk I/O utilization, which causes QPS to drop precipitously, which causes an outage. Or, MySQL uses 100% of memory and is killed by the operating system kernel, which causes the ultimate rate decrease: to zero. This relationship is an expression of the USL (recall Equation 4-1) because utilization increases contention (α) and coherency (β), which are in the divisor of the equation.

What happens at *or near* 100% utilization? MySQL waits. In Figure 6-4, this is indicated by the arrow between *Utilization* and *Wait*—the utilization-wait relationship. The arrow is labeled *Stall* because query execution waits, then resumes—perhaps many times. I emphasize *or near* because, as discussed in "Performance Destabilizes at the Limit" on page 125, stalls can occur before 100% utilization.

Stalls are anti-stable but unavoidable for two reasons: MySQL load is usually greater than hardware capacity; and latency is inherent in all systems, especially hardware. The first reason can be ameliorated by reducing load (optimizing the workload) or increasing hardware capacity. The second reason is difficult to address but not impossible. If, for example, you still use spinning disks, upgrading to NVMe storage will dramatically reduce storage latency.

Wait

Wait metrics indicate idle time during query execution. Waits occur when query execution stalls due to contention and coherency. (Waits also occur due to MySQL bugs or performance regressions, but these are exceedingly rare enough not to raise concern.)

Wait metrics are calculated as rates or response times (depending on the metric), but they merit a separate class because they reveal when MySQL is *not working* (idle), which is the opposite of performance. *Not working* is why the wait class in Figure 6-4 is darker: MySQL has gone dark.

Waits are unavoidable. Eliminating waits is not the goal; the goal is reducing and stabilizing them. When waits are stabilized and reduced to an acceptable level, they effectively disappear, blending into response time as an inherent part of query execution.

When MySQL waits too long, it times out—the wait-error relationship. The most important, high-level MySQL waits have configurable timeouts:

- MAX_EXECUTION_TIME (*https://oreil.ly/H0fwi*) (SQL statement optimizer hint)
- max_execution_time (*https://oreil.ly/2rdKw*)
- lock_wait_timeout (*https://oreil.ly/WD6p7*)
- innodb_lock_wait_timeout (*https://oreil.ly/4uT4F*)
- connect_timeout (*https://oreil.ly/R7HwC*)
- wait_timeout (*https://oreil.ly/C7M9a*)

Use these but don't rely on them because, for example, take a guess at the default value for lock_wait_timeout. The default value for lock_wait_timeout is 31,536,000 seconds—365 days. Establishing default values is not easy, so we must give MySQL some leeway, but wow—365 days. Consequently, applications should always employ code-level timeouts, too. Long-running transactions and queries are a common problem because MySQL is fast but, perhaps, too patient.

Error

Error metrics indicate errors. (I allow myself one tautological statement in this book; there it is.) Wait timeouts are one type of error, and there are many more (see "MySQL Error Message Reference" (*https://oreil.ly/Jtpqd*) for more). I don't need to enumerate MySQL errors because, with respect to server performance and MySQL metrics, the point is simple and clear: an abnormal error rate is bad. Like waits, errors are also calculated as rates, but they merit a separate class because they indicate when MySQL or the client (the application) has failed, which is why the error class in Figure 6-4 is darker.

To reiterate a point about errors from "Key Performance Indicators" on page 181: don't expect a zero error rate because, for example, there's nothing you, the application, or MySQL can do if a client aborts a connection.

Access Pattern

Access pattern metrics indicate how the application uses MySQL. These metrics relate to "Data Access Patterns" on page 131. For example, MySQL has metrics for each type of SQL statement (Com_select, Com_insert, and so on) that relate to "Read/Write" on page 133.

As indicated in Figure 6-4, access pattern metrics underlie higher level metrics. The Com_select access pattern metric counts the number of SELECT statements executed. This can be represented as a rate (SELECT QPS) or a utilization (% SELECT); either way, it reveals something deeper about server performance that helps explain higher level metrics. For example, if response time is abysmal and the access pattern metric Select_full_join is high, that's a smoking gun (see "Select full join" on page 21).

Internal

There's a seventh class of metrics shown in Figure 6-5: internal metrics.

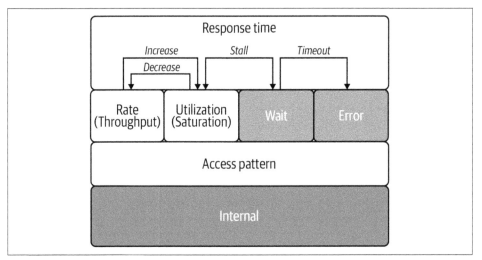

Figure 6-5. Field of metrics with internal metrics

I didn't mention this class at the beginning of "Field of Metrics" on page 182 because, as engineers and users of MySQL, we're not supposed to know or care about it. But it's the most interesting—if not arcane—part of the field, and I want you to be fully informed in case you need or want to fathom the depths of MySQL. Down here, things are esoteric.

Of course, *esoteric* is subjective. What I consider to be an internal metric might be the most favorite and useful rate metric for another engineer. But metrics like `buffer_page_read_index_ibuf_non_leaf` make a strong case for the internal class of metrics. That metric indicates the number of non-leaf index pages read in the change buffer. Not exactly your daily bread.

Spectra

Prepare yourself for another journey: into the penumbra of MySQL metrics. This section examines over 70 MySQL metrics divided into 11 spectra, some of which have sub-spectra. I organize MySQL metrics into spectra for two reasons:

- Spectra give the journey waypoints. Without them, we face a vast and unorganized universe swirling with nearly *one thousand* metrics from different sources that vary by MySQL version, distribution, and configuration.

- Spectra reveal important areas of MySQL to understand and monitor with respect to performance.

Even with spectra illuminating a path through the darkness, we need a metric naming convention to talk clearly and precisely about the MySQL metrics and system variables that constitute each spectrum. The reason is simple: MySQL does not have a metric naming convention, and there is no industry standard, either. Table 6-1 is the MySQL metric naming convention that I use in this book.

Table 6-1. MySQL metric naming convention

Example	Refers to
`Threads_running`	Global status variables
`var.max_connections`	Global system variables
`innodb.log_lsn_checkpoint_age`	InnoDB metrics
replication lag	Derived metrics

Most metrics are global status variables that you have likely seen or used by executing SHOW GLOBAL STATUS (*https://oreil.ly/NacuT*): `Aborted_connects`, `Queries`, `Threads_running`, and so forth. In MySQL and this book, global status variable names begin with a single uppercase letter followed by lowercase letters, even if the first word is an acronym: `Ssl_client_connects`, *not* `SSL_client_connects`. (This is one aspect of MySQL metrics that is consistent.) By contrast, global system variables are lowercase; and to make them more distinct, I prefix them with `var.`, which is important given the next convention. InnoDB metrics are also lowercase, like lock_timeouts. Since that can look like a global system variable, I prefix InnoDB metrics with innodb., like innodb.lock_timeouts. Derived metrics are ubiquitous in monitoring but not native to MySQL. *Replication lag*, for example, is a metric that nearly every monitor will emit, but the precise metric name depends on the monitor, which is why I use a descriptive name without underscore characters rather than a specific technical name.

 The InnoDB metrics in this section require enabling certain counters or modules. For example, starting MySQL with innodb_monitor_enable=module_log,module_buffer,mod ule_trx. See var.innodb_monitor_enable (*https://oreil.ly/nFKFT*) and "InnoDB INFORMATION_SCHEMA Metrics Table" (*https://oreil.ly/e0wpA*) in the MySQL manual.

Second to last bit of mental equipment: *global* refers to the entire MySQL server: all clients, all users, all queries, and so on—combined. By contrast, there are *session* and *summary* metrics. Session metrics are global metrics scoped to a single client connection. Summary metrics are usually a subset of global metrics scoped to a variety of aspects: account, host, thread, transaction, and so on. This chapter looks only at global metrics since they underlie all metrics. (Global metrics are also the original: in ancient times, MySQL had only global metrics; then it added session metrics; then it added summary metrics.)

Last bit of mental equipment before we begin the journey: most MySQL metrics are simple counters, and only a few are gauges. I explicitly note the gauges; otherwise, counter is implied. Let's begin!

Query Response Time

Global query response time is one of the four "Key Performance Indicators" on page 181. Surprisingly, MySQL did not have this metric until version 8.0. As of MySQL 8.0.1, you can obtain the 95th percentile (P95) global query response time in milliseconds from the Performance Schema (*https://oreil.ly/dj06D*) by executing the query in Example 6-1.

Example 6-1. Global 95th percentile query response time

```
SELECT
  ROUND(bucket_quantile * 100, 1) AS p,
  ROUND(BUCKET_TIMER_HIGH / 1000000000, 3) AS ms
FROM
  performance_schema.events_statements_histogram_global
WHERE
  bucket_quantile >= 0.95
ORDER BY bucket_quantile LIMIT 1;
```

That query returns a percentile very close to—but not exactly—the P95: 95.2% instead of 95.0%, for example.[1] The difference is negligible and does not affect monitoring.

You can replace `0.95` in the query to return a different percentile: `0.99` for P99, or `0.999` for P999. I prefer and advise P999 for the reasons stated in "Average, Percentile, and Maximum" on page 25.

The rest of this section is for MySQL 5.7 and older—skip it if you're running MySQL 8.0 or newer.

MySQL 5.7 and older
> MySQL 5.7 and older do not expose a global query response time metric. Only query metrics include response time (see "Query time" on page 12), but that is per-query response time. To calculate global response time, you would need to aggregate it from every query. That's possible, but there are two better alternatives: upgrade to MySQL 8.0; or, switch to Percona Server or MariaDB, which have a plug-in to capture global response time.

Percona Server 5.7
> Way back in 2010, Percona Server (*https://oreil.ly/Gyq8J*) introduced a plug-in to capture global response time called Response Time Distribution (*https://oreil.ly/PE5kh*). It's easy to install the plug-in, but it takes work to configure and use because it's a histogram of response time ranges, which means you need to set `var.query_response_time_range_base`—a global system variable that the plug-in creates—to configure the histogram bucket ranges, then compute a percentile from the bucket counts. MySQL 8.0 global response time is also a histogram, but the bucket ranges and percentiles are preset and precomputed, which is why the query in Example 6-1 works out of the box. It's not that difficult to set up; it only sounds complicated. The benefit of having global response time is well worth the effort.

MariaDB 10.0
> MariaDB (*https://oreil.ly/oeGJO*) uses the same plug-in from Percona but it has a slightly different name: Query Response Time Plugin (*https://oreil.ly/kb4gA*). Although introduced in MariaDB 10.0, it was not marked stable until MariaDB 10.1.

Before MySQL 8.0, obtaining global query response time is not trivial, but it's worth the effort if you're running Percona Server or MariaDB. If you're running MySQL in the cloud, check the cloud provider metrics because some provide a response

---

1 The MySQL worklog 5384 (*https://oreil.ly/2kFWK*) explains how response time quantiles are implemented in the Performance Schema.

time metric (which the cloud provider might call *latency*). If nothing else, frequently review the query profile to keep an eye on response times.

Errors

Errors are one of the four "Key Performance Indicators" on page 181. As of MySQL 8.0.0, it's easy to obtain a count of *all* errors from the Performance Schema (*https://oreil.ly/glJUC*) by executing the query in Example 6-2.

Example 6-2. Global error count

```
SELECT
  SUM(SUM_ERROR_RAISED) AS global_errors
FROM
  performance_schema.events_errors_summary_global_by_error
WHERE
  ERROR_NUMBER NOT IN (1287);
```

 Error number 1287, excluded in the WHERE clause in Example 6-2, is for deprecation warnings: when a query uses a feature that is deprecated, MySQL issues a warning. Including this error number is likely to make the global error count too noisy, which is why I exclude it.

Since MySQL has so many errors and warnings, there's no telling what your global error rate will be. Don't expect or try to achieve a zero error rate. That's essentially impossible because clients can cause errors, and there's nothing you, the application, or MySQL can do to prevent that. The goal is to establish the normal error rate for the application. If the query in Example 6-2 is too noisy—which means it produces a high rate of errors but you are certain the application is functioning normally—then fine tune the query by excluding additional error numbers. MySQL error codes are documented in the "MySQL Error Message Reference" (*https://oreil.ly/wKfnV*).

Before MySQL 8.0, you cannot obtain a global error count from MySQL, but you can obtain a count of all *query* errors from the Performance Schema (*https://oreil.ly/QiHj8*) by executing the query in Example 6-3.

Example 6-3. Query error count

```
SELECT
  SUM(sum_errors) AS query_errors
FROM
  performance_schema.events_statements_summary_global_by_event_name
WHERE
  event_name LIKE 'statement/sql/%';
```

Since this works in all distributions as of MySQL 5.6, there is no reason not to monitor all query errors. Granted, the application should report query errors, too; but if it also retries on error, it might hide a certain amount of errors. By contrast, this will expose all query errors, potentially revealing a problem that application retries are masking.

The last error metrics are client connection errors:

- `Aborted_clients`
- `Aborted_connects`
- `Connection_errors_%`

The first two metrics are commonly monitored to ensure that there are no issues *while connecting* or *already connected* to MySQL. That wording is precise: if the application cannot make a network connection to MySQL, then MySQL does not see the client and does not report a client connection error because, from the MySQL point of view, there is no client connection yet. Low-level network connection issues should be reported by the application. However, if the application cannot connect, you're likely to see a drop in the other three KPIs (QPS, threads running, and response time) because the application isn't executing queries.

> The `%` character in `Connection_errors_%` is a MySQL wildcard; several metrics exist with the prefix `Connection_errors_`. To list them, execute `SHOW GLOBAL STATUS LIKE Connection_errors_%;`.

Before moving on to the next spectrum, let's address a problem that's also not a problem—at least not for MySQL. If the application begins to spew errors but MySQL does not and the other three KPIs are normal, then the problem is with the application or the network. MySQL has many quirks, but lying is not one of them. If MySQL KPIs are thumbs up (all okay and normal), then you can trust that MySQL is working normally.

Queries

Metrics related to queries reveal how fast MySQL is working and what type of work it's doing—at a very high level. These metrics reveal two access pattern traits: throughput and read/write (see "Throughput" and "Read/Write" on page 133).

QPS

QPS is one of the four "Key Performance Indicators" on page 181. The underlying metric is aptly named:

- Queries

That metric is a counter, but QPS is a rate, so technically QPS equals the difference of two Queries measurements divided by the number of seconds between the measurements: QPS = (Queries @ T1 – Queries @ T0) / (T1 – T0), where T0 is the time of the first measurement and T1 is the time of the second measurement. Metric graphing systems (like Grafana (*https://grafana.com*)) convert counters to rates by default. As a result, you should not need to convert Queries or any other counters to rates. Just be aware that most MySQL metrics are counters, but they are converted to and expressed as rates.

Metric graphing systems convert counters to rates by default.

QPS receives a lot of attention because it indicates overall MySQL throughput—how fast MySQL is executing queries—but don't fixate on it. As mentioned in "Less QPS Is Better" on page 96, QPS reveals nothing qualitative about the queries or performance in general. If QPS is incredibly high but response time is also incredibly high, then QPS indicates a problem, not great performance. Other metrics reveal more about MySQL performance than QPS.

When everything is running normally, QPS fluctuates with application usage. When there is a problem, QPS fluctuations correlate with other metrics. To analyze performance or diagnose a problem, I glance at QPS to see where (in a chart) its value is abnormal. Then I correlate that period (time along the X axis of the chart) with other, more specific metrics in the spectra. As a KPI, QPS indicates a problem, but other metrics pinpoint the problem.

All abnormal changes in QPS are suspect and worth investigating. Most, if not all, engineers know that a drop in QPS is bad, but an abnormal increase in QPS can be equally bad or worse. Also bad but more rare is flatline QPS—a nearly constant QPS value—because minor fluctuations are normal. When QPS changes abnormally, the first question is usually: what's the cause? I address that later in this chapter (see "Cause and Effect" on page 228).

MySQL exposes another closely related metric: Questions. (The term *question* is only used for this metric; it's not used for anything else inside MySQL.) Questions counts only queries sent by clients, not queries executed by stored programs. For example, queries executed by a trigger do *not* count in Questions because a client did not send them; but they do count in Queries. Since Questions is a subset of Queries, the difference is only informational, and monitoring Questions is optional. For QPS, always use Queries.

TPS

If the application relies on explicit, multistatement transactions, then transactions per second (TPS) is as important as QPS. For some applications, a database transaction represents a unit of work in the application, so TPS is a better rate than QPS because the application unit of work is all or nothing, which is why it's executed in an explicit transaction.

 An *implicit transaction* is a single SQL statement with autocommit (*https://oreil.ly/zrjQK*) enabled, which is the default. An *explicit transaction* starts with BEGIN or START TRANSACTION and ends with either COMMIT or ROLLBACK, regardless of autocommit.

In MySQL, explicit transaction throughput is revealed by three metrics:

- Com_begin
- Com_commit
- Com_rollback

Normally, the rate of Com_begin and Com_commit are the same because every transaction must begin and successful transactions must commit. When there's a problem that causes transactions to stall (one of the "Common Problems" on page 282), the rate of Com_begin exceeds the other two metrics.

Use Com_commit to measure TPS because transaction throughput implies successful transactions.

A transaction rollback is supposed to indicate an error—since transactions are all or nothing—but the ROLLBACK statement is also commonly used for cleanup: it ensures that the previous transaction—if any—is closed before starting the next transaction. Consequently, the rollback rate might not be zero. As with most metrics, normal and stable is the goal (see "Normal and Stable: The Best Database Is a Boring Database" on page 180).

Another gauge metric that indicates the current number of active transactions is innodb.trx_active_transactions.

BEGIN starts a transaction, but a transaction is not *active* until, generally speaking, a query accesses a table. For example, BEGIN; SELECT NOW(); starts a transaction that is not active because no query accesses a table.

SHOW ENGINE INNODB STATUS

InnoDB metrics are exposed in the information_schema.innodb_metrics table. (See "InnoDB INFORMATION_SCHEMA Metrics Table" (*https://oreil.ly/GHalc*) for details.) Before this table was mainstream, InnoDB metrics were exposed using the SHOW ENGINE INNODB STATUS command, but the output is a long blob of text. The text is divided into sections, which makes it a little easier for humans to read, but it's programmatically unorganized: it requires parsing and pattern matching to extract specific metric values. Some MySQL monitors still use SHOW ENGINE INNODB STATUS, but avoid this if you can because using the Information Schema (and Performance Schema) is the best practice.

I no longer consider SHOW ENGINE INNODB STATUS authoritative. For example, with respect to active transactions, BEGIN; SELECT col FROM tbl; does *not* show as active in SHOW ENGINE INNODB STATUS, but it correctly shows as active in innodb.trx_active_transactions.

Read/write

There are nine read/write metrics named according to a type of SQL statement:

- Com_select
- Com_delete
- Com_delete_multi
- Com_insert
- Com_insert_select
- Com_replace
- Com_replace_select
- Com_update
- Com_update_multi

For example, Com_select is a counter for the number of SELECT statements. The _multi suffix in Com_delete_multi and Com_update_multi refers to queries that reference multiple tables. A multitable DELETE increments only Com_delete_multi, whereas a single-table DELETE only updates Com_delete. The same is true for UPDATE statements with respect to Com_update_multi and Com_update.

Read/write metrics reveal the important types and throughputs of queries that constitute Queries. These metrics do not fully account for Queries; they are only the most important metrics with respect to performance.

Monitor these metrics as individual rates and percentages of Queries:

- Com_select indicates the read percentage of the workload:

    (Com_select / Queries) × 100.

- The sum of the other eight metrics indicates the write percentage of the workload.[2]

The read and write percentages will *not* equal 100% because Queries accounts for other types of SQL statements: SHOW, FLUSH, GRANT, and many more. If the remaining percentage is suspiciously high (more than 20%), it probably won't affect performance, but it's worth investigating: examine other Com_ metrics to account for other types of SQL statements.

Admin

Admin metrics refer to commands that, typically, only database administrators invoke:

- Com_flush
- Com_kill
- Com_purge
- Com_admin_commands

The first three metrics refer to FLUSH (*https://oreil.ly/O6j77*), KILL (*https://oreil.ly/fMbiY*), and PURGE (*https://oreil.ly/czxYb*), respectively. These commands could affect performance, but they should be very rare. If not, ask your DBA or cloud provider what they're doing.

The last metric, Com_admin_commands, is an oddity. It refers to other admin commands for which there are not specific Com_ status variables. For example, the MySQL protocol has a ping command that is commonly used by MySQL client drivers to test the connection. This is harmless in moderation, but problems can result from a

---

2 Com_insert_select and Com_replace_select are technically both reads and writes, but for simplicity I count them as writes.

lack of moderation. Don't expect `Com_admin_commands` to indicate any problems, but monitoring it is still a best practice.

SHOW

MySQL has over 40 `SHOW` (*https://oreil.ly/u7Xzs*) statements, most of which have a corresponding `Com_show_` metric. `SHOW` commands never change MySQL or modify data, so in that sense they're harmless. But they are queries, which means they use a thread, time, and resources in MySQL. `SHOW` commands can stall, too. `SHOW GLOBALS STATUS`, for example, can take a full second or more on a busy server. Consequently, it's a best practice to monitor at least the following 10 metrics:

- `Com_show_databases`
- `Com_show_engine_status`
- `Com_show_errors`
- `Com_show_processlist`
- `Com_show_slave_status`
- `Com_show_status`
- `Com_show_table_status`
- `Com_show_tables`
- `Com_show_variables`
- `Com_show_warnings`

As of MySQL 8.0.22, monitor `Com_show_replica_status` instead of `Com_show_slave_status`.

Don't expect `SHOW` metrics to indicate any problems, but don't be surprised if one does because it wouldn't be the first time.

Threads and Connections

`Threads_running` is one of the four "Key Performance Indicators" on page 181. It indicates how hard MySQL is working because it's directly connected to active query execution (when a client connection is not executing a query, its thread is idle), and it's effectively limited by the number of CPU cores. Let's come back to `Threads_running` after looking at related metrics.

Threads and connections are one spectrum because they are directly related: MySQL runs one thread per client connection. The four most important metrics for threads and connections are:

- Connections
- Max_used_connections
- Threads_connected
- Threads_running

Connections is the number of connection attempts to MySQL, both successful and failed. It reveals the stability of the application connection pool to MySQL. Usually, application connections to MySQL are long-lived, where *long* is at least a few seconds, if not minutes or hours. Long-lived connections avoid the overhead of establishing a connection. When the application and MySQL are on the same local network, the overhead is negligible: 1 millisecond or less. But network latency between the application and MySQL adds up quickly when multiplied by hundreds of connections and multiplied again by the connection rate. (Connections is a counter but expressed as a rate: connections/second.) MySQL can easily handle hundreds of connections per second, but if this metric reveals an abnormally high rate of connections, find and fix the root cause.

Max_used_connections as a percentage of var.max_connections (*https://oreil.ly/MVZaQ*) reveals connection utilization. The default value for var.max_connections is 151, which is probably too low for most applications but *not* because the application needs more connections for performance. The application needs more connections only because each application instance has its own connection pool. (I presume the application is scaled out.) If the connection pool size is 100 and there are 3 application instances, then the application (all instances) can create 300 connections to MySQL. That is the main reason why 151 max connections is not sufficient.

A common misconception is that the application needs thousands of connections to MySQL for performance or to support thousands of users. This is patently not true. The limiting factor is threads, not connections—more on Threads_running in a moment. A single MySQL instance can easily handle thousands of connections. I've seen 4,000 connections in production and more in benchmarks. But for most applications, several hundred connections (total) is more than sufficient. If your application demonstrably requires several thousand connections, then you need to shard (see Chapter 5).

The real problem to monitor and avoid is 100% connection utilization. If MySQL runs out of available connections, an application outage is essentially guaranteed. If connection utilization rises suddenly, approaching 100%, the cause is always an external problem, or bug, or both. (MySQL cannot connect to itself, so the cause must be external.) In response to an external problem—like a network issue, for example—the application creates more connections than normal. Or, a bug causes the application not to close connections—commonly known as a *connection leak*. Or, an external problem triggers a bug in the application—I've seen it happen. Either way, the underlying cause is always external: something outside MySQL is connecting to MySQL and using all the connections.

As clients connect and disconnect, MySQL increments and decrements the Threads_connected gauge metric. The name of this metric is a little misleading since *clients* are connected, not threads, but it reflects that MySQL runs one thread per client connection.

Threads_running is a gauge metric and an implicit utilization relative to the number of CPU cores. Although Threads_running can spike into the hundreds and thousands, performance will degrade sharply at much lower values: around twice the number of CPU cores. The reason is simple: one CPU core runs one thread. When the number of threads running is greater than the number of CPU cores, it means that some threads are stalled—waiting for CPU time. This is analogous to rush hour traffic: thousands of cars in gridlock on the highway, engines running but barely moving. (Or, for electric cars: batteries running but barely moving.) Consequently, it's normal for Threads_running to be quite low: less than 30. Bursts lasting seconds or less are possible with good hardware and an optimized workload, but sustained (normal and stable) Threads_running should be as low as possible. As in "Less QPS Is Better" on page 96, less Threads_running is better too.

High throughput (QPS) with very low threads running is a strong indication of efficient performance because there is only one way to achieve both: very fast query response time. Table 6-2 lists threads running and QPS from five real (and different) applications.

Table 6-2. Threads running and QPS

Threads running	QPS
4	8,000
8	6,000
8	30,000
12	23,000
15	33,000

The second and third rows highlight how profoundly the application workload affects performance: with one workload, 6,000 QPS needs 8 threads running; but another workload achieves 5x QPS (30,000) with the same number of threads. For the last row, 33,000 QPS is not exceptionally high, but that database is sharded: total QPS across all shards exceeds one million. Empirically, high throughput is possible with few threads running.

Temporary Objects

Temporary objects are temporary files and tables that MySQL uses for various purposes: sorting rows, large joins, and so on. Three metrics count the number of temporary tables on disk, temporary tables in memory, and temporary files (on disk) created:

- `Created_tmp_disk_tables`
- `Created_tmp_tables`
- `Created_tmp_files`

These metrics are rarely zero because temporary objects are common and harmless as long as the rates are stable. The most impactful metric is `Created_tmp_disk_tables`, which is the reciprocal of `Created_tmp_tables`. When MySQL needs a temporary table to execute a query (for `GROUP BY`, for example), it starts with an in-memory temporary table and increments `Created_tmp_tables`. This shouldn't impact performance because it's in memory. But if that temporary table grows larger than `var.tmp_table_size` (*https://oreil.ly/4plVm*)—the system variable that determines the in-memory temporary table size—then MySQL writes the temporary table to disk and increments `Created_tmp_disk_tables`. In moderation, this probably won't impact performance, but it certainly doesn't help, either, because storage is significantly slower than memory. The same is true for `Created_tmp_files`: acceptable in moderation, but not helping performance.

> As of MySQL 8.0, `Created_tmp_disk_tables` does *not* count temporary tables created on disk. This is due to the new storage engine used for internal temporary tables: `TempTable`. The corresponding metric is a Performance Schema memory instrument: `memory/temptable/physical_disk`. (A related instrument is `memory/temptable/physical_ram`, which tracks `TempTable` memory allocation for in-memory temporary tables.) If you're using MySQL 8.0, talk with your DBA to ensure that this metric is collected and reported correctly.

Since temporary objects are side effects of queries, these metrics are most revealing when a change in one correlates to a change in KPIs. For example, a sudden increase in `Created_tmp_disk_tables` coupled with a sudden increase in response time screams "Look at me!"[3]

Prepared Statements

Prepared statements are a double-edged sword: used properly, they increase efficiency; but used improperly (or unknowingly), they increase waste. The proper and most efficient way to use prepared statements is to prepare once and execute many times, which is counted by two metrics:

- `Com_stmt_prepare`
- `Com_stmt_execute`

`Com_stmt_execute` should be significantly greater than `Com_stmt_prepare`. If it isn't, then prepared statements are increasing waste due to extra queries to prepare and close the statement. The worst case is when these metrics are one-to-one, or close to it, because a single query incurs two wasted roundtrips to MySQL: one to prepare and another to close the statement. When MySQL and the application are on the same local network, two extra roundtrips might not be noticeable, but they are pure waste multiplied by QPS. For example, an extra 1 millisecond at 1,000 QPS is a wasted second—a second during which another 1,000 queries could have been executed.

Aside from the performance implications, you should monitor these prepared statement metrics because the application might be using prepared statements unintentionally. For example, the MySQL driver for the Go programming language defaults to using prepared statements for security: to avoid SQL injection vulnerabilities. At first glance (or any number of glances), you would not think that the Go code in Example 6-4 uses a prepared statement, but it does.

Example 6-4. Hidden prepared statement

```
id := 75
db.QueryRow("SELECT col FROM tbl WHERE id = ?", id)
```

Check the documentation for the MySQL driver that the application uses. If it does not explicitly mention if and when it uses prepared statements, then verify manually: on a development instance of MySQL (your laptop, for example), enable the general query log (*https://oreil.ly/1Vczu*) and write a test program to execute SQL statements using the same methods and function calls that the application uses. The general log indicates when prepared statements are used:

---

3 "I'm Mr. Meeseeks, look at me!"

```
2022-03-01T00:06:51.164761Z    32 Prepare    SELECT col FROM tbl WHERE id=?
2022-03-01T00:06:51.164870Z    32 Execute    SELECT col FROM tbl WHERE id=75
2022-03-01T00:06:51.165127Z    32 Close stmt
```

Finally, the number of open prepared statements is limited to `var.max_prepared_stmt_count` (*https://oreil.ly/K2MWz*), which is 16,382 by default. (Even 1,000 prepared statements is a lot for one application, unless the application is programmatically generating statements.) This gauge metric reports the current number of open prepared statements:

- `Prepared_stmt_count`

Don't let `Prepared_stmt_count` reach `var.max_prepared_stmt_count`, else the application will stop working. If this happens, it's an application bug due to leaking (not closing) prepared statements.

Bad SELECT

Four metrics count the occurrence of `SELECT` statements that are usually bad for performance:[4]

- `Select_scan`
- `Select_full_join`
- `Select_full_range_join`
- `Select_range_check`

`Select_scan` and `Select_full_join` are described in Chapter 1: "Select scan" on page 20 and "Select full join" on page 21, respectively. The only difference here is that these two metrics apply globally (all queries).

`Select_full_range_join` is the lesser evil of `Select_full_join`: instead of a full table scan to join a table, MySQL uses an index to do a range scan. It's possible that the range is limited and response time for the `SELECT` is acceptable, but it's bad enough to warrant its own metric.

`Select_range_check` is similar to but worse than `Select_full_range_join`. It's easiest to explain with a simple query: `SELECT * FROM t1, t2 WHERE t1.id > t2.id`. When MySQL joins tables `t1` and `t2` (in that order), it does *range checks* on `t2`: for every value from `t1`, MySQL checks if it can use an index on `t2` to do a range scan or index merge. Rechecking every value from `t1` is necessary because, given the

---

4 See my blog post "MySQL Select and Sort Status Variables" (*https://oreil.ly/OpJvS*) for an in-depth explanation of all `Select_%` and `Sort_%` metrics.

query, MySQL cannot know t1 values ahead of time. But rather than do the worst possible execution plan—Select_full_join—MySQL keeps trying to use an index on t2. In the EXPLAIN output, the Extra field for t2 lists "Range checked for each record," and Select_range_check is incremented once for the table. The metric is *not* incremented for each range change; it's incremented once to signal that a table was joined by doing range checks.

Bad SELECT metrics should be zero or virtually zero (if you round down). A few Select_scan or Select_full_range_join are inevitable, but the other two—Select_full_join and Select_range_check—should be found and fixed immediately if not zero.

Network Throughput

The MySQL protocol is very efficient and rarely uses any noticeable amount of network bandwidth. Usually, it's the network affecting MySQL rather than MySQL affecting the network. Nevertheless, it's good to monitor network throughput as recorded by MySQL:

- Bytes_sent
- Bytes_received

Since these metrics count network bytes sent and received, respectively, convert the values to network units: Mbps or Gbps, whichever matches the link speed of the server running MySQL. Gigabit links are most common, even in the cloud.

 Metric graphing systems convert counters to rates by default, but you probably need to multiply these metrics by eight (8 bits per byte) and set the graph unit to bits to display as Mbps or Gbps.

I have seen MySQL saturate a network only once. The cause was related to a system variable that's not usually a problem: var.binlog_row_image (*https://oreil.ly/tboxy*). This system variable is related to replication that Chapter 7 addresses in more detail, but the short version is: this system variable controls whether or not BLOB and TEXT columns are logged in the binary logs and replicated. The default value is full, which logs and replicates BLOB and TEXT columns. Normally, that's not a problem, but one application created a perfect storm by having all of the following attributes at once:

- Using MySQL as a queue
- Huge BLOB values
- Write-heavy

- High throughput

These access patterns combined to replicate a small flood of data, causing major replication lag. The solution was changing var.binlog_row_image to noblob to stop replicating the BLOB values, which didn't need to be replicated. This true story leads to the next spectrum: replication.

Replication

Lag is the bane of replication: the delay between a write on the source MySQL instance and when that write is applied on a replica MySQL instance. When replication (and the network) is working normally, replication lag is subsecond, limited only by network latency.

 Before MySQL 8.0.22, the replica lag metric and command were Seconds_Behind_Master and SHOW SLAVE STATUS, respectively. As of MySQL 8.0.22, the metric and command are Seconds_Behind_Source and SHOW REPLICA STATUS. I use the current metric and command in this book.

MySQL has an infamous gauge metric for replication lag: Seconds_Behind_Source. This metric is infamous because it's not wrong but it's also not what you expect. It can jump between zero and a high value, which is as amusing as it is confusing. Consequently, the best practice is to ignore this metric and, instead, use a tool like pt-heartbeat (*https://oreil.ly/VMg4c*) to measure true replication lag. Then you have to configure your MySQL monitor software (or service) to measure and report *replication lag* from pt-heartbeat. Since pt-heartbeat has been around for so long, some MySQL monitors support it natively; and there's a good chance that the engineers who manage your MySQL instances are already using it.

MySQL exposes one metric related to replication that is not infamous: Binlog_cache_disk_use. Chapter 7 clarifies the following details; for now, a high level explanation is sufficient. For each client connection, a in-memory binary log cache buffers writes before they're written to the binary log files—from which the writes replicate to replicas. If the binary log cache is too small to hold all the writes for a transaction, the changes are written to disk and Binlog_cache_disk_use is incremented. In moderation, this is acceptable, but it shouldn't be frequent. If it becomes frequent, you can alleviate it by increasing the binary log cache size: var.binlog_cache_size (*https://oreil.ly/0TEIJ*).

From the example in the previous section, we know that var.binlog_row_image affects the binary log cache, too: full row images can require a lot of space if the table has BLOB or TEXT columns.

Data Size

Chapter 3 explains why less data is more performance. Monitoring data size is important because it's common for databases to grow larger than expected. If data growth is due to application growth—the application is becoming increasingly popular—then it's a good problem to have, but it's a problem nevertheless.

It's also easy to overlook because MySQL performance scales effortlessly as data grows, but not forever. A database can grow from 10 GB to 300 GB—a 30x increase—and not encounter performance issues if queries and access patterns are optimized well. But another 30x increase to 9 TB? Not possible. Even a 3x increase to 900 GB is asking too much—it could happen if the access patterns are exceptionally favorable, but don't bet on it.

MySQL exposes table sizes (and other table metadata) in an Information Schema table: `information_schema.tables` (*https://oreil.ly/PqATu*). The query in Example 6-5 returns the size of each database in gigabytes.

Example 6-5. Database sizes (GB)

```
SELECT
  table_schema AS db,
  ROUND(SUM(data_length + index_length) / 1073741824 , 2) AS 'size_GB'
FROM
  information_schema.tables
GROUP BY table_schema;
```

The query in Example 6-6 returns the size of each table in gigabytes.

Example 6-6. Table sizes (GB)

```
SELECT
  table_schema AS db,
  table_name as tbl,
  ROUND((data_length + index_length) / 1073741824 , 2) AS 'size_GB'
FROM
  information_schema.tables
WHERE
    table_type = 'BASE TABLE'
  AND table_schema != 'performance_schema';
```

There is no standard for database and table size metrics. Query and aggregate values from `information_schema.tables` to suit your needs. At a bare minimum, collect database sizes (Example 6-5) every hour. It's better to be more precise and collect table sizes every 15 minutes.

Be sure that, wherever you store or send MySQL metrics, you can retain data size metrics for at least a year. Near-term data growth trending is used to estimate when the disk will run out of space; or, in the cloud, when more storage will need to be provisioned. Long-term data growth trending is used to estimate when sharding (Chapter 5) becomes necessary, as covered in "Practice: Four-Year Fit" on page 173.

InnoDB

InnoDB (*https://oreil.ly/4b5qP*) is complex.

However, since it is the default MySQL storage engine, we must steel ourselves to embrace it. A deep dive is not necessary—or even possible within the limits of this book. Although this section is long, it barely breaks the surface of InnoDB internals. Nevertheless, the following InnoDB metrics reveal some of the inner workings of the storage engine responsible for reading and writing data.

History list length (metric)

History list length (HLL) is a curious metric because every engineer that uses MySQL learns what it *means*, but very few know what it *is*. When HLL increases significantly over a period of minutes or hours, it means that InnoDB is keeping a significant number of old row versions instead of purging them because one or more long-running transaction has not committed or was abandoned without being rolled back due to an undetected lost client connection. All of that, which I explain later in "History List Length" on page 280, is revealed by one gauge metric:

- `innodb.trx_rseg_history_len`

A normal value for `innodb.trx_rseg_history_len` is less than 1,000. You should monitor and alert if HLL is greater than 100,000. Contrary to "Wild Goose Chase (Thresholds)" and "Alert on User Experience and Objective Limits" later in this chapter, this is a reliable threshold and actionable alert. The action: find and terminate the long-running or abandoned transaction.

History list length does not directly affect performance, but it is a harbinger of trouble—do not ignore it. The trouble relates to the fact that, since InnoDB is a transactional storage engine, every query on an InnoDB table is a transaction. Transactions incur overhead, and the HLL metric reveals when a long-running or abandoned transaction is causing InnoDB to handle an unreasonable amount of overhead. Some overhead is necessary—even beneficial—but too much amounts to waste, and waste is antithetical to performance.

There's so much more to say about transactions and HLL that it won its own chapter: Chapter 8. For now, let's stay focused on metrics because we've only begun with InnoDB.

Deadlock

A deadlock occurs when two (or more) transactions hold row locks that the other transaction needs. For example, transaction *A* holds a lock on row 1 and needs a lock on row 2, and transaction *B* holds a lock on row 2 and needs a lock on row 1. MySQL automatically detects and rolls back one transaction to resolve the deadlock, and increments one metric:

- `innodb.lock_deadlocks`

Deadlocks should not occur. A prevalence of deadlocks is related to the concurrency access pattern trait (see "Concurrency" on page 138). Highly concurrent data access must be designed (in the application) to avoid deadlocks by ensuring that different transactions accessing the same rows (or nearby rows) examine the rows in roughly the same order. In the earlier example of transaction *A* and transaction *B*, they access the same two rows in opposite order, which can lead to a deadlock when the transactions execute at the same time. To learn more about deadlocks, read "Deadlocks in InnoDB" (*https://oreil.ly/UpX0r*) in the MySQL manual.

Row lock

Row lock metrics reveal *lock contention*: how quickly (or not) queries acquire row locks to write data. The most fundamental row lock metrics are:

- `innodb.lock_row_lock_time`
- `innodb.lock_row_lock_current_waits`
- `innodb.lock_row_lock_waits`
- `innodb.lock_timeouts`

The first metric, `innodb.lock_row_lock_time`, is a rare type: the total number of milliseconds spent acquiring row locks. It's in the class of response time metrics (see "Response Time" on page 182), but unlike "Query Response Time" on page 188, it is collected as a running total rather than a histogram. Consequently, it's not possible to report `innodb.lock_row_lock_time` as a percentile, which would be ideal. And reporting it as a rate (see "Rate" on page 183) is nonsensical: milliseconds per second. Instead, this metric must be reported as a difference: if 500 milliseconds at time T1 and 700 milliseconds at time T2, then report T2 value – T1 value = 200 ms. (Use maximum for the chart rollup function. Don't average the data points because it's better to see the worst case.) As a response time metric, lower is better. The value of `innodb.lock_row_lock_time` cannot be zero (unless the workload is read-only and never needs to acquire a single row lock) because it takes a nonzero amount of time to acquire locks. The goal, as always, is that the metric is normal and stable. When it's not, the other row lock metrics will not be normal either.

`innodb.lock_row_lock_current_waits` is a gauge metric for the current number of queries waiting to acquire a row lock. `innodb.lock_row_lock_waits` is a count of the number of queries that waited to acquire a row. The two variables are essentially the same: the former is a current gauge, and the latter is a historical counter and rate. When the rate of row lock waits increases, it's a sure sign of trouble because MySQL does not wait by accident: something must cause it to wait. In this case, the cause will be concurrent queries accessing the same (or nearby) rows.

`innodb.lock_timeouts` is incremented when a row lock wait times out. The default row lock wait timeout is 50 seconds, configured by `var.innodb_lock_wait_timeout` (*https://oreil.ly/4kCLg*), and applies *per row lock*. This is far too long for any normal application to wait; I advise a much lower value: 10 seconds or less.

InnoDB locking is sophisticated and nuanced. As a result, lock contention is *not* a common problem unless the workload exhibits three particular access patterns:

- Write-heavy ("Read/Write" on page 133)
- High throughput ("Throughput" on page 133)
- High concurrency ("Concurrency" on page 138)

That would be a very particular application and workload. But lock contention can become a problem for any application and workload (even with low throughput and concurrency), so always monitor rock lock metrics.

Data throughput

Data throughput in bytes per seconds is measured by two metrics:

- `Innodb_data_read`
- `Innodb_data_written`

Data throughput is rarely an issue: SSD is fast; PCIe and NVMe made it even faster. Regardless, monitoring data throughput is a best practice because storage throughput is limited, especially in the cloud. Do not expect to achieve published storage throughput rates because published rates are measured under ideal conditions: data straight to (or from) disk. InnoDB is super fast and efficient, but it's still a complex layer of software between the data and the disk that inherently precludes achieving published storage throughput rates.

 Be careful about throughput in the cloud: storage is unlikely to be locally attached, which limits throughput to network speeds. 1 Gbps equals 125 MB/s, which is throughput similar to spinning disks.

IOPS

InnoDB has a deep and sometimes complicated relationship with storage I/O capacity, measured in IOPS. But first, the easy part: InnoDB read and write IOPS are counted by two metrics, respectively:

- `innodb.os_data_reads`
- `innodb.os_data_writes`

These metrics are counters, so like other counters, they are converted to and expressed as rates by metric graphing systems. Be sure to set the graph unit to IOPS for each.

The performance raison d'être of InnoDB is to optimize and reduce storage I/O. Although high IOPS are impressive from an engineering point of view, they are the bane of performance because storage is slow. But storage is required for durability—persisting data changes to disk—so InnoDB goes to great lengths to be fast *and* durable. Consequently, as in "Less QPS Is Better" on page 96, fewer IOPS are better.

But don't underutilize IOPS, either. If your company runs its own hardware, the maximum number of storage IOPS is determined by the storage device—check the device specifications, or ask the engineers who manage the hardware. In the cloud, storage IOPS are allocated or provisioned, so it's usually easier to tell the maximum because you purchase the IOPS—check the storage settings, or ask the cloud provider. If InnoDB never uses more than 2,000 IOPS, for example, then don't purchase (or provision) 40,000 IOPS: InnoDB simply won't use the excess IOPS. By contrast, if InnoDB constantly uses the maximum number of storage IOPS, then either the application workload needs to be optimized to reduce storage I/O (see Chapters 1–5), or InnoDB legitimately needs more IOPS.

InnoDB I/O capacity for *background tasks* is largely configured by `var.inno db_io_capacity` (*https://oreil.ly/zU6iW*) and `var.innodb_io_capacity_max` (*https://oreil.ly/LiilY*), two system variables that default to 200 and 2,000 IOPS, respectively. (There are other variables, but I must gloss over them to stay focused on metrics. To learn more, read "Configuring InnoDB I/O Capacity" (*https://oreil.ly/G9Bcw*) in the MySQL manual.) Background tasks include page flushing, change buffer merging, and more. In this book, I cover only page flushing, which is arguably the single most important background task. Limiting background task storage I/O ensures that InnoDB does not overwhelm the server. It also allows InnoDB to optimize and stabilize storage I/O rather than bombard the storage device with erratic access. By contrast, foreground tasks do not have any configurable I/O capacities or limits: they use as many IOPS as necessary and available. The primary foreground task is executing queries, but this does not mean queries use high or excessive IOPS because, remember, the performance raison d'être of InnoDB is to optimize and reduce storage

I/O. For reads, the buffer pool purposefully optimizes and reduces IOPS. For writes, page flushing algorithms and the transaction log purposefully optimize and reduce storage I/O. The following sections reveal how.

InnoDB can achieve high IOPS, but can the application? Probably not because there are many layers between the application and the IOPS that preclude the former from achieving a high number of the latter. In my experience, applications use hundreds to thousands of IOPS, and exceptionally optimized applications that are "going viral" push around 10,000 IOPS on a single MySQL instance. Recently, I was benchmarking MySQL in the cloud and hit a ceiling at 40,000 IOPS. The cloud provider publishes 80,000 IOPS as the maximum and allows me to provision that, but their storage system is capped at 40,000 IOPS. Point being: InnoDB can achieve high IOPS, but everything around it is a different question.

> ### Millions of IOPS
>
> High end storage is capable of over one million IOPS. This class of storage is used in bare metal (physical) servers designed to host many virtual servers. The same is true for high-end CPUs and memory: it's too much hardware for one application.

This section is only a primer on InnoDB I/O because it underlies the final three InnoDB spectra that consume IOPS: "Buffer pool efficiency" on page 210, "Page flushing" on page 212, and "Transaction log" on page 219.

To learn more InnoDB I/O, start by reading "Configuring InnoDB I/O Capacity" (*https://oreil.ly/w9MOg*) in the MySQL manual. To really dive into the nitty-gritty details of InnoDB I/O, read an illuminating three-part blog post by renowned MySQL experts Yves Trudeau and Francisco Bordenave: "Give Love to Your SSDs: Reduce innodb_io_capacity_max!" (*https://oreil.ly/q0L61*), "InnoDB Flushing in Action for Percona Server for MySQL" (*https://oreil.ly/ZY2Xe*), and "Tuning MySQL/InnoDB Flushing for a Write-Intensive Workload" (*https://oreil.ly/P03EX*). But finish this chapter first because it's a great foundation for those blog posts.

InnoDB works with data in memory, not on disk. It reads data from disk when necessary, and it writes data to disk to make changes durable, but these are lower level operations into which the next three sections delve. At a higher level, InnoDB works with data in memory because storage is too slow—even with a million IOPS. Consequently, there is not a direct correlation between queries, rows, and IOPS. Writes always consume IOPS (for durability). Reads can execute without consuming any IOPS, but it depends on buffer pool efficiency.

Buffer pool efficiency

The InnoDB buffer pool is an *in-memory* cache of table data and other internal data structures. From "InnoDB Tables Are Indexes" on page 41, you know that the buffer pool contains index pages—more on pages in the next section. InnoDB certainly understands rows, but internally it's far more concerned with pages. At this depth of MySQL performance, the focus changes from rows to pages.

At a high level, InnoDB accesses (reads and writes) all data by pages in the buffer pool. (Low-level writes are more complicated and addressed in the last InnoDB section: "Transaction log" on page 219.) If data is not in the buffer pool when accessed, InnoDB reads it from storage and saves it in the buffer pool.

Buffer pool efficiency is the percentage of data accessed from memory, calculated from two metrics:

- `Innodb_buffer_pool_read_request`
- `Innodb_buffer_pool_reads`

`Innodb_buffer_pool_read_request` counts all requests to access data in the buffer pool. If the requested data is *not* in memory, InnoDB increments `Innodb_buffer_pool_reads` and loads the data from disk. Buffer pool efficiency equals (`Innodb_buffer_pool_read_request` / `Innodb_buffer_pool_reads`) × 100.

The word *read* in these metrics does not mean `SELECT`. InnoDB reads data from the buffer pool for all queries: `INSERT`, `UPDATE`, `DELETE`, and `SELECT`. For example, on `UPDATE`, InnoDB reads the row from the buffer pool. If not in the buffer pool, it loads the row from disk into the buffer pool.

Buffer pool efficiency will be very low when MySQL starts. This is normal; it's called a *cold buffer pool*. Loading data warms the buffer pool—like throwing logs on a fire. It usually takes several minutes to fully warm the buffer pool, which is indicated when buffer pool efficiency reaches its normal and stable value.

Buffer pool efficiency should be extremely close to 100%—ideally 99.0% or greater—but don't fixate on the value. Technically, this metric is a cache hit ratio, but that's not how it's used. A cache hit ratio reveals little beyond the metric: values are cached, or they're not. On the contrary, buffer pool efficiency reveals how well InnoDB is able to keep frequently accessed data—the working set—in memory while balancing speed and durability. To put it colorfully, buffer pool efficiency is how well InnoDB can keep a match lit in a hurricane. The working set is the flame; durability is the rain (it dampens throughput);[5] the application is the wind.

 In a bygone era, performance equated to cache hit ratios. Today, that is no longer true: performance is query response time. If buffer pool efficiency is extremely low but response time is great, then performance is great. That probably won't happen, but the point is not to lose focus—recall "North Star" on page 3.

If total data size is less than available memory, then all data can fit in the buffer pool at once. (Buffer pool size is configured by `var.innodb_buffer_pool_size` (*https:// oreil.ly/N4lnI*). Or, as of MySQL 8.0.3, enabling `var.innodb_dedicated_server` (*https://oreil.ly/I5KaC*) automatically configures buffer pool size and other related system variables.) In this case, buffer pool efficiency is a nonissue and performance bottlenecks—if any—will occur in CPU or storage (since all data is in memory). But this case is the exception, not the norm. The norm is total data size being *far greater* than available memory. In this (normal) case, buffer pool efficiency has three primary influences:

Data access
> Data access brings data into the buffer pool. The data age access pattern trait (see "Data Age" on page 134) is the primary influence because only new data needs to be loaded into the buffer pool.

Page flushing
> Page flushing allows data to be evicted from the buffer pool. Page flushing is necessary for new data to be loaded into the buffer pool. The next section goes into more detail.

Available memory
> The more data that InnoDB keeps in memory, the less it needs to load or flush data. In the exceptional case previously mentioned, when all data fits in memory, buffer pool efficiency is a nonissue.

Buffer pool efficiency reveals the combined effect of those three influences. As a combined effect, it cannot pinpoint one cause. If its value is lower than normal, the cause could be one, two, or all three influences. You must analyze all three to determine which is the greatest *or* the most feasible to change. For example, as detailed in Chapter 4, changing access patterns is a best practice for improving performance, but if you're page-deep in MySQL performance, you've probably already done that. In that case, more memory or faster storage (more IOPS) might be more feasible—

---

5 You can disable durability, but that's a terrible idea.

and more justified since you've already optimized the workload. Although buffer pool efficiency cannot give you answers, it tells you where to look: access patterns (especially "Data Age" on page 134), page flushing, and memory size.

InnoDB buffer pool efficiency is the tip of the iceberg. Underneath, page flushing is the internal machinery that keeps it afloat.

Page flushing

This spectrum is large and complicated, so it's further subdivided into *Pages* and *Flushing*, which are inextricable.

Pages. As mentioned in the previous section, the buffer pool contains index pages. There are four types of pages:

Free pages
> These contain no data; InnoDB can load new data into them.

Data pages
> These contain data that has not been modified; also called *clean pages*.

Dirty pages
> These contain modified data that has not been flushed to disk.

Misc pages
> These contain miscellaneous internal data not covered in this book.

Since InnoDB keeps the buffer pool full of data, monitoring the number of data pages is not necessary. Free and dirty pages are the most revealing with respect to performance, especially when viewed with flushing metrics in the next section. Three gauges and one counter (the last metric) reveal how many free and dirty pages are sloshing around in the buffer pool:

- `innodb.buffer_pool_pages_total`
  - `innodb.buffer_pool_pages_dirty`
  - `innodb.buffer_pool_pages_free`
    - `innodb.buffer_pool_wait_free`

`innodb.buffer_pool_pages_total` is the total number of pages in the buffer pool (total page count), which depends on the buffer pool size (`var.innodb_buffer_pool_size` (*https://oreil.ly/fXHQ4*)). (Technically, this is a gauge metric because, as of MySQL 5.7.5, the InnoDB buffer pool size is dynamic. But frequently changing the buffer pool size is not common because it's sized according to system memory, which cannot change quickly—even cloud instances require a few minutes to resize.) Total page count calculates the percentage of free and dirty pages:

`innodb.buffer_pool_pages_free` and `innodb.buffer_pool_pages_dirty` divided by total pages, respectively. Both percentages are gauge metrics, and the values change frequently due to page flushing.

To ensure that free pages are available when needed, InnoDB maintains a nonzero balance of free pages that I call the *free page target*. The free page target is equal to the product of two system variables: the system variable `var.innodb_lru_scan_depth` (*https://oreil.ly/TG9hj*) multiplied by `var.innodb_buffer_pool_instances` (*https://oreil.ly/srIHw*). The name of the former system variable is somewhat misleading, but it configures the number of free pages that InnoDB maintains in *each* buffer pool instance; the default is 1024 free pages. Until now, I have written about *the buffer pool* as one logical part of InnoDB. Under the hood, the buffer pool is divided into multiple *buffer pool instances*, each with its own internal data structures to reduce contention under heavy load. The default for `var.innodb_buffer_pool_instances` is 8 (or 1 if the buffer pool size is less than 1 GB). Therefore, with defaults for both system variables, InnoDB maintains 1024 × 8 = 8192 free pages. Free pages should hover around the free page target.

 Reducing `var.innodb_lru_scan_depth` is a best practice because, with default values, it yields 134 MB of free page size: 8192 free pages × 16 KB/page = 134 MB. That is excessive given that rows are typically hundreds of bytes. It's more efficient for free pages to be as low as possible without hitting zero and incurring free page waits (explained in the next paragraph). It's good to be aware of this, but it's MySQL tuning, which is beyond the scope of this book. The default does not hinder performance; MySQL experts just abhor inefficiency.

If free pages are consistently near zero (below the free page target), that's fine as long as `innodb.buffer_pool_wait_free` remains zero. When InnoDB needs a free page but none is available, it increments `innodb.buffer_pool_wait_free` and waits. This is called a *free page wait* and it should be exceptionally rare—even when the buffer pool is full of data—because InnoDB actively maintains the free page target. But under very heavy load, it might not be able to flush and free pages fast enough. Simply put: InnoDB is reading new data faster than it can flush old data. Presuming that the workload is already optimized, there are three solutions to free page waits:

Increase free page target
    If your storage can provide more IOPS (or you can provision more IOPS in the cloud), then increasing `var.innodb_lru_scan_depth` causes InnoDB to flush and free more pages, which requires more IOPS (see "IOPS" on page 208).

Better storage system

If your storage cannot provide more IOPS, upgrade to better storage, then increase the free page target.

More memory

The more memory, the bigger the buffer pool, and the more pages can fit in memory without needing to flush and evict old pages to load new pages. There's one more detail about free page waits that I clarify later when explaining LRU flushing.

 Remember from "Buffer pool efficiency" on page 210: *read* doesn't mean SELECT. InnoDB reads new data from the buffer pool for all queries: INSERT, UPDATE, DELETE, and SELECT. When data is accessed but not in the buffer pool (in memory), InnoDB reads it from disk.

If free pages are consistently much higher than the free page target, or never decrease to the target, then the buffer pool is too large. For example, 50 GB of data fills only 39% of 128 GB of RAM. MySQL is optimized to use only the memory that it needs, so giving it an overabundance of memory will not increase performance—MySQL simply won't use the excess memory. Don't waste memory.

Dirty pages as a percentage of total pages varies between 10% and 90% by default. Although dirty pages contain modified data that has not been flushed to disk, the data changes have been flushed to disk in the transaction log—more on this in the next two sections. Even with 90% dirty pages, all data changes are guaranteed durable—persisted to disk. It's completely normal to have a high percentage of dirty pages. In fact, it's expected unless the workload is exceptionally read-heavy (recall access pattern trait "Read/Write" on page 133) and simply does not modify data very often. (In this case, I would consider whether another data store is better suited to the workload.)

Since a high percentage of dirty pages is expected, this metric is used to corroborate other metrics related to page flushing (next section), the transaction log ("Transaction log" on page 219), and disk I/O ("IOPS" on page 208). For example, writing data causes dirty pages, so a spike in dirty pages corroborates a spike in IOPS and transaction log metrics. But a spike in IOPS without a corresponding spike in dirty pages cannot be caused by writes; it must be another issue—maybe an engineer manually executed an ad hoc query that dredged up a mass of old data that hadn't seen the light of day in eons, and now InnoDB is reading it from disk in a maelstrom of IOPS. Ultimately, dirty pages rise and fall with the gentle tides of page flushing.

Page flushing. *Page flushing* cleans dirty pages by writing the data modifications to disk. Page flushing serves three closely related purposes: durability, checkpointing, and page eviction. For simplicity, this section focuses on page flushing with respect to page eviction. "Transaction log" on page 219 clarifies how page flushing serves durability and checkpointing.

From "Buffer pool efficiency" on page 210, you know that page flushing makes space for new data to be loaded into the buffer pool. More specifically, page flushing makes dirty pages clean, and clean pages can be evicted from the buffer pool. Thus, the circle of page life is complete:

- A free page becomes a clean (data) page when data is loaded
- A clean page becomes a dirty page when its data is modified
- A dirty page becomes a clean page again when the data modifications are flushed
- A clean page becomes a free page again when it's evicted from the buffer pool

The implementation of page flushing is complex and varies among distributions (Oracle MySQL, Percona Server, and MariaDB Server), so you might want to reread the following information to fully absorb the many intricate details. Figure 6-6 depicts the high-level components and flow of InnoDB page flushing from committing transactions in the transaction log (at top) to flushing and evicting pages from the buffer pool (at bottom).

Figuratively, InnoDB page flushing works top to bottom in Figure 6-6, but I'm going to explain it from the bottom up. In the buffer pool, dirty pages are dark, clean (data) pages are white, and free pages have a dotted outline.

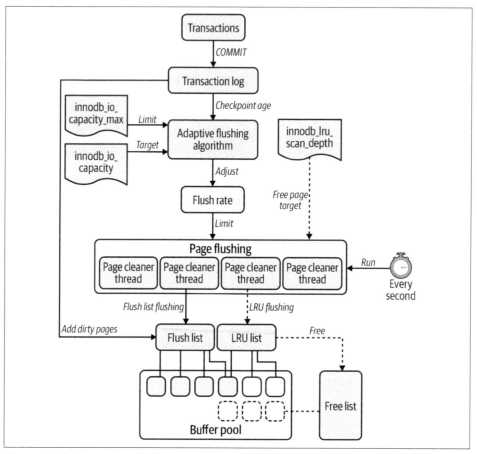

Figure 6-6. InnoDB page flushing

Dirty pages are recorded in two internal lists (for each buffer pool instance):

Flush list
Dirty pages from writes committed in the transaction log.

LRU list
Clean and dirty pages in the buffer pool ordered by data age.

Strictly speaking, the LRU list tracks all pages with data, and that just happens to include dirty pages; whereas the flush list explicitly tracks only dirty pages. Either way, MySQL uses both lists to find dirty pages to flush. (In Figure 6-6, the LRU list is connected to [tracking] only one dirty page, but this only a simplification to avoid a clutter of lines.)

Once every second, dirty pages are flushed from both lists by background threads aptly named *page cleaner threads*. By default, InnoDB uses four page cleaner threads, configured by `var.innodb_page_cleaners` (*https://oreil.ly/ELUoy*). Each page cleaner flushes both lists; but for simplicity, Figure 6-6 shows one page cleaner flushing one list.

Two flushing algorithms are primarily responsible for flush list flushing and LRU list flushing, respectively:

Adaptive flushing

Adaptive flushing determines the rate at which page cleaners flush dirty pages from the flush list.[6] The algorithm is *adaptive* because it varies the page flush rate based on the rate of transaction log writes. Faster writes, faster page flushing. The algorithm responds to write load, but it's also finely tuned to produce a stable rate of page flushing under varying write loads.

Page flushing by page cleaners is a background task, therefore the page flush rate is limited by the configured InnoDB I/O capacity explained in "IOPS" on page 208, specifically: `var.innodb_io_capacity` and `var.innodb_io_capacity_max`. Adaptive flushing does a fantastic job of keeping the flush rate (in terms of IOPS) between these two values.

The purpose of adaptive flushing is to allow checkpointing to reclaim space in the transaction logs. (Actually, this is the purpose of flush list flushing in general; algorithms are just different methods of accomplishing it.) I explain checkpointing in "Transaction log" on page 219, but I mention it here to clarify that, although flushing makes pages clean and candidates for eviction, that is not the purpose of adaptive flushing.

The intricate details of the adaptive flushing algorithm are beyond the scope of this book. The important point is: adaptive flushing flushes dirty pages from the flush list in response to transaction log writes.

LRU flushing

LRU flushing flushes dirty pages from the tail of the LRU list, which contains the oldest pages. Simply put: LRU flushing flushes and evicts old pages from the buffer pool.

LRU flushing happens in the background and the foreground. Foreground LRU flushing happens when a user thread (a thread executing a query) needs a free page but there are none. This is not good for performance because it's a wait—it increases query response time. When it occurs, MySQL increments `innodb.buffer_pool_wait_free`, which is the "one more detail about free page waits" mentioned earlier.

---

6 The MySQL adaptive flushing algorithm was created in 2008 by renowned MySQL expert Yasufumi Kinoshita while working at Percona. See his blog post "Adaptive checkpointing" (*https://oreil.ly/8QG6X*).

Page cleaners handle background LRU flushing (because page cleaners are background threads). When a page cleaner flushes a dirty page from the LRU list, it also frees the page by adding it to the free list. This is primarily how InnoDB maintains the free page target (see "Pages" on page 212) and avoids free page waits.

Although background LRU flushing is a background task, it is *not* limited by the configured InnoDB I/O capacity explained (var.innodb_io_capacity and var.innodb_io_capacity_max).[7] It's effectively limited (per buffer pool instance) by var.innodb_lru_scan_depth (*https://oreil.ly/fGGjJ*). For various reasons beyond the scope of this book, this is not a problem in terms of excessive background storage I/O.

The purpose of LRU flushing is to flush and free (evict) the oldest pages. *Old*, as detailed in "Data Age" on page 134, means the least recently used pages, hence *LRU*. The intricate details of LRU flushing, the LRU list, and how it all relates to the buffer pool are beyond the scope of this book; but if you're curious, start by reading "Buffer Pool" (*https://oreil.ly/OyBeI*) in the MySQL manual. The important point is that LRU flushing frees pages and its maximum rate is the free page target (per second), not the configured InnoDB I/O capacity.

Idle Flushing and Legacy Flushing

There are two more flushing algorithms in addition to adaptive flushing and LRU flushing: idle flushing and legacy flushing.

Idle flushing occurs when InnoDB is not processing any writes (the transaction log is not being written to). In this rare situation, InnoDB flushes dirty pages from the flush list at the configured I/O capacity (see "IOPS" on page 208). Idle flushing also flushes the change buffer (*https://oreil.ly/uKb08*) and handles flushing when MySQL shuts down.

Legacy flushing is my term for the simple algorithm that InnoDB employed before adaptive flushing became the standard.[8] InnoDB flushes dirty pages when the percentage of dirty pages is between var.innodb_max_dirty_pages_pct_lwm (*https://oreil.ly/OSqCZ*) and var.innodb_max_dirty_pages_pct (*https://oreil.ly/zsCWL*). Although this algorithm is still active in MySQL 8.0, it's essentially never used, and you can ignore it.

---

7 For proof and a deep dive, read my blog post "MySQL LRU Flushing and I/O Capacity" (*https://oreil.ly/YHEcj*).

8 *Legacy flushing* is also called *dirty pages percentage flushing*, but I prefer my term because it's simpler and frames it more accurately: *legacy* implies that it's no longer current, which is true.

With that crash course on InnoDB flushing, the following four metrics are now intelligible:

- `innodb.buffer_flush_batch_total_pages`
- `innodb.buffer_flush_adaptive_total_pages`
- `innodb.buffer_LRU_batch_flush_total_pages`
- `innodb.buffer_flush_background_total_pages`

All four metrics are counters that, when converted to rates, reveal page flush rates for each algorithm. `innodb.buffer_flush_batch_total_pages` is the total page flush rate for all algorithms. It's a high-level rate that's useful as a KPI for InnoDB: the total page flush rate should be normal and stable. If not, one of the metrics indicates which part of InnoDB is not flushing normally.

`innodb.buffer_flush_adaptive_total_pages` is the number of pages flushed by adaptive flushing. `innodb.buffer_LRU_batch_flush_total_pages` is the number of pages flushed by background LRU flushing. Given the earlier explanation of these flushing algorithms, you know which parts of InnoDB they reflect: the transaction log and free pages, respectively.

`innodb.buffer_flush_background_total_pages` is included for completeness: it is the number of pages flushed by other algorithms described in "Idle Flushing and Legacy Flushing" on page 218. If the rate of background page flushing is problematic, you will need to consult a MySQL expert because that's not supposed to happen.

Although different flushing algorithms have different rates, the storage system underlies all of them because flushing requires IOPS. If you're running MySQL on spinning disks, for example, the storage system (both the storage bus and the storage device) simply do not provide many IOPS. If you run MySQL on high-end storage, then IOPS may never be an underlying issue. And if you're running MySQL in the cloud, you can provision as many IOPS as you need, but the cloud uses network-attached storage, which is slow. Also remember that IOPS have latency—especially in the cloud—ranging from microseconds to milliseconds. This is deep knowledge verging on expert-level internals, but let's keep going because it's powerful knowledge worth learning.

Transaction log

The final and perhaps most important spectrum: the transaction log, also known as the redo log. For brevity, it's called *the log* when the context is clear and unambiguous, as it is here.

The transaction log guarantees durability. When a transaction commits, all data changes are recorded in the transaction log and flushed to disk—which makes the data changes durable—and corresponding dirty pages remain in memory. (If MySQL crashes with dirty pages, the data changes are not lost because they were already flushed to disk in the transaction log.) Transaction log flushing is *not* page flushing. The two processes are separate but inextricable.

The InnoDB transaction log is a fixed-size ring buffer on disk, as shown in Figure 6-7. By default, it comprises two physical log files. The size of each is configured by `var.innodb_log_file_size` (*https://oreil.ly/ItAxz*). Or, as of MySQL 8.0.3, enabling `var.innodb_dedicated_server` (*https://oreil.ly/gv38o*) automatically configures the log file size and other related system variables.

The transaction log contains data changes (technically, *redo logs*), not pages; but the data changes are linked to dirty pages in the buffer pool. When a transaction commits, its data changes are written to the head of the transaction log and flushed (synced) to disk, which advances the head clockwise, and the corresponding dirty pages are added to the flush list shown earlier in Figure 6-6. (In Figure 6-7, the head and tail move clockwise, but this is only an illustration. Unless you have spinning disks, the transaction log does not literally move.) Newly written data changes overwrite old data changes for which the corresponding pages have been flushed.

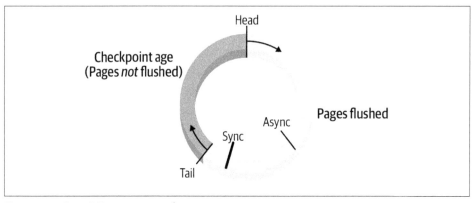

Figure 6-7. InnoDB transaction log

 A simplified illustration and explanation of the InnoDB transaction log makes it appear serialized. But that is only an artifact of simplifying a complex process. The actual low-level implementation is highly concurrent: many user threads are committing changes to the transaction log in parallel.

Checkpoint age is the length of the transaction log (in bytes) between the head and the tail. *Checkpointing* reclaims space in the transaction log by flushing dirty pages from the buffer pool, which allows the tail to advance. Once dirty pages have been flushed, the corresponding data changes in the transaction log can be overwritten with new data changes. Adaptive flushing implements checkpointing in InnoDB, which is why the checkpoint age is an input to the adaptive flushing algorithm shown in Figure 6-6.

 By default, all data changes (redo logs) in the transaction log are durable (flushed to disk), but corresponding dirty pages in the buffer pool are not durable until flushed by checkpointing.

Checkpointing advances the tail to ensure that the checkpoint age does not become too old (which really means *too large* because it's measured in bytes, but *too old* is the more common phrase). But what happens if the checkpoint age becomes so old that the head meets the tail? Since the transaction log is a fixed-size ring buffer, the head can wrap around and meet the tail if the write rate consistently exceeds the flush rate. InnoDB won't let this happen. There are two safeguard points called *async* and *sync*, as shown in Figure 6-7. *Async* is the point at which InnoDB begins asynchronous flushing: writes are allowed, but the page flushing rate is increased to near maximum. Although writes are allowed, flushing will use so much InnoDB I/O capacity that you can (and should) expect a noticeable drop in overall server performance. *Sync* is the point at which InnoDB begins synchronous flushing: *all writes stop*, and page flushing takes over. Needless to say, that's terrible for performance.

InnoDB exposes metrics for the checkpoint age and the async flush point, respectively:

- `innodb.log_lsn_checkpoint_age`
- `innodb.log_max_modified_age_async`

`innodb.log_lsn_checkpoint_age` is a gauge metric measured in bytes, but the raw value is meaningless to humans (it ranges from zero to the log file size). What is meaningful to humans and critical to monitor is how close the checkpoint age is to the async flush point, which I call *transaction log utilization*:

$$(\text{innodb.log\_lsn\_checkpoint\_age} / \text{innodb.log\_max\_modified\_age\_async}) \times 100$$

Transaction log utilization is conservative because the async flush point is at 6/8 (75%) of the log file size. Therefore, at 100% transaction log utilization, 25% of the log is free to record new writes, but remember: server performance drops noticeably at the async flush point. It's important to monitor and know when this point is reached. If you want to live dangerously, InnoDB exposes a metric for the sync flush point (which is at 7/8 [87.5%] of the log file size) that you can substitute for the async flush point metric (or monitor both): `innodb.log_max_modified_age_sync`.

There's one small but important detail about how queries log data changes to the transaction log: data changes are first written to an in-memory *log buffer* (not to be confused with the *log file* that refers to the actual on-disk transaction log), then the log buffer is written to the log file, and the log file is synced. I'm glossing over myriad details, but the point is: there's an in-memory log buffer. If the log buffer is too small and a query has to wait for free space, InnoDB increments:

- `innodb.log_waits`

`innodb.log_waits` should be zero. If it isn't, the log buffer size is configured by `var.innodb_log_buffer_size` (*https://oreil.ly/2I1cq*). The default 16 MB is usually more than sufficient.

Since the transaction log comprises two physical files on disk (two files, but one logical log), writing and syncing data changes to disk are the most fundamental tasks. Two gauge metrics report how many of those tasks are pending—waiting to be completed:

- `innodb.os_log_pending_writes`
- `innodb.os_log_pending_fsyncs`

Since writes and syncs are supposed to happen extremely quickly—nearly all write performance depends on it—these metrics should always be zero. If not, they indicate a low-level problem with either InnoDB or, more likely, the storage system—presuming other metrics are normal or were normal before pending writes and syncs. Don't expect problems at this depth, but monitor it.

Last but not least, a simple but important metric that counts the number of bytes written to the transaction log:

- `innodb.os_log_bytes_written`

It's best practice to monitor total log bytes written per hour as a basis for determining log file size. Log file size is the product of system variables `var.inno db_log_file_size` (*https://oreil.ly/sinUV*) and `var.innodb_log_files_in_group` (*https://oreil.ly/0hYp1*). Or, as of MySQL 8.0.14, enabling `var.innodb_dedica ted_server` (*https://oreil.ly/f2UqB*) automatically configures both system variables. The default log file size is only 96 MB (two log files at 48 MB each). As an engineer using MySQL, not a DBA, I presume whoever is managing your MySQL has properly configured these system variables, but it's wise to verify.

We made it: the end of InnoDB metrics. The spectrum of InnoDB metrics is much wider and deeper than presented here; these are only the most essential InnoDB metrics for analyzing MySQL performance. Moreover, significant changes were made to InnoDB from MySQL 5.7 to 8.0. For example, the internal implementation of the transaction log was rewritten and improved as of MySQL 8.0.11. There are other parts of InnoDB not covered here: double-write buffer, change buffer, adaptive hash index, and so on. I encourage you to learn more about InnoDB, for it is a fascinating storage engine. You can begin that journey at "The InnoDB Storage Engine" (*https:// oreil.ly/s0PZk*) in the MySQL manual.

Monitoring and Alerting

MySQL metrics reveal the spectrum of MySQL performance, and they're also great for waking engineers in the middle of the night—otherwise known as monitoring and alerting.

Monitoring and alerting are external to MySQL, so they cannot affect its performance, but I am compelled to address the following four topics because they are related to metrics and important to success with MySQL.

Resolution

Resolution means the frequency at which metrics are collected and reported: 1 second, 10 seconds, 30 seconds, 5 minutes, and so on. Higher resolution entails higher frequency: 1 second is higher resolution than 30 seconds. Like a television, the higher the resolution, the more detail you see. And since "seeing is believing," let's see three charts of the same data over 30 seconds. The first chart, Figure 6-8, shows QPS values at maximum resolution: 1 second.

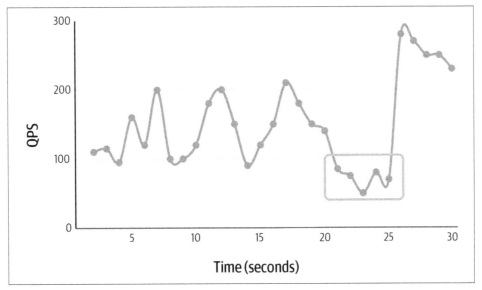

Figure 6-8. QPS at 1-second resolution

In the first 20 seconds, QPS is normal and stable, bouncing between 100 and 200 QPS. From 20 to 25 seconds, there is a 5-second stall (the 5 data points below 100 QPS in the box). For the last five seconds, QPS spikes to an abnormally high value, which is common after a stall. This chart isn't dramatic, but it's realistic and it begins to illustrate a point that the next two charts bring into focus.

The second chart, Figure 6-9, is the exact same data but at 5-second resolution.

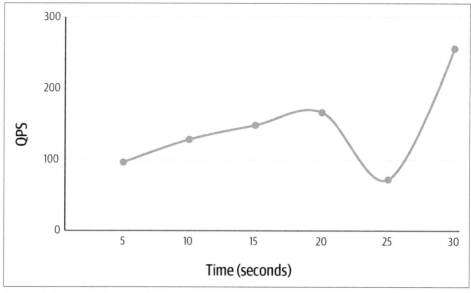

Figure 6-9. QPS at 5-second resolution

At 5-second resolution, some fine detail is lost, but critical details remain: normal and stable QPS in the first 20 seconds; the stall around 25 seconds; and the spike after the stall. This chart is acceptable for daily monitoring—especially considering that collecting, storing, and charting metrics at 1-second resolution is so difficult that it's almost never done.

The third chart, Figure 6-10, is the exact same data but at 10-second resolution.

At 10-second resolution, nearly all detail is lost. According to the chart, QPS is stable and normal, but it's misleading: QPS destabilized and was not normal for 10 seconds (five second stall and five second spike).

At the very least, collect KPIs (see "Key Performance Indicators" on page 181) at 5-second resolution or better. If possible, collect most of the metrics in "Spectra" on page 187 at 5-second resolution too, with the following exceptions: Admin, SHOW, and bad SELECT metrics can be collected slowly (10, 20, or 30 seconds), and data size can be collected very slowly (5, 10, or 20 minutes).

Strive for the highest resolution possible because, unlike query metrics that are logged, MySQL metrics are either collected or gone for all eternity.

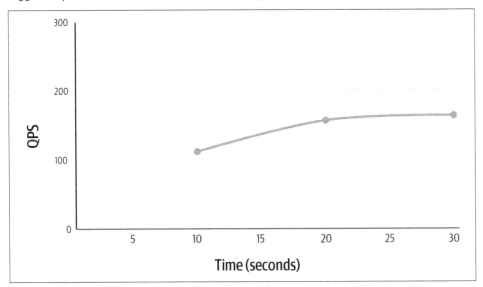

Figure 6-10. QPS at 10-second resolution

Wild Goose Chase (Thresholds)

A *threshold* is a static value past which a monitoring alert triggers, often times paging the engineer who's on-call. Thresholds seem like a good and reasonable idea, but they don't work. That's a very strong claim, but it's closer to the truth than the opposite—claiming that thresholds work.

The problem is that a threshold also needs a *duration*: how long the metric value must remain past the threshold until the alert triggers. Consider the chart in Figure 6-8 from the previous section (QPS at 1-second resolution). Without a duration, a threshold at QPS less than 100 would trigger seven times in 30 seconds: the five second stall, and the third and thirteenth data points. That's "too noisy" in the parlance of monitoring and alerting, so what about a threshold at QPS less than 50? Surely, a 50% drop in QPS—from 100 QPS to 50 QPS—signals a problem worth alerting a human. Sorry, the alert never triggers: the lowest data point is 50 QPS, which is not *less than* 50 QPS.

This example seems contrived but it's not, and it gets worse. Suppose you add a 5-second duration to the alert, and reset the threshold to QPS less than 100. Now the alert only triggers after the five-second stall. But what if the stall wasn't a stall? What if there was a network blip that caused packet loss during those five seconds, so the problem was neither MySQL nor the application? The poor on-call human who was alerted is on a wild goose chase.

I know it seems like I'm tailoring the example to suit my point, but all joking aside: thresholds are notoriously difficult to perfect, where *perfect* means that it alerts only on truly legitimate problems—no false-positives.

Alert on User Experience and Objective Limits

There are two proven solutions that work in lieu of thresholds:

- Alert on what users experience
- Alert on *objective* limits

From "North Star" on page 3 and "Key Performance Indicators" on page 181, there are only two MySQL metrics that users experience: response time and errors. These are reliable signals not only because users experience them, but because they cannot be false-positive. A change in QPS might be a legitimate change in user traffic. But a change in response time can only be explained by a change in response time. The same is true for errors.

 With microservices, the user might be another application. In that case, normal response times could be very low (tens of milliseconds), but the monitoring and alerting principles are the same.

Thresholds and duration are simpler for response time and errors, too, because we can imagine the abnormal conditions past the thresholds. For example, presume the normal P99 response time for an application is 200 milliseconds, and the normal error rate is 0.5 per second. If P99 response time increased to 1 second (or more) for a full a minute, would that be a bad user experience? If yes, then make those the threshold and duration. If errors increased to 10 per second for a full 20 seconds, would that be a bad user experience? If yes, then make those the threshold and duration.

For a more concrete example, let's clarify the implementation of the previous example where 200 milliseconds is the normal P99 response time. Measure and report P99 response time every five seconds (see "Query Response Time" on page 188). Create a rolling one minute alert on the metric that triggers when the last 12 values are greater than one second. (Since the metric is reported every five seconds, there are 60 / 5 seconds = 12 values/minute.) From a technical point of view, a sustained 5x increase in query response time is drastic and merits investigation—it's probably an early warning that a larger problem is brewing and, if ignored, will cause an application outage. But the intention of the alert is more practical than technical: if users are used to subsecond responses from the application, then one-second responses are noticeably sluggish.

Objective limits are minimum or maximum values that MySQL cannot pass. These are common objective limits external to MySQL:

- Zero free disk space
- Zero free memory
- 100% CPU utilization
- 100% storage IOPS utilization
- 100% network utilization

MySQL has many *max* system variables, but these are the most common ones that affect applications:

- max_connections (*https://oreil.ly/0ODxA*)
- max_prepared_stmt_count (*https://oreil.ly/jqNuk*)
- max_allowed_packet (*https://oreil.ly/qM3R5*)

There's one more object limit that has surprised more than one engineer: maximum AUTO_INCREMENT (*https://oreil.ly/tkXWP*) value. MySQL does not have a native metric or method for checking if an AUTO_INCREMENT column is approaching its maximum value. Instead, common MySQL monitoring solutions create a metric by executing a SQL statement similar to Example 6-7, which was written by renowned MySQL expert Shlomi Noach in "Checking for AUTO_INCREMENT capacity with single query" (*https://oreil.ly/LJ64E*).

Example 6-7. SQL statement that checks maximum AUTO_INCREMENT

```
SELECT
  TABLE_SCHEMA,
  TABLE_NAME,
  COLUMN_NAME,
  DATA_TYPE,
  COLUMN_TYPE,
  IF(
    LOCATE('unsigned', COLUMN_TYPE) > 0,
    1,
    0
  ) AS IS_UNSIGNED,
  (
    CASE DATA_TYPE
      WHEN 'tinyint' THEN 255
      WHEN 'smallint' THEN 65535
      WHEN 'mediumint' THEN 16777215
      WHEN 'int' THEN 4294967295
      WHEN 'bigint' THEN 18446744073709551615
    END >> IF(LOCATE('unsigned', COLUMN_TYPE) > 0, 0, 1)
```

```
  ) AS MAX_VALUE,
  AUTO_INCREMENT,
  AUTO_INCREMENT / (
    CASE DATA_TYPE
      WHEN 'tinyint' THEN 255
      WHEN 'smallint' THEN 65535
      WHEN 'mediumint' THEN 16777215
      WHEN 'int' THEN 4294967295
      WHEN 'bigint' THEN 18446744073709551615
    END >> IF(LOCATE('unsigned', COLUMN_TYPE) > 0, 0, 1)
  ) AS AUTO_INCREMENT_RATIO
FROM
  INFORMATION_SCHEMA.COLUMNS
  INNER JOIN INFORMATION_SCHEMA.TABLES USING (TABLE_SCHEMA, TABLE_NAME)
WHERE
  TABLE_SCHEMA NOT IN ('mysql', 'INFORMATION_SCHEMA', 'performance_schema')
  AND EXTRA='auto_increment'
;
```

What about the other two key performance indicators: QPS and threads running? Monitoring QPS and threads running is a best practice, but alerting on them is not. These metrics are pivotal when investigating a legitimate problem signaled by response time or errors, but otherwise they fluctuate too much to be reliable signals.

If this approach seems radical, remember: these are alerts for engineers using MySQL, not DBAs.

Cause and Effect

I won't mince words: when MySQL is slow to respond, the application is the cause the vast majority (maybe 80%) of the time—in my experience—because the application drives MySQL. Without it, MySQL is idle. If the application isn't the cause, there are a few other common causes of slow MySQL performance. Another application—any application, not just MySQL—is a likely culprit maybe 10% of the time, as I discuss later in "Noisy Neighbors" on page 301. Hardware, which includes the network, causes problems a mere 5% of the time because modern hardware is quite reliable (especially enterprise-grade hardware, which lasts longer [and costs more] than consumer-grade hardware). Last and least: I estimate only a 1% chance that MySQL is the root cause of its own slowness.

Once identified, the cause is presumed to be the root cause, not a side effect of some prior, unseen cause. For example, application causes presume something like a poorly written query that, once deployed in production, immediately causes a problem in MySQL. Or, hardware causes presume something like a degraded storage system that's working but significantly slower than usual, which causes MySQL to respond slowly. When this presumption is false—the identified cause is *not* the root cause—an especially pernicious situation occurs. Consider the following sequence of events:

1. A network issue lasting 20 seconds causes significant packet loss or low-level network retries.

2. The network issue causes query errors or timeouts (due to packet loss or retries, respectively).

3. Both the application and MySQL log errors (query errors and client errors, respectively).

4. The application retries queries.

5. While retrying old queries, the application continues executing new queries.

6. QPS increases due to executing new and old queries.

7. Utilization increases due to QPS increasing.

8. Waits increase due to utilization increasing.

9. Timeouts increase due to waits increasing.

10. The application retries queries again, which creates a feedback loop.

By the time you step into this situation, the problem is apparent but the root cause is not. You know that everything was normal and stable before the problem: no application changes or deployments; MySQL key performance indicators were normal and stable; and DBAs confirm that no work was done on their side. That's what makes this situation especially pernicious: as far as you can tell, it shouldn't be happening, but there's no denying that it is.

Technically speaking, all causes are knowable because computers are finite and discrete. But practically speaking, causes are only as knowable as monitoring and logging allow. In this example, if you have exceptionally good networking monitoring and application logging (and access to the MySQL error log), you can figure out the root cause: the 20-second network blip. But that's a lot easier said than done because in the midst of this situation—your application is down, customers are calling, and it's 4:30 p.m. on a Friday—engineers are focused on fixing the problem, not elucidating its root cause. When focused on fixing the problem, it's easy to see MySQL as the cause that needs to be fixed: make MySQL run faster and the application will be OK. But there is no way to fix MySQL in this sense—recall, "MySQL Does Nothing" on page 124. Since everything was normal before the problem, the goal is to return to that normal, starting with the application because it drives MySQL. The correct solution depends on the application, but common tactics are: restarting the application, throttling incoming application requests, and disabling application features.

I'm not favoring MySQL. The simple reality is that MySQL is a mature database with more than 20 years in the field. Moreover, as an open source database, it has been scrutinized by engineers from all over the world. At this juncture in the storied life of

MySQL, inherent slowness is not its weakness. Rather than ask why MySQL is slow, a more powerful and effective question that leads to a root cause or immediate fix is "What is causing MySQL to run slowly?"

Summary

This chapter analyzed the spectra of MySQL metrics that are the most important for understanding the nature of the workload, which accounts for MySQL performance. The illuminating takeaway points are:

- MySQL performance has two sides: query performance and server performance.
- Query performance is input; server performance is output.
- Normal and stable are whatever performance MySQL exhibits for your application on a typical day when everything is working properly.
- Stability does not limit performance; it ensures that performance—at any level—is sustainable.
- MySQL KPIs are response time, errors, QPS, and threads running.
- The field of metrics comprises six classes of metrics: response time, rate, utilization, wait, error, and access pattern (seven, if you count internal metrics).
- Metric classes are related: rate increases utilization; utilization pushes back to decrease rate; high (maximum) utilization incurs wait; wait timeout incurs error.
- The spectra of MySQL metrics are vast; see "Spectra" on page 187.
- *Resolution* means the frequency at which metrics are collected and reported.
- High resolution metrics (5 seconds or less) reveal important performance details that are lost in low resolution metrics.
- Alert on what users experience (like response time) and objective limits.
- Application issues (your application or another) are the most likely cause of slow MySQL performance.
- MySQL server performance is revealed through a spectrum of metrics that are the figurative refraction of the workload through MySQL.

The next chapter investigates replication lag.

Practice: Review Key Performance Indicators

The goal of this practice is to know the normal and stable values of the four KPIs for MySQL, as addressed in "Key Performance Indicators" on page 181. To make this practice interesting first, write down what you think the KPI values are for your application. You probably have a good idea about QPS; what about response time (P99 or P999), errors, and threads running?

Start collecting the four "Key Performance Indicators" on page 181, if you're not already. Your method depends on the software (or service) that you use to collect MySQL metrics. Any decent MySQL monitor should collect all four; if your current solution does not, seriously consider a better MySQL monitor because if it doesn't collect key performance indicators, it's unlikely to collect many of the metrics detailed in "Spectra" on page 187.

Review at least one full day of KPI metrics. Are the real values close to what you thought? If response time is higher than you thought, then you know where to begin: "Query profile" on page 9. If the rate of errors is higher than you thought, then query table `performance_schema.events_errors_summary_global_by_error` to see which error numbers are occurring. Use "MySQL Error Message Reference" (*https://oreil.ly/F9z9W*) to look up the error code. If threads running is higher than you thought, diagnosis is tricky because a single thread executes different queries (presuming the application uses a connection pool). Start with the slowest queries in the query profile. If your query metric tool reports query load, focus on queries with the highest load; otherwise, focus on queries with the highest total query time. If necessary, investigate using the Performance Schema `threads` table (*https://oreil.ly/ZgtGW*).

Review the KPIs for different periods throughout the day. Are the values stable all day, or do they decrease in the middle of the night? Are there periods when the values are abnormal? Overall, what are the normal and stable KPI values for your application?

Practice: Review Alerts and Thresholds

The goal of this practice is to help you sleep at night. Whereas charts for MySQL metrics are front and center, alerts—and configuration of those alerts—are usually hidden away. Consequently, engineers—especially newly hired engineers—do not know what alerts lurk in the darkness, waiting to page them while they sleep. Take a morning or afternoon to shine a light on all your alerts and how they are configured—their thresholds, if any. And while you're at it: document the alerts (or update the current documentation). Review "Wild Goose Chase (Thresholds)" on page 225 and "Alert on User Experience and Objective Limits" on page 226, and adjust or remove superfluous alerts.

The goal for alerting is simple: every page is legitimate and actionable. *Legitimate* means that something is already broken, or certain to break very soon, and it requires fixing right now. *Actionable* means that the engineer (who was paged) has the knowledge, skills, and access to fix it. This is possible with MySQL. Say *no* to the wild goose chase and *yes* to a good night's sleep.

## CHAPTER 7

Replication Lag

Replication lag is the delay between the time when a write occurs on a source MySQL instance and the time when that write is applied on a replica MySQL instance. Replication lag is inherent to all database servers because replication across a network incurs network latency.

I'm glad that, as an engineer using MySQL, you don't have to set up, configure, and maintain a MySQL replication topology because MySQL replication has become complex. Instead, this chapter investigates replication lag with respect to performance: what it is, why it happens, what risk it poses, and what you can do about it.

Simple Replication Won the Internet

Simple replication is one reason that MySQL became the most popular open source relational database server in the world. In the early 2000s, the internet was reemerging from the dot-com bubble of the '90s and online companies were growing fast. Since replication is required for high availability and also used to scale out reads, simple replication in early versions of MySQL (v3.23 through v5.5) helped it win the internet in those heedless days. Early versions of MySQL used single-threaded *statement-based replication* (SBR): the source MySQL instance would log the SQL statements that it executed—yes, the actual SQL statements—and replica instances would simply re-execute those SQL statements. Replication doesn't get simpler than that. Yes, it worked, and yes, it had problems and gotchas. But sometimes the simplest solution really is the best. Now, more than 20 years later, MySQL replication is complex, but it still supports statement-based replication.

Technically, yes, replication decreases performance, but you don't want to run MySQL without it. It's not hyperbole to say that replication prevents businesses from failing—from data loss so catastrophic that, if replication did not prevent it, the company would go out of business. MySQL runs everywhere from hospitals to banks, and replication keeps invaluable data safe despite inevitable failures. Although replication decreases performance and lag is a risk, these costs are cancelled by the overwhelming benefits of replication.

This chapter investigates replication lag. There are six major sections. The first introduces basic MySQL replication terminology and traces the technical origins of replication lag—why it happens despite fast databases and networks. The second discusses the main causes of replication lag. The third explains the risk of replication lag: data loss. The fourth provides a conservative configuration for enabling a multithreaded replica, which dramatically reduces lag. The fifth looks at monitoring replication lag with high precision. The sixth explains why replication lag is slow to recover.

Foundation

MySQL has two types of replication:

Source to replica

> *Source to replica replication* is the fundamental type of replication that MySQL has used for more than 20 years. Its venerable status means that *MySQL replication* (*https://oreil.ly/A8fTn*) implies source to replica replication. MySQL replication is old, but make no mistake: it's fast, reliable, and still widely used today.

Group Replication

> *Group Replication* (*https://oreil.ly/TASM9*) is the new type of replication that MySQL has supported as of MySQL 5.7.17 (released December 12, 2016). Group Replication creates a MySQL cluster of primary and secondary instances that use a group consensus protocol to synchronize (replicate) data changes and manage group membership. That's a long way of saying that Group Replication is MySQL clustering, and it is the future of MySQL replication and high availability.

This chapter covers only traditional MySQL replication: source to replica. Group Replication is the future, but I defer coverage to the future because, at the time of this writing, neither I nor any DBAs that I know have significant experience operating Group Replication at scale. Moreover, another innovation built on top of Group Replication is becoming the standard: InnoDB Cluster (*https://oreil.ly/BFqu9*).

Additionally, Percona XtraDB Cluster (*https://oreil.ly/fWNfb*) and MariaDB Galera Cluster (*https://oreil.ly/LMhEC*) are database cluster solutions similar to MySQL Group Replication in purpose but different in implementation. I defer coverage of these solutions, too, but keep them in mind if you're running a Percona or MariaDB distribution of MySQL and looking for a database cluster solution.

MySQL source to replica replication is ubiquitous. Although the inner workings of replication are beyond the scope of this book, understanding the foundation illuminates the causes of replication lag, the risk that it poses, and how to reduce both.

Replication terminology changed as of MySQL 8.0.22 and 8.0.26–released in 2020 and 2021, respectively. For a summary of the changes, see "MySQL Terminology Updates" (*https://oreil.ly/ wrzfU*). I use the current terminology, metrics, variables, and commands in this book.

Source to Replica

Figure 7-1 illustrates the foundation of MySQL source to replica replication.

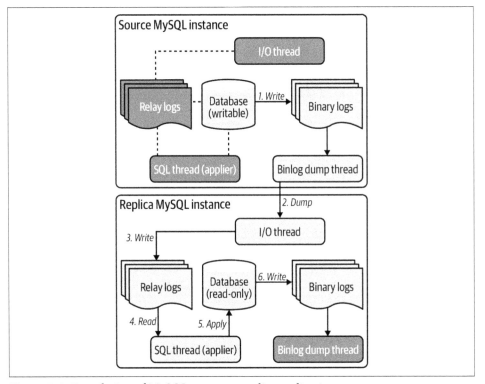

Figure 7-1. Foundation of MySQL source to replica replication

A *source MySQL instance* (or *source* for short) is any MySQL server to which clients (the application) write data. MySQL replication supports multiple writable sources, but this is rare due to the difficulty of handling write conflicts. Consequently, a single writable source is the norm.

A *replica MySQL instance* (or *replica* for short) is any MySQL server that replicates data changes from a source. *Data changes* are modifications to rows, indexes, schemas, and so forth. Replicas should always be read-only to avoid split-brain (see "Split-Brain Is the Greatest Risk" on page 297). Usually, a replica replicates from a single source, but multisource replication (*https://oreil.ly/GeaVQ*) is an option.

Arrows in Figure 7-1 represent the flow of data changes from the source to a replica:

1. During transaction commit, data changes are written to *binary logs* (or *binlogs* for short) on the source: on-disk files that record data changes in *binary log events* (see "Binary Log Events" on page 237).

2. An *I/O thread* on the replica dumps (reads) binary log events from the source binary logs. (A *binlog dump thread* on the source is dedicated to this purpose.)

3. The I/O thread on the replica writes the binary log events to *relay logs* on the replica: on-disk files that are a local copy of the source binary logs.

4. A *SQL thread* (or *applier thread*) reads binary log events from the relay log.

5. The SQL thread applies the binary log events to the replica data.

6. The replica writes the data changes (applied by the SQL thread) to its binary logs.

By default, MySQL replication is asynchronous: on the source, the transaction completes after step 1 and the remaining steps happen asynchronously. MySQL supports semisynchronous replication: on the source, the transaction completes after step 3. That is not a typo: MySQL semisynchronous replication commits after step 3; it does *not* wait for step 4 or 5. "Semisynchronous Replication" on page 244 goes into more detail.

Replicas are not required to write binary logs (step 6), but it's standard practice for high availability because it allows a replica to become the source. This is how a database *failover* works: when the source dies or is taken down for maintenance, a replica is promoted to become the new source. Let's call the instances *old source* and *new source*. Eventually, a DBA will restore the old source (or clone a new instance to replace it) and make it replicate from the new source. In the old source, the previously idle I/O thread, relay logs, and SQL threads (shaded darkly in Figure 7-1) start working. (The I/O thread in the old source will connect to the new source, which activates its previously idle binlog dump thread.) From the new source binary logs, the old source replicates writes that it missed while it was offline. While doing so, the old source reports replication lag, but this is a special case addressed in "Post-Failure Rebuild" on page 241. That's failover in a nutshell; but of course, it's more complex in practice.

Binary Log Events

Binary log events are a low-level detail that you probably won't encounter (even DBAs don't often mess around in binary logs), but they are a direct result of transactions executed by the application. Therefore, it's important to understand what the application is trying to flush through the plumbing of replication.

 The following presumes row-based replication (RBR), which is the default binlog_format (*https://oreil.ly/rtKm0*) as of MySQL 5.7.7.

Replication focuses on transactions and binary log events, not individual writes, because data changes are committed to binary logs during transaction commit, at which point writes have already completed. At a high level, the focus is transactions because they are meaningful to the application. At a low level, the focus is binary log events because they are meaningful to replication. Transactions are logically represented and delineated in binary logs as events, which is how multithread replicas can apply them in parallel—more on this in "Reducing Lag: Multithreaded Replication" on page 246. To illustrate, let's use a simple transaction:

```
BEGIN;
UPDATE t1 SET c='val' WHERE id=1 LIMIT 1;
DELETE FROM t2 LIMIT 3;
COMMIT;
```

The table schemas and data do not matter. What's important is that the UPDATE changes one row in table t1, and the DELETE deletes three rows from table t2. Figure 7-2 illustrates how that transaction is committed in a binary log.

Four contiguous events constitute the transaction:

- An event for BEGIN
- An event for the UPDATE statement with one row image
- An event for the DELETE statement with three row images
- An event for COMMIT

At this low level, SQL statements essentially disappear and replication is a stream of events and row images (for events that modify rows). A *row image* is a binary snapshot of a row before and after modification. This is an important detail because a single SQL statement can generate countless row images, which yields a large transaction that might cause lag as it flows through replication.

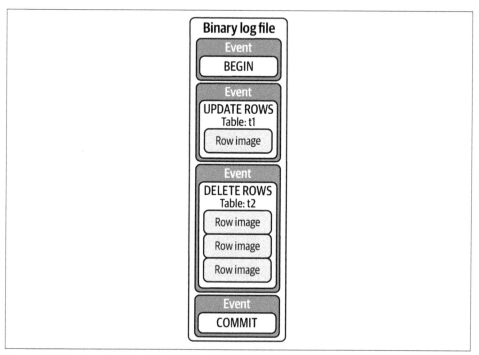

Figure 7-2. Binary log events for a transaction

Let's stop here because we're a little deeper into MySQL internals than we should be for this book. Although brief, this introduction to binary log events makes the following sections more intelligible because now you know what's flowing through the plumbing of replication and why the foci are transactions and binary log events.

Replication Lag

Referring back to Figure 7-1, replication lag occurs when applying changes on a replica (step 5) is slower than committing changes on the source (step 1). The steps in between are rarely a problem (when the network is working properly) because MySQL binary logs, the MySQL network protocol, and typical networks are very fast and efficient.

 Apply changes is short for *apply transactions* or *apply events*, depending on the context.

The I/O thread on a replica can write binary log events to its relay logs at a high rate because this is a relatively easy process: read from network, write sequentially to disk.

But a SQL thread has a much more difficult and time-consuming process: applying the changes. Consequently, the I/O thread outpaces the SQL thread, and replication lag looks like Figure 7-3.

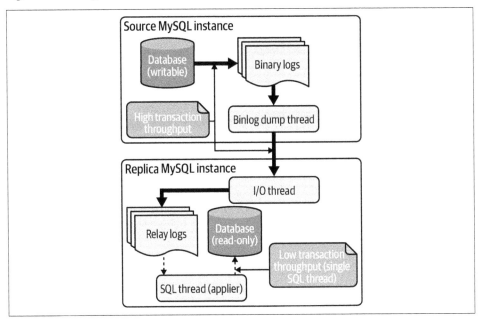

Figure 7-3. MySQL replication lag

Strictly speaking, a single SQL thread does not cause replication lag, it's only the limiting factor. The cause, in this case, is high transaction throughput on the source, which is a good problem if the application is busy, but a problem nonetheless. More on causes in the next section. The solution is more SQL threads, which is covered later in "Reducing Lag: Multithreaded Replication" on page 246.

Semisynchronous replication does not solve or preclude replication lag. When semisynchronous replication is enabled, for each transaction, MySQL waits for a replica to acknowledge that it has written the binary log events for the transaction to its relay logs—step 3 in Figure 7-1. On a local network, replication lag as depicted in Figure 7-3 can still occur. If semisynchronous reduces replication lag, it's only a side-effect of network latency throttling transaction throughput on the source. "Semisynchronous Replication" on page 244 goes into more detail.

Lag is inherent to replication, but make no mistake: MySQL replication is very fast. A single SQL thread can easily handle thousands of transactions per second. The first reason is simple: replicas do not execute the full workload that the source executes. Notably, replicas do not execute reads (presuming replicas aren't used to serve reads). The second reason requires a few lines to explain. As noted in "Binary Log Events" on page 237, this chapter presumes row-based replication (RBR). Consequently, replicas do not execute SQL statements: they apply binary log events. That saves replicas a lot of time because they're given the end result—data changes—and told where to apply them. That can be significantly faster than finding the matching rows to update, which is what the source had to do. As a result of these two reasons, replicas can be nearly idle even while the source is very busy. Nevertheless, three causes can overwhelm replication.

Causes

Replication lag has three main causes: transaction throughput, post-failure rebuilds, and network issues. A section for each follows.

Transaction Throughput

Transaction throughput causes replication lag when the rate on the source is greater than the rate at which SQL (applier) threads on the replica can apply changes. When this happens because the application is legitimately busy, it's usually not feasible to reduce the rate on the source. Instead, the solution is to increase the rate on the replica by running more SQL (applier) threads. Focus on improving replica performance by tuning multithreaded replication, as outlined in "Reducing Lag: Multithreaded Replication" on page 246.

Large transactions—ones that modify an inordinate number of rows—have a greater impact on replicas than the source. On the source, a large transaction that takes two seconds to execute, for example, most likely does not block other transactions because it runs (and commits) in parallel. But on a single-threaded replica, that large transactions blocks all other transactions for two seconds (or however long it takes to execute on the replica—it might be less due to less contention). On a multithreaded replica, other transactions continue to execute, but that large transaction still blocks one thread for two seconds. The solution is smaller transactions. More on this in "Large Transactions (Transaction Size)" on page 282.

Transaction throughput is not always driven by the application: backfilling, deleting, and archiving data are common operations that can cause massive replication lag if they don't control the batch size, as forewarned in "Batch Size" on page 115. In addition to proper batch size, these operations should monitor replication lag and slow down when replicas begin to lag. It's better for an operation to take one day than to lag a replica by one second. "Risk: Data Loss" on page 241 explains why.

At some point, transaction throughput will exceed the capacity of a single MySQL instance—source or replica. To increase transaction throughput, you must scale out by sharding the database (see Chapter 5).

Post-Failure Rebuild

When MySQL or hardware fails, the instance is fixed and put back into the replication topology. Or a new instance is cloned from an existing instance and takes the place of the failed instance. Either way, the replication topology is rebuilt to restore high availability.

 Replicas are used for several purposes, but this chapter discusses only replicas used for high availability.

The fixed (or new) instance will take minutes, hours, or days to *catch up*: to replicate all the binary log events that it missed while it was offline. Technically, this is replication lag, but in practice you can ignore it until the fixed instance has caught up. Once caught up, any lag is legitimate.

Since failure is inevitable and catching up takes time, the only solution is to be aware that the replication lag is due to a post-failure rebuild and wait.

Network Issues

Network issues cause replication lag by delaying the transfer of binary log events from source to replica—step 2 in Figure 7-1. Technically, the network—not replication—is lagging, but quibbling about semantics doesn't change the end result: the replica is *behind the source*—a long way of saying *lagged*. In this case, you must enlist network engineers to fix the root cause: the network.

The risk caused by a network issue is mitigated by communication and teamwork: talk with the network engineers to ensure that they know what's at stake for the database when there's a network issue—it's quite possible they don't know because they're not DBAs or engineers using MySQL.

Risk: Data Loss

Replication lag is data loss.

This is true by default for MySQL because the default is asynchronous replication. Fortunately, semisynchronous replication is an option that will not lose any committed transactions. Let's first examine the risk with asynchronous replication, then it will be clear how semisynchronous replication mitigates the risk.

As noted in "Foundation" on page 234, I defer Group Replication to the future. Moreover, the synchronicity of Group Replication requires careful explanation.[1]

Asynchronous Replication

Figure 7-4 shows the point in time at which the source crashed.

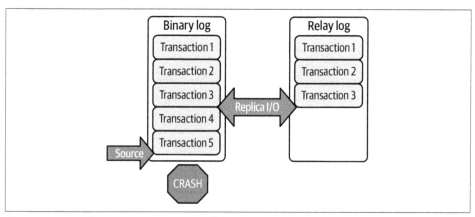

Figure 7-4. Crash on MySQL source with asynchronous replication

Before crashing, the source committed five transactions to its binary logs. But when it crashed, the replica I/O thread had only fetched the first three transactions. Whether or not the last two transactions are lost depends on two factors: the cause of the crash, and whether a DBA must failover.

If MySQL is the cause of the crash (most likely due to a bug), then it will automatically restart, perform crash recovery, and resume normal operations. (By default, replicas automatically reconnect and resume replication, too.) And since MySQL is truly durable when properly configured, the committed transactions 4 and 5 are not lost. There's just one problem: crash recovery can take several minutes *or hours* to complete—it depends on several factors outside the scope of this book. If you can wait, crash recovery is the ideal solution because no committed transactions are lost.

If hardware or operating system is the cause of the crash, or if the crashed MySQL instance cannot be recovered quickly enough for any reason, then a DBA will failover—promote a replica to the source—and transactions 4 and 5 are lost. This is not an ideal solution, but it's standard practice because the alternative is worse: a long

---

1 "MySQL Group Replication...Synchronous or Asynchronous Replication?" (*https://oreil.ly/Gv6GR*) by renowned MySQL expert Frédéric Descamps explains the synchronicity of Group Replication.

outage (downtime) while recovering the crashed MySQL instance, which requires exacting data forensics that could take hours or days.

 No data is lost when DBAs failover for maintenance (operations). And since nothing has failed, some DBAs call this *successover*.

This example is not contrived to prove the point that *replication lag is data loss*; it's inevitable with asynchronous replication because all hardware and software (including MySQL) fails eventually.

The only mitigation is a strict adherence to minimizing replication lag. Do not, for example, disregard 10 seconds of replication as "not too far behind." Instead, treat it as "we're at risk of losing the last 10 seconds of customer data." The odds are in your favor that MySQL or the hardware won't fail at the worst possible moment—when the replica is lagging—but let me relate a cautionary tale about hardware failure.

One week when I was on-call, I received an alert around 9 a.m. That's not too early; I was already done with my first cup of coffee. One alert quickly turned into thousands. Database servers everywhere—in multiple, geographically distributed data centers— were failing. It was so bad that I immediately knew: the problem was not hardware or MySQL, because the odds of that many simultaneous but unrelated failures was infinitesimal. Long story short, one of the most experienced engineers in the company had not had his coffee that morning. He had written and run a custom script that went terribly awry. The script didn't simply reboot servers at random, it turned them off. (In data centers, server power is programmatically controlled through a backplane called Intelligent Platform Management Interface.) Killing power is akin to hardware failure.

The moral of that story is: failure can be caused by human error. Be prepared.

Asynchronous replication is not a best practice because virtually unmitigated data loss is antithetical to the purpose of a persistent data store. Countless companies around the world have been successful with asynchronous replication for more than 20 years. (But "common practice" doesn't necessarily mean "best practice.") If you run asynchronous replication, MySQL DBAs and experts will not scoff as long as the following three conditions are true:

- You monitor replication lag with a heartbeat (see "Monitoring" on page 250).
- You are alerted any time (not just during business hours) when replication lag is too high.
- You treat replication lag as data loss and fix it immediately.

Many successful companies use asynchronous MySQL replication, but there's a higher standard to strive for: semisynchronous replication.

Semisynchronous Replication

When semisynchronous (or *semisync*) replication is enabled, the source waits for at least one replica to acknowledge each transaction. *Acknowledge* means that the replica has written the binary log events for the transaction to its relay logs. Therefore, the transaction is safely on disk on the replica, but the replica hasn't applied it yet. (Consequently, replication lag still occurs with semisync replication, as mentioned in "Replication Lag" on page 238.) Acknowledgment when received, not when applied, is why it's called *semi*synchronous, not fully synchronous.

Let's replay the source crash from "Asynchronous Replication" on page 242, but now with semisynchronous replication enabled. Figure 7-5 shows the point in time at which the source crashed.

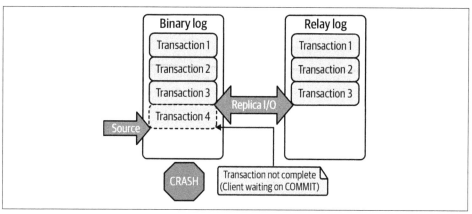

Figure 7-5. Crash on MySQL source with semisynchronous replication

With semisynchronous replication, every committed transaction is guaranteed to have replicated to at least one replica. *Committed transaction* in this context means that the COMMIT statement executed by the client has returned—the transaction is complete from the client's point of view. That's the usual, high-level understanding of a committed transaction, but down in the plumbing of replication, the technical details differ. The following four steps are an extreme simplification of how a transaction commits when binary logging and semisynchronous replication are enabled:

1. Prepare transaction commit

2. Flush data changes to binary log

3. Wait for acknowledgment from at least one replica

4. Commit transaction

An InnoDB transaction commit is a two-phase commit. In between the two phases (steps 1 and 4), data changes are written and flushed to the binary logs, and MySQL waits for at least one replica to acknowledge the transaction.[2]

In Figure 7-5, the dashed outline of the fourth transaction indicates that at least one replica has *not* acknowledged it. The source crashed after step 2, so the transaction is in the binary logs, but the commit did not complete. The client COMMIT statement will return an error (not from MySQL because it has crashed; it will probably receive a network error).

Whether or not the fourth transaction is lost depends on the same two factors as before ("Asynchronous Replication" on page 242): the cause of the crash, and whether a DBA must failover. The important difference is that only one uncommitted transaction per connection can be lost when semisynchronous replication is enabled. Since the transaction did not complete and the client received an error, the potential loss of the uncommitted transaction is less worrisome. The keyword is *less* worrisome: there are edge cases that mean you cannot simply disregard the lost transaction. For example, what if a replica acknowledges the transaction but the source crashes before it receives the acknowledgment? The answer would descend further into replication plumbing than we need to go. The point is: semisynchronous replication guarantees that all committed transactions have replicated to at least one replica, and only one uncommitted transaction per connection can be lost on failure.

The fundamental purpose of a persistent data store is to persist data, not lose it. So why isn't semisynchronous the default for MySQL? It's complicated.

There are successful companies that operate MySQL at scale using semisynchronous replication. One notable company is GitHub, the former employer of renowned MySQL expert Shlomi Noach who wrote a blog post about their use of semisynchronous replication: "MySQL High Availability at GitHub" (*https://oreil.ly/6mLug*).

Semisynchronous replication *reduces* availability—that's not a typo. Although it safeguards transactions, that safeguard means that the current transaction for every connection might stall, timeout, or fail on COMMIT. By contrast, COMMIT with asynchronous replication is essentially instant and guaranteed as long as the storage on the source is working.

By default, semisynchronous replication reverts to asynchronous when there are not enough replicas or the source times out waiting for an acknowledgment. This can be effectively disabled by configuration, but the best practice is to allow it because the alternative is worse: a complete outage (the application cannot write to the source).

---

2 I presume sync_binlog = 1 (*https://oreil.ly/lbfwm*).

Performance with semisynchronous replication requires that the source and replicas are on a fast, local network because network latency implicitly throttles transaction throughput on the source. Whether or not this is an issue depends on the local network where you run MySQL. A local network should have submillisecond latency, but that must be verified and monitored, else transaction throughput will suffer the whims of network latency.

Whereas asynchronous replication works without any special configuration, semisynchronous requires specific configuration and tuning. Neither is burdensome for a DBA, but they are careful work nevertheless.

 I think semisynchronous replication is the best practice because data loss is never acceptable—full stop. I advise you to learn more about semisync replication, test and verify it on your network, and use it if possible. Start by reading "Semisynchronous Replication" (*https://oreil.ly/JnxUJ*) in the MySQL manual. Or, if you want to be truly prepared for the future, look into Group Replication (*https://oreil.ly/5ZWHQ*) and InnoDB Cluster (*https://oreil.ly/JrrYd*): the future of MySQL replication and high availability. Although semisynchronous replication and Group Replication elicit debate among MySQL experts, one point garners universal agreement: preventing data loss is a virtue.

Reducing Lag: Multithreaded Replication

By default, MySQL replication is asynchronous *and* single-threaded: one SQL thread on the replica. Even semisynchronous replication is single-threaded by default. The single SQL thread does not cause replication lag—"Causes" on page 240 are the three main causes—but it is the limiting factor. The solution is *multithreaded replication* (or *parallel replication*): multiple SQL threads applying transactions in parallel. On a multithreaded replica, the SQL threads are called *applier threads*.[3] You can still call them SQL threads if you want—the terms are synonymous—but the MySQL manual uses *applier* in the context of multithreaded replication.

The solution is simple for us as engineers using MySQL, but it's not simple for MySQL. As you can imagine, transactions cannot be applied in random order: there might be dependencies among transactions. For example, if one transaction inserts a new row, and second transaction updates that row, obviously the second transaction must run after the first. *Transaction dependency tracking* is the art and science (and magic) of determining which transactions—from a serialized record

---

3 In the MySQL manual, the full term is *applier worker thread*, but I think *worker* is redundant since every thread is a worker of some type.

(the binary logs)—can be applied in parallel. It's both fascinating and impressive, but it's beyond the scope of this book, so I encourage you to watch the video "MySQL Parallel Replication (LOGICAL_CLOCK): all the 5.7 (and some of the 8.0) details" (*https://oreil.ly/Q8aJv*) by renowned MySQL expert Jean-François Gagné.

Strictly speaking, one system variable enables multithreaded replication, but I suspect that you are not going to be surprised when I tell you: it's more complicated in practice. Configuring MySQL replication is beyond the scope of this book, but multi-threaded replication is too important not to give you a *conservative starting point*. A conservative starting point means that the following configuration might not yield the full performance of multithreaded replication. Consequently, you (or DBAs) must tune multithreaded replication—as in "MySQL Tuning" on page 39—to maximize its potential while at the same time taking into account the various ramifications of parallel replication.

> The rest of this section is nontrivial MySQL configuration that should only be done by an engineer with experience configuring MySQL in high performance, high availability environments. The system variables in Table 7-1 will *not* affect data integrity or dura-bility in any way, but they will affect performance on source and replica instances. Be aware that:
>
> - Replication affects high availability.
> - Global transaction identifiers (*https://oreil.ly/xYtq3*) and `log-replica-updates` (*https://oreil.ly/wAOMO*) must be enabled.
> - Configuring MySQL requires elevated MySQL privileges.
> - System variables change between MySQL versions and distributions.
> - MariaDB uses different system variables: see "Parallel Replica-tion" (*https://oreil.ly/F5n6J*) in the MariaDB documentation.
>
> Be very careful when configuring MySQL, and thoroughly read the relevant sections of the manual for your version and distribution of MySQL.

Table 7-1 lists three system variables as a conservative starting point for enabling and configuring multithreaded replication. Variable names changed as of MySQL 8.0.26, so the table lists old and new variable names, followed by a recommended value. I do not recommend using multithreaded replication in MySQL older than 5.7.22 because certain replication features from 8.0 were backported into this version.

Table 7-1. System variables to enable multithreaded replication

MySQL 5.7.22 through 8.0.25	MySQL 8.0.26 and newer	Value
slave_parallel_workers (*https://oreil.ly/82SBV*)	replica_parallel_workers (*https://oreil.ly/kFqAz*)	4
slave_parallel_type (*https://oreil.ly/s5NOE*)	replica_parallel_type (*https://oreil.ly/mlft5*)	LOGICAL_CLOCK
slave_preserve_commit_order (*https://oreil.ly/oKRSy*)	replica_preserve_commit_order (*https://oreil.ly/QGBB1*)	1

Set all three variables on all MySQL instances in the replication topology that are used for high availability (that can be promoted to source).

Setting `replica_parallel_workers` greater than zero is the one system variable that enables multithreaded replication. Four applier threads is a good start; you must tune to find the optimized number of applier threads for your workload and hardware. But, like a magic spell, it must be invoked with `replica_parallel_type` to conjure the full performance of multithreaded replication. Even as of MySQL 8.0.26, the default for `replica_parallel_type` is DATABASE, which only applies transactions in parallel for different databases—effectively, only one applier thread per database. This is historical: it was the first type of parallelization. But today, the best practice is `replica_parallel_type` = LOGICAL_CLOCK because it has no drawbacks when `replica_preserve_commit_order` is enabled, and it provides better parallelization because it applies transactions in parallel regardless of database.

`replica_preserve_commit_order` is disabled by default, but I do not think that is a best practice because it allows a multithreaded replica to *commit out of order*: commit transactions in a different order than they were committed on the source. For example, transactions 1, 2, 3 committed in that order on the source might commit in order 3, 1, 2 on the replica. Multithreaded replication only commits out of order when safe (when there are no ordered dependencies among transactions), and table data is (eventually) the same, but committing out of order has consequences that you and especially the DBAs managing MySQL must understand and handle. "Replication and Transaction Inconsistencies" (*https://oreil.ly/Bf04z*) in the MySQL manual documents the consequences. When `replica_preserve_commit_order` is enabled, transactions are still applied in parallel, but some transactions might wait for earlier transactions to commit first—this is how commit order is preserved. Although `replica_preserve_commit_order` reduces the effectiveness of parallelization, it's the best practice until you and the DBAs verify that its consequences are acceptable and handled.

Multithreaded replication works the same for Group Replication.

Since Table 7-1 is a conservative starting point for enabling multithreaded replication, it does not enable the latest transaction dependency tracking: WRITESET. MySQL transaction dependency tracking is determined by the system variable binlog_transaction_dependency_tracking (*https://oreil.ly/5SMUG*). The default is COMMIT_ORDER, but the latest is WRITESET. Benchmarks show that WRITESET achieves greater parallelization than COMMIT_ORDER. At the time of this writing, WRITESET is less than four years old: it was introduced in MySQL 8.0 which became GA on April 19, 2018. As a matter of technology, you should use WRITESET because it achieves better performance on multithread replicas. But as a matter of policy, it's up to you (or your DBA) to decide when a feature has matured enough to be used in production. To use WRITESET on MySQL 5.7, you must enable system variable trans action_write_set_extraction (*https://oreil.ly/3lKGX*). On MySQL 8.0 this system variable is enabled by default but deprecated as of MySQL 8.0.26.

 Create a new replica to test and tune multithreaded replica. A new replica poses little to no risk since it does not serve the application or high availability.

There's one more system variable that you should experiment with: binlog_ group_commit_sync_delay (*https://oreil.ly/YMXoI*). By default, this variable is disabled (zero) because, as its name suggests, it adds an artificial delay to group commit. Delays are usually bad for performance, but group commit delay is a rare exception—sometimes. On the source, transactions are committed to a binary log in groups, which is an internal optimization aptly named *group commit*. Adding a delay to group commit creates larger groups: more transactions committed per group. Multithreaded replication does not depend on group commit, but it can benefit from larger group commits because more transactions at once helps transaction dependency tracking find more opportunities for parallelization. To experiment with binlog_group_commit_sync_delay, start with a value of 10000: the unit is microseconds, so that's 10 milliseconds. This will increase transaction commit response time by 10 milliseconds on the source, but it should also increase transaction throughput on the replica. Tuning group commit size with respect to multithreaded replica applier transaction throughput is not easy due to a lack of MySQL metrics. If you go this route, read "A Metric for Tuning Parallel Replication in MySQL 5.7" (*https://oreil.ly/QG4E1*) by renowned MySQL expert Jean-François Gagné.

Multithreaded replication is a best practice, but it requires nontrivial MySQL configuration and possibly tuning to achieve maximum performance. Benchmarks and real-world results vary, but multithreaded replication can more than double transaction throughput on replicas. For performance gains like that, it's well worth the effort. But most importantly: multithreaded replication significantly reduces replication lag, which is critical when using asynchronous replication.

Monitoring

The best practice for monitoring replication lag is to use a purpose-built tool. But first, let's examine the infamous MySQL metric for replication lag: Seconds_Behind_Source, as reported by SHOW REPLICA STATUS.

 Before MySQL 8.0.22, the replica lag metric and command were Seconds_Behind_Master and SHOW SLAVE STATUS, respectively. As of MySQL 8.0.22, the metric and command are Seconds_Behind_Source and SHOW REPLICA STATUS. I use the current metric and command in this book.

Seconds_Behind_Source equals the current time on the replica minus the timestamp of the binary log event that the SQL thread is executing.[4] If the current time on the replica is T = 100 and the SQL thread is executing a binary log event with timestamp T = 80, then Seconds_Behind_Source = 20. When everything is working (replication lag notwithstanding), Seconds_Behind_Source is relatively accurate, but it's notorious for three problems:

- The first problem occurs when everything is not working. Since Seconds_Behind_Source relies solely on binary log event timestamps, it does not figuratively see (or care about) any issues before the binary log events arrive. If the source or network has a problem that causes binary log events not to arrive, or to arrive slowly, then the SQL thread applies all binary log events and Seconds_Behind_Source reports zero lag because, from the SQL thread point of view, that is technically correct: zero events, zero lag. But from our point of view, we know that's wrong: not only is there replication lag, there's an issue before the replica, too.

- The second problem is that Seconds_Behind_Source is notorious for flapping between zero and a nonzero value. For example, one moment Seconds_Behind_Source reports 500 seconds of lag, the next moment it reports

---

4 Technically, it's the event timestamp plus its execution time. Also, the clock skew between source and replica is subtracted from Seconds_Behind_Source when it's reported by SHOW REPLICA STATUS.

zero lag, and a moment later it reports 500 seconds of lag again. This problem is related to the first problem: when events trickle into the relay logs because of an issue before the replica, the SQL thread oscillates noticeably between working (applying the latest event) and waiting (for the next event). That causes Seconds_Behind_Source to flap between a value (SQL thread is working) and zero (SQL thread is waiting).

- The third problem is that Seconds_Behind_Source does not precisely answer the question that engineers really want to know: *when will the replica catch up?* When will replica lag be effectively zero because it's applying the latest transactions from the source? Presuming everything is working (replication lag notwithstanding), the value of Seconds_Behind_Source only indicates how long ago the current event being applied was executed on the source; it does *not* precisely indicate how long until the replica catches up to the source. The reason is that replicas apply transactions at a different rate than the source.

  For example, suppose that 10 transactions execute concurrently on the source, and each transaction takes 1 second. The total execution time is 1 second and the rate is 10 TPS because the transactions executed concurrently on the source. On a single-threaded replica, which applies each transaction serially, the worst-case total execution time and rate *could be* 10 seconds and 1 TPS, respectively. I emphasize *could be* because it's also possible that the replica applies all 10 transactions significantly faster because the replica isn't burdened with the full workload and it doesn't execute SQL statements (it applies binary log events). This could happen if the 1 second execution time per transaction on the source was due to a terrible WHERE clause that accessed a million rows but only matched and updated a single row. The lucky replica updates that single row in almost no time. On a multithreaded replica (see "Reducing Lag: Multithreaded Replication" on page 246), the total execution time and rate vary based on at least two factors: the number of applier threads and whether the transactions can be applied in parallel. Either way, the point is: replicas apply transactions at a different rate than the source, and since there's no way to know the difference, Seconds_Behind_Source cannot—and does not—precisely indicate when a replica will catch up.

Despite these problems, Seconds_Behind_Source provides value: it's a ballpark estimate of how long until the replica catches up to the source: seconds, minutes, hours, days? More on recovery time in the next section.

MySQL 8.0 introduced significantly better visibility into MySQL replication, including replication lag. There's just one catch: it provides primitives, not ready-to-use metrics like Seconds_Behind_Source. If you're using MySQL 8.0, talk with your DBA about Performance Schema replication tables (*https://oreil.ly/xDKOd*) that expose a new wealth of information about MySQL replication. Otherwise, the best practice for monitoring replication lag is to use a purpose-built tool. Instead of relying on binary log event timestamps, tools use their own timestamps. A tool writes timestamps at regular intervals to a table, then reports replication lag as the difference of the current time on a replica minus the latest timestamp in the table. Fundamentally, the approach is similar to how MySQL calculates Seconds_Behind_Source, but there are three important differences when using a tool:

- A tool writes timestamps at regular intervals, which means that it's not susceptible to the first problem of Seconds_Behind_Source. If there's any issue before the binary log events arrive, replication lag from a tool will immediately begin to increase because its timestamp (written to a table) stops incrementing.

- A tool precludes the second problem of Seconds_Behind_Source: replication lag from a tool does not flap; it can only be (effectively) zero if its timestamp is (effectively) equal to the current time.

- A tool can measure replication lag and write timestamps at subsecond intervals (every 200 milliseconds, for example). A single second of replication lag is too much for high performance applications—or any application when using asynchronous replication.

The de facto tool for monitoring MySQL replication is pt-heartbeat (*https://oreil.ly/sTvro*). (Timestamps written by replication lag monitoring tools are called *heartbeats*.) This venerable tool has seen more than a decade of use and success because it's simple and effective. Use it to start monitoring replication lag, or use it to learn how to write your own tool.

Recovery Time

When a replica has a significant amount of lag, the most pressing question is often "When will it recover?" When will the replica catch up to the source so that it's executing (applying) the latest transactions? There's no precise answer. But replication lag always recovers after the cause is fixed. I return to this notion at the end of the section. Until then, there's one more characteristic of replication lag to understand.

Another common and important characteristic of replication lag is the inflection point between increasing lag and when the replica begins to recover (decreasing lag). In Figure 7-6, the inflection point is marked by the dotted line at time 75.

When replication lag begins, the situation looks increasingly dire as lag increases. But this is normal. Presuming the replica isn't broken, the SQL threads are working hard, but the cause has not been fixed yet, so the backlog of binary log events continues to increase. As long as the cause persists, replication lag will increase. But again: this is normal. Very soon after the cause is fixed, the proverbial tide will turn, creating an inflection point in the graph of replication lag, as shown in Figure 7-6 at time 75. The replica is still lagged, but it's applying binary log events faster than the I/O thread is dumping them into the relay logs. Post–inflection point, replica lag usually decreases with noticeable and satisfying haste.

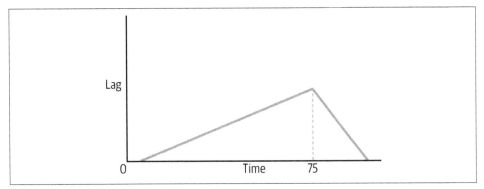

Figure 7-6. Inflection point in graph of replication lag

Recovery time is not very meaningful before the inflection point because, in theory, if the cause is never fixed, then the replica will never recover. When replication lag is increasing steadily (pre–inflection point), don't be distracted by the value; instead, focus on fixing the cause. Lag will increase until the cause is fixed.

Recovery time is more meaningful after the inflection point and it's usually faster than `Seconds_Behind_Source` or the value reported by tools. As explained in "Monitoring" on page 250, despite replication lag, a single SQL thread is very fast because the replica doesn't have to execute the full workload that besets the source. As a result, replicas often apply transactions faster than the source, which is how replicas eventually catch up.

In my experience, if replication lag is measured in days, it often recovers in hours (post–inflection point)—perhaps many hours, but hours nevertheless. Likewise, several hours of lag often recovers in a few hours, and several minutes of lag often recovers before you can finish a cup of coffee.

Returning to the notions that there's no precise answer and lag always recovers, the end result is that a precise recovery time is not as useful or meaningful as it first seems. Even if you could know the exact time that a replica will recover, you cannot do anything but wait. MySQL replication is remarkably dogged. As long as the replica doesn't break, MySQL *will* recover—it always does. Fix the cause as quickly as possible, wait for the inflection point, then replication lag indicates a worst case recovery time: MySQL usually recovers more quickly because SQL threads are fast.

Summary

This chapter investigated MySQL replication lag. Replication is the foundation of MySQL high availability, and replication lag is data loss. The main takeaways are:

- MySQL has three types of replication: asynchronous, semisynchronous, and Group Replication.
- Asynchronous (async) replication is the default.
- Asynchronous replication can lose numerous transactions on failure.
- Semisynchronous (semisync) replication does not lose any committed transactions on failure, only one uncommitted transaction per client connection.
- Group Replication is the future of MySQL replication and high availability (but not covered in this chapter or book): it turns MySQL instances into a cluster.
- The foundation of MySQL async and semisync replication is sending transactions, encoded as binary log events, from a source to a replica.
- Semisync replication makes a transaction commit on the source wait for at least one replica to acknowledge receiving and saving (not applying) the transaction.
- A replica has an I/O thread that fetches binary log events from the source and stores them in local relay logs.
- A replica has, by default, one SQL thread that executes binary log events from the local relay logs.
- Multithreaded replication can be enabled to run multiple SQL threads (applier threads).
- Replication lag has three main causes: (high) transaction throughput on the source, a MySQL instance catching up after failure and rebuild, or network issues.
- SQL (applier) threads are the limiting factor in replication lag: more SQL threads reduce lag by applying transaction in parallel.
- Semisync replication can incur replication lag.
- Replication lag is data loss, especially with asynchronous replication.
- Enabling multithreaded replication is the best way to reduce replication lag.
- The MySQL metric for replication lag, `Seconds_Behind_Source`, can be misleading; avoid relying on it.
- Use a purpose-built tool to measure and report MySQL replication lag at subsecond intervals.

- Recovery time from replication lag is imprecise and difficult to calculate.
- MySQL will recover, eventually—it always does once the cause is fixed.

The next chapter examines MySQL transactions.

Practice: Monitor Subsecond Lag

The goal of this practice is to monitor subsecond replication lag and determine: is your replica lagging beyond the 1-second resolution that `Seconds_Behind_Source` can report? For example, is your replica lagging by 800 milliseconds (which is far greater than network latency)? A tool is needed to monitor subsecond lag: `pt-heartbeat` (*https://oreil.ly/sTvro*).

To complete this practice, you need:

- A compute instance to run `pt-heartbeat` that can connect to the source and a replica
- MySQL `SUPER` or `GRANT OPTION` privileges to create a user; or ask your DBA to create the user
- MySQL `CREATE` privileges to create a database; or ask your DBA to create the database

Every MySQL configuration and environment is different, so adapt the following example as needed.

1. Create a database for `pt-heartbeat` to use:

   ```
   CREATE DATABASE IF NOT EXISTS `percona`;
   ```

   You can use a different database name; I just chose `percona` as an example. If you change the database name, be sure to change it in the following commands.

2. Create a MySQL user for `pt-heartbeat` and grant it the privileges that it needs:

   ```
   CREATE USER 'pt-heartbeat'@'%' IDENTIFIED BY 'percona';
   GRANT CREATE, INSERT, UPDATE, DELETE, SELECT ON `percona`.`heartbeat`
     TO 'pt-heartbeat'@'%';
   GRANT REPLICATION CLIENT ON *.* TO 'pt-heartbeat'@'%';
   ```

   You can use a different MySQL username and password; I just chose `pt-heartbeat` and `percona` (respectively) as an example. You should definitely change the password if running this in production. (The password is set by the `IDENTIFIED BY` clause.)

3. Run pt-heartbeat in update-mode to write heartbeats to a table in the percona database:

```
pt-heartbeat         \
  --create-table     \
  --database percona \
  --interval 0.2     \
  --update           \
  h=SOURCE_ADDR,u=pt-heartbeat,p=percona
```

A quick breakdown of those command-line arguments:

--create-table
> Automatically create the heartbeat table in the specified database, if needed. The first GRANT statement allows the pt-heartbeat user to CREATE the table. If not using this option, read the pt-heartbeat documentation to learn how to create the heartbeat table manually.

--database
> Specify the database to use. pt-heartbeat requires this option.

--interval
> Write heartbeats every 200 milliseconds. This option determines the maximum resolution of pt-heartbeat, which is the smallest amount of lag that it can detect. The default is 1.0 second, which is not subsecond. The maximum resolution is 0.01 seconds (10 milliseconds). Therefore, 0.2 seconds is a little conservative, so experiment with lower values (high resolution).

--update
> Write heartbeats to heartbeat table in --database every --interval seconds.

h=SOURCE_ADDR,u=pt-heartbeat,p=percona
> The data source name (DSN) to connect to MySQL. The h specifies the hostname. Change SOURCE_ADDR to the hostname of the source instance. The u specifies the username. The p specifies the password.

> Read the pt-heartbeat documentation (*https://oreil.ly/sTvro*) for further details on command-line options and the DSN.

> If the command is successful when run, it prints nothing and runs silently. Else, it prints an error and exits.

4. Run `pt-heartbeat` again but in monitor mode to print replication lag:

```
pt-heartbeat           \
   --database percona \
   --interval 0.5      \
   --monitor           \
   h=REPLICA_ADDR,u=pt-heartbeat,p=percona
```

Change REPLICA_ADDR in the DSN to the hostname of a replica instance.

In monitor mode, `--interval` is how often to check and print replication lag. The update mode instance of `pt-heartbeat` is writing heartbeats every 0.2 seconds (200 milliseconds), but the monitor mode instance of `pt-heartbeat` checks and prints replication lag a little more slowly (every 0.5 seconds) for easy reading.

If the command in step four is successful when run, it prints lines like:

```
0.00s [  0.00s,  0.00s,  0.00s ]
0.20s [  0.00s,  0.00s,  0.00s ]
0.70s [  0.01s,  0.00s,  0.00s ]
0.00s [  0.01s,  0.00s,  0.00s ]
```

The first field is the current replication lag. The three fields between the brackets are moving averages for the last 1, 5, and 15 minutes of replication lag.

In this example, the first line shows zero lag. Then I intentionally lagged my replica for 1.1 seconds. Consequently, the second line shows 200 milliseconds of replication lag, which is the maximum resolution because the update-mode instance of `pt-heartbeat` is running with `--interval 0.2`. Half a second later (due to the monitor-mode instance of `pt-heartbeat` running with `--interval 0.5`), the tool reports 0.7 seconds (700 milliseconds) of replication lag on the third line. But then my fake 1.1 seconds of lag ends, so the last (fourth) line correctly reports zero lag.

This example is contrived, but it demonstrates how `pt-heartbeat` can monitor and report subsecond replication lag. Try it on your network—the tool is safe to use.

## CHAPTER 8

Transactions

MySQL has nontransactional storage engines, like MyISAM, but InnoDB is the default and the presumptive norm. Therefore, practically speaking, every MySQL query executes in a transaction by default, even a single SELECT statement.

 This chapter does not apply if you happen to be using another storage engine, like Aria or MyRocks. But more than likely, you're using InnoDB, in which case: every MySQL query is a transaction.

From our point of view as engineers, transactions appear conceptual: BEGIN, execute queries, and COMMIT. Then we trust MySQL (and InnoDB) to uphold the ACID properties: atomicity, consistency, isolation, and durability. When the application workload—queries, indexes, data, and access patterns—is well optimized, transactions are a nonissue with respect to performance. (Most database topics are a nonissue when the workload is well optimized.) But behind the scenes, transactions invoke a whole new world of considerations because upholding ACID properties while maintaining performance is not an easy feat. Fortunately, MySQL shines at executing transactions.

As with replication lag in the previous chapter, the inner workings of transactions are beyond the scope of this book, but understanding a few basic concepts is pivotal to avoiding common problems that hoist transactions from the lowest levels of MySQL to the tops of engineers' minds. A little understanding avoids a lot of problems.

This chapter examines MySQL transactions with respect to avoiding common problems. There are five major sections. The first descends into row locking with respect to transaction isolation levels. The second examines how InnoDB manages concurrent data access while guaranteeing ACID properties: MVCC and the undo logs. The third describes the history list length and how it indicates problematic transactions.

The fourth enumerates common problems with transactions to avoid. The fifth is a foray into reporting transaction details in MySQL.

Row Locking

Reads do not lock rows (except for SELECT...FOR SHARE and SELECT...FOR UPDATE), but writes always lock rows. That's simple and expected, but the tricky question is: which rows must be locked? Of course, the rows being written must be locked. But in a REPEATABLE READ transaction, InnoDB can lock significantly more rows than it writes. This section illustrates and explains why. But first, we must shift terminology into the vernacular of InnoDB data locking.

Since tables are indexes (recall "InnoDB Tables Are Indexes" on page 41), rows are index *records*. InnoDB row locking is discussed in terms of *locking records*, not locking rows, because of index record gaps. A *gap* is a range of values between two index records, as illustrated in Figure 8-1: a primary key with two records, two pseudo-records (infimum and supremum), and three gaps.

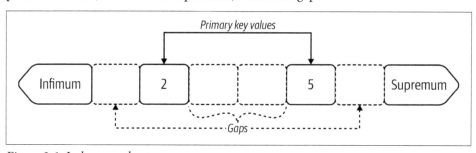

Figure 8-1. Index record gaps

Records are depicted as solid squares with index values inside: 2 and 5 in this example. Pseudo-records are depicted as solid arrows on each end of the index: *infimum* and *supremum*. Every InnoDB B-tree index has these two pseudo-records: infimum represents all index values less than the minimum record (2 in this example); supremum represents all index values greater than the maximum record (5 in this example). Index records don't begin at 2 or end at 5; technically, they begin and end at the infimum and supremum, and examples in this section reveal the importance of this detail. Gaps are depicted as dashed squares with no index value. If the primary key is a single unsigned four-byte integer, then the three gaps are (in interval notation):

- [0, 2)
- (2, 5)
- (5, 4294967295]

When discussing row locking, the term *record* is used instead of *row* because records have gaps, but it could be misleading to say that rows have gaps. For example, if the application has two rows with values 2 and 5, that does not entail a gap in the rows comprising values 3 and 4 because maybe these aren't valid values for the application. But with respect to an index, between record values 2 and 5, values 3 and 4 constitute a valid record gap (presuming an integer column). To put it succinctly: the application deals in rows; InnoDB row locking deals in records. Examples in this section demonstrate that gap locks are surprisingly pervasive and arguably more important than individual record locks.

The term *data locks* refers to all types of locks. There are many types of data locks, but Table 8-1 lists the fundamental InnoDB data locks.

Table 8-1. Fundamental InnoDB data locks

Lock type	Abbreviation	Locks gap	Locks
Record lock	REC_NOT_GAP		Locks a single record
Gap lock	GAP	✓	Locks the gap before (less than) a record
Next-key lock		✓	Locks a single record and the gap before it
Insert intention lock	INSERT_INTENTION		Allows INSERT into gap

The best way to understand the fundamental InnoDB data locks is with real transactions, real locks, and illustrations.

> As of MySQL 8.0.16, data locks are easy to examine using Performance Schema tables `data_locks` and `data_lock_waits`. The following examples use these Performance Schema tables.
>
> In MySQL 5.7 and older, you must first SET GLOBAL innodb_sta tus_output_locks=ON, which requires SUPER MySQL privileges, then execute SHOW ENGINE INNODB STATUS and shift through the output to find the relevant transaction and locks. It's not easy—even experts strain to carefully parse the output. Since MySQL 5.7 is not the current release, I do not use its output in this section; but since MySQL 5.7 is still widely used, refer to my blog post "MySQL Data Locks: Mapping 8.0 to 5.7" (*https://oreil.ly/pIAM6*) for an illustrated guide to mapping data lock output from MySQL 5.7 to MySQL 8.0.

Let's reuse the tried and true table `elem` but simplified as shown in Example 8-1.

Example 8-1. Table `elem` simplified

```
CREATE TABLE `elem` (
  `id` int unsigned NOT NULL,
  `a`  char(2) NOT NULL,
  `b`  char(2) NOT NULL,
  `c`  char(2) NOT NULL,
  PRIMARY KEY (`id`),
  KEY `idx_a` (`a`)
) ENGINE=InnoDB;

+----+-----+----+----+
| id | a   | b  | c  |
+----+-----+----+----+
|  2 | Au  | Be | Co |
|  5 | Ar  | Br | C  |
+----+-----+----+----+
```

The table `elem` is nearly the same as before, but now the nonunique index `idx_a` only covers column `a`, and there are only two rows, which create two primary key values as shown earlier in Figure 8-1. Since row locks are really index record locks and there are no indexes on columns `b` and `c`, you can ignore these two columns; they're shown only for completeness and the nostalgia of simpler chapters, like Chapter 2 when row locks were just rows locks.

Since `autocommit` (*https://oreil.ly/86J7d*) is enabled by default, the following examples begin with `BEGIN` to start an explicit transaction. Locks are released when a transaction ends; therefore, the transaction is kept active—no `COMMIT` or `ROLLBACK`—to examine the data locks that the SQL statement following `BEGIN` has acquired (or is waiting to acquire). At the end of each example, data locks are printed by querying the table `performance_schema.data_locks`.

Record and Next-Key Locks

An `UPDATE` on table `elem` using the primary key to match rows acquires four data locks in the default transaction isolation level, `REPEATABLE READ`:

```
BEGIN;
UPDATE elem SET c='' WHERE id BETWEEN 2 AND 5;


SELECT index_name, lock_type, lock_mode, lock_status, lock_data
FROM   performance_schema.data_locks
WHERE  object_name = 'elem';
```

```
+-------------+-----------+---------------+-------------+-----------------------+
| index_name  | lock_type | lock_mode     | lock_status | lock_data             |
+-------------+-----------+---------------+-------------+-----------------------+
| NULL        | TABLE     | IX            | GRANTED     | NULL                  |
| PRIMARY     | RECORD    | X,REC_NOT_GAP | GRANTED     | 2                     |
| PRIMARY     | RECORD    | X             | GRANTED     | supremum pseudo-record|
| PRIMARY     | RECORD    | X             | GRANTED     | 5                     |
+-------------+-----------+---------------+-------------+-----------------------+
```

Before illustrating and explaining these data locks, I will briefly describe what each row means:

- The first row is a *table lock*, as indicated by the lock_type column. InnoDB is a row-level locking storage engine, but MySQL also requires table locks—refer back to "Lock time" on page 13. There will be a table lock for every table referenced by queries in the transaction. I include table locks for completeness, but ignore them since we're focusing on record locks.

- The second row is a *record lock* on primary key value 2, as indicated by all the columns. The cryptic column is lock_mode: X means an exclusive lock (S [not shown] means a shared lock), and REC_NOT_GAP means a record lock.

- The third row is a *next-key lock* on the supremum pseudo-record. In column lock_mode, a solitary X or S means an exclusive or shared next-key lock, respectively. Imagine it as X,NEXT_KEY.

- The fourth row is a *next-key lock* on primary key value 5. Again, the solitary X in column lock_mode means an exclusive next-key lock. Imagine it as X,NEXT_KEY.

Figure 8-2 illustrates the impact of these data locks.

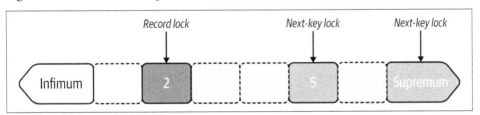

Figure 8-2. Record and next-key locks on primary key, REPEATABLE READ transaction

Locked records are shaded; unlocked records are white. The record lock on primary key value 2 is shaded darkly. This record is locked because its corresponding row matches the table condition: id BETWEEN 2 AND 5.

The next-key lock on primary key value 5 is shaded medium-dark, and the gap before it is shaded lightly. This record is locked because its corresponding row matches the table condition, too. The gap before this record is locked because it's a next-key lock.

The gap comprises the nonexistent primary key values 3 and 4 (to which there are no corresponding rows).

Similarly, the next-key lock on the supremum pseudo-record is shaded medium-dark, and the gap before it is shaded lightly. The gap comprises all primary key values greater than 5. The intriguing question is: why lock the supremum pseudo-record, which *includes* all primary key values greater than 5, when the table condition *excludes* primary key values greater than 5? The answer is equally intriguing, but I must defer it until "Gap Locks" on page 266.

Let's confirm that the gaps are locked by trying to insert a row (using another transaction with autocommit enabled):

```
mysql> INSERT INTO elem VALUES (3, 'Au', 'B', 'C');
ERROR 1205 (HY000): Lock wait timeout exceeded; try restarting transaction

+------------+-----------+------------------------+-------------+-----------+
| index_name | lock_type | lock_mode              | lock_status | lock_data |
+------------+-----------+------------------------+-------------+-----------+
| PRIMARY    | RECORD    | X,GAP,INSERT_INTENTION | WAITING     | 5         |
....

mysql> INSERT INTO elem VALUES (6, 'Au', 'B', 'C');
ERROR 1205 (HY000): Lock wait timeout exceeded; try restarting transaction

+------------+-----------+--------------------+-------------+------------------ ----+
| index_name | lock_type | lock_mode          | lock_status | lock_data        |
+------------+-----------+--------------------+-------------+------------------+
| PRIMARY    | RECORD    | X,INSERT_INTENTION | WAITING     | supremum pseudo... |
...
```

The first INSERT times out trying to acquire an insert intention lock on the gap between values 2 and 5, which is where the new value (3) would be inserted. Although column lock_data lists value 5, this record is *not* locked because this not a record or next-key lock: it's an insert intentions lock, which is a special type of gap lock (for INSERT); therefore, it locks the gap before the value 5. More on insert intention locks in "Insert Intention Locks" on page 273.

The second INSERT times out trying to acquire a next-key lock on the supremum pseudo-record because the new value, 6, is greater than the current maximum value, 5, so it would be inserted between the maximum record and the supremum pseudo-record.

These INSERT statements prove that Figure 8-2 is not wrong: nearly the entire index is locked except for values less than 2. Why does InnoDB use next-key locks that lock the gaps instead of record locks? Because the transaction isolation level is REPEATABLE READ, but that's only part of the answer. The complete answer is not straightforward, so bear with me for a moment. By locking the gaps before the affected records, next-key locks isolate the entire range of records that the query accesses, which is the *I* in ACID: isolation. That prevents a phenomenon called *phantom rows* (*https://oreil.ly/DYs9L*) (or *phantom reads*) when, at a later time, a transaction reads rows that it did not read at an earlier time. The new rows are *phantoms* because, like a ghost, they appear mysteriously. (*Phantom* is the actual term in the ANSI SQL-92 standard.) Phantom rows violate the principle of isolation, which is why certain transaction isolation levels forbid them. Now the truly mysterious part of this explanation: the ANSI SQL-92 standard *allows* phantom rows in REPEATABLE READ but InnoDB prevents them with next-key locking. But let's not go down the proverbial rabbit hole by asking why InnoDB prevents phantom rows in REPEATABLE READ. Knowing why doesn't change the fact, and it's not uncommon for database servers to implement transaction isolation levels differently than the standard.[1] For completeness, however, know that the ANSI SQL-92 standard forbids phantom rows only in the highest transaction isolate level: SERIALIZABLE. InnoDB supports SERIALIZABLE, but I don't cover it in this chapter because it's not commonly used. REPEATABLE READ is the default in MySQL and InnoDB uses next-key locks to prevent phantom rows in REPEATABLE READ.

Transaction isolation level READ COMMITTED disables gap locking, which includes next-key locks. To prove it, change the transaction isolation level to READ COMMITTED:

```
SET TRANSACTION ISOLATION LEVEL READ COMMITTED;
BEGIN;
UPDATE elem SET c='' WHERE id BETWEEN 2 AND 5;


SELECT index_name, lock_type, lock_mode, lock_status, lock_data
FROM   performance_schema.data_locks
WHERE  object_name = 'elem';
+------------+-----------+----------------+-------------+-----------+
| index_name | lock_type | lock_mode      | lock_status | lock_data |
+------------+-----------+----------------+-------------+-----------+
| NULL       | TABLE     | IX             | GRANTED     | NULL      |
| PRIMARY    | RECORD    | X,REC_NOT_GAP  | GRANTED     | 2         |
| PRIMARY    | RECORD    | X,REC_NOT_GAP  | GRANTED     | 5         |
+------------+-----------+----------------+-------------+-----------+
```

SET TRANSACTION applies once to the next transaction. After the next transaction, subsequent transactions use the default transaction isolation level. See SET TRANSACTION (*https://oreil.ly/46zcp*) for details.

---

[1] To go down the rabbit hole, follow "A Critique of ANSI SQL Isolation Levels" (*https://oreil.ly/WF6NT*): a classic read on the subject of ANSI SQL-92 isolation levels.

The same UPDATE statement in a READ COMMITTED transaction acquires records locks only on the matching rows, as illustrated in Figure 8-3.

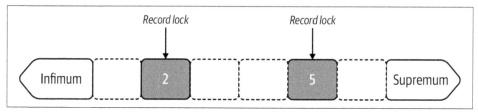

Figure 8-3. Record locks on primary key, READ COMMITTED transaction

Why not use READ COMMITTED? That question relates to an access pattern trait ("Transaction Isolation" on page 136) that makes it entirely application-specific, even query-specific. In a transaction, READ COMMITTED has two important side effects:

- The same read statement can return different rows if re-executed.
- The same write statement can affect different rows if re-executed.

These side effects explain why InnoDB does not need to use a consistent snapshot for reads or lock the gaps for writes: READ COMMITTED allows the transaction to read or write different records (for committed changes) at different times. ("MVCC and the Undo Logs" on page 276 defines *consistent snapshot*.) Carefully consider these side effects with respect to your application. If you are certain they will not cause a transaction to read, write, or return incorrect data, then READ COMMITTED reduces locks and undo logs, which helps improve performance.

Gap Locks

Gap locks are purely prohibitive: they prevent other transactions from inserting rows into the gap. That's all they do.

Multiple transactions can lock the same gap because all gaps locks are compatible with other gap locks. But since gap locks prevent *other* transactions from inserting rows into the gap, only one transaction can insert rows into a gap when it's the only transaction locking the gap. Two or more locks on the same gap prevent all transactions from inserting rows into the gap.

The purpose of a gap lock is narrow: prevent other transactions from inserting rows into the gap. But the creation of a gap lock is wide: any query that accesses the gap. Reading nothing can create a gap lock that blocks inserting rows:

```
BEGIN;
SELECT * FROM elem WHERE id = 3 FOR SHARE;
```

```
SELECT index_name, lock_type, lock_mode, lock_status, lock_data
FROM    performance_schema.data_locks
WHERE   object_name = 'elem';
+------------+-----------+-----------+-------------+-----------+
| index_name | lock_type | lock_mode | lock_status | lock_data |
+------------+-----------+-----------+-------------+-----------+
| NULL       | TABLE     | IS        | GRANTED     | NULL      |
| PRIMARY    | RECORD    | S,GAP     | GRANTED     | 5         |
+------------+-----------+-----------+-------------+-----------+
```

Prima facie, that SELECT seems innocuous: a SELECT in REPEATABLE READ uses a consistent snapshot, and FOR SHARE only creates shared locks, so it won't block other reads. More importantly, the SELECT doesn't match any rows: table elem has primary key values 2 and 5, not 3. No rows, no locks—right? Wrong. By accessing the gap with READ REPEATABLE and SELECT...FOR SHARE, you summon a lone gap lock: Figure 8-4.

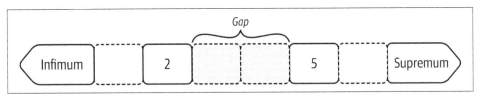

Figure 8-4. Lone gap lock

I call it a *lone* gap lock because it doesn't accompany a next-key lock or insert intention lock; it stands alone. All gap locks—shared or exclusive—prevent other transactions from inserting rows into the gap. That innocuous SELECT statement is actually an insidious INSERT blocker. The larger the gap, the larger the block, which the next section illustrates with a secondary index.

The easy creation of gap locks by any access to the gap is part of the answer to the intriguing question in "Record and Next-Key Locks" on page 262: why lock the supremum pseudo-record, which *includes* all primary key values greater than 5, when the table condition *excludes* primary key values greater than 5? First, let me dial the intrigue to maximum. Here's the original query and its data locks:

```
BEGIN;
UPDATE elem SET c='' WHERE id BETWEEN 2 AND 5;

+------------+-----------+---------------+-------------+------------------------+
| index_name | lock_type | lock_mode     | lock_status | lock_data              |
+------------+-----------+---------------+-------------+------------------------+
| NULL       | TABLE     | IX            | GRANTED     | NULL                   |
| PRIMARY    | RECORD    | X,REC_NOT_GAP | GRANTED     | 2                      |
| PRIMARY    | RECORD    | X             | GRANTED     | supremum pseudo-record |
| PRIMARY    | RECORD    | X             | GRANTED     | 5                      |
+------------+-----------+---------------+-------------+------------------------+
```

Now, here's the same query but with an IN clause instead of a BETWEEN clause:

```
BEGIN;
UPDATE elem SET c='' WHERE id IN (2, 5);
```

```
+------------+-----------+---------------+-------------+-----------+
| index_name | lock_type | lock_mode     | lock_status | lock_data |
+------------+-----------+---------------+-------------+-----------+
| NULL       | TABLE     | IX            | GRANTED     | NULL      |
| PRIMARY    | RECORD    | X,REC_NOT_GAP | GRANTED     | 2         |
| PRIMARY    | RECORD    | X,REC_NOT_GAP | GRANTED     | 5         |
+------------+-----------+---------------+-------------+-----------+
```

Both transactions are REPEATABLE READ, and both queries have the exact same EXPLAIN plan: range access on primary key. But the new query acquires record locks only on the matching rows. What is this magic? Figure 8-5 shows what's happening for each query.

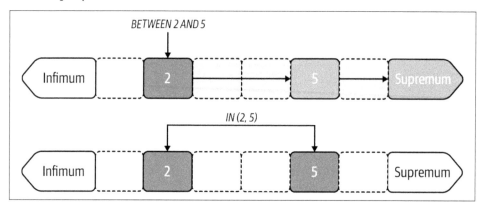

Figure 8-5. Range access for BETWEEN versus IN, REPEATABLE READ transaction

Row access for BETWEEN happens as you might expect: from 2 to 5 and everything between. In simplistic terms, the sequence of row access for BETWEEN is:

1. Read row at index value 2
2. Row matches: record lock
3. Next index value: 5
4. Traverse the gap from 2 to 5
5. Read row at index value 5
6. Row matches: next-key lock
7. Next index value: supremum

---

8. Traverse the gap from 5 to supremum

9. End of the index: next-key lock

But the sequence of row access for `IN` is much simpler:

1. Read row at index value 2

2. Row matches: record lock

3. Read row at index value 5

4. Row matches: record lock

Despite having the exact same EXPLAIN plan and matching the same rows, the queries access rows differently. The original query (`BETWEEN`) accesses the gaps; therefore, it uses next-key locks to lock the gaps. The new query (`IN`) does not access the gaps; therefore, it uses record locks. But make no mistake: the `IN` clause does not preclude gap locking. If the new query table condition is `IN (2, 3, 5)`, that accesses the gap between value 2 and 5 and causes a gap lock (not a next-key lock):

```
BEGIN;
UPDATE elem SET c='' WHERE id IN (2, 3, 5);
```

```
+------------+-----------+----------------+-------------+-----------+
| index_name | lock_type | lock_mode      | lock_status | lock_data |
+------------+-----------+----------------+-------------+-----------+
| NULL       | TABLE     | IX             | GRANTED     | NULL      |
| PRIMARY    | RECORD    | X,REC_NOT_GAP  | GRANTED     | 2         |
| PRIMARY    | RECORD    | X,REC_NOT_GAP  | GRANTED     | 5         |
| PRIMARY    | RECORD    | X,GAP          | GRANTED     | 5         |
+------------+-----------+----------------+-------------+-----------+
```

You have a lone gap lock: `X,GAP`. But notice: there is no next-key lock on the supremum pseudo-record because `IN (2, 3, 5)` does not access that gap. Mind the gap.

Gap locking is easy to disable by using `READ COMMITTED`. A `READ COMMITTED` transaction doesn't need gap locks (or next-key locks) because records in the gap are allowed to change, and each query accesses the latest latest changes (committed rows) when it executes. Even the lone gap lock summoned by `SELECT * FROM elem WHERE id = 3 FOR SHARE` is quashed by `READ COMMITTED`.

Secondary Indexes

Secondary indexes introduce potentially wide-ranging consequences with respect to row locking, especially nonunique indexes. Recall that simplified table `elem` (Example 8-1) has a nonunique secondary index on column `a`. With that in mind, let's see how the following UPDATE in a REPEATABLE READ transaction locks records on the secondary index and the primary key:

```
BEGIN;
UPDATE elem SET c='' WHERE a BETWEEN 'Ar' AND 'Au';


SELECT    index_name, lock_type, lock_mode, lock_status, lock_data
FROM      performance_schema.data_locks
WHERE     object_name = 'elem'
ORDER BY index_name;
+------------+-----------+----------------+-------------+----------------------+
| index_name | lock_type | lock_mode      | lock_status | lock_data            |
+------------+-----------+----------------+-------------+----------------------+
| NULL       | TABLE     | IX             | GRANTED     | NULL                 |
| a          | RECORD    | X              | GRANTED     | supremum pseudo-record |
| a          | RECORD    | X              | GRANTED     | 'Au', 2              |
| a          | RECORD    | X              | GRANTED     | 'Ar', 5              |
| PRIMARY    | RECORD    | X,REC_NOT_GAP  | GRANTED     | 2                    |
| PRIMARY    | RECORD    | X,REC_NOT_GAP  | GRANTED     | 5                    |
+------------+-----------+----------------+-------------+----------------------+
```

Figure 8-6 illustrates those six records locks: four on the secondary index and two on the primary key.

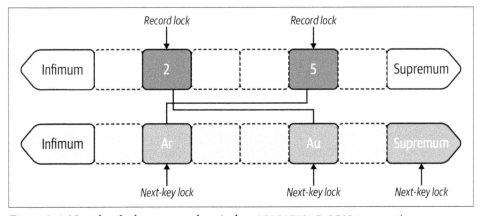

Figure 8-6. Next-key locks on secondary index, REPEATABLE READ transaction

The UPDATE only matches two rows, but it locks the entire secondary index, which prevents inserting any values. The locks on the secondary index are similar to those in Figure 8-2. But now there is a next-key lock on the first record in the secondary index record: tuple ('Ar', 5), where 5 is the corresponding primary key value. This next-key lock isolates the range from new duplicate "Ar" values. For example, it prevents inserting the tuple ('Ar', 1), which sorts before ('Ar', 5).

Normally, InnoDB does not lock an entire secondary index. That happens in these examples only because there are only two index records (in both the primary key and the nonunique secondary index). But recall "Extreme Selectivity" on page 86: the lower the selectivity, the larger the gaps. As an extreme example, if a nonunique index has 5 unique values evenly distributed over 100,000 rows, that is 20,000 records per row (100,000 rows / 5 cardinality), or 20,000 records per gap.

The lower the index selectivity, the larger the record gaps.

READ COMMITTED avoids gap locking, even for nonunique secondary indexes because only matching rows are locked with record locks. But let's not make it too easy on ourselves; let's keep examining InnoDB data locks on nonunique secondary indexes for different kinds of data changes.

At the end of the previous section, changing the BETWEEN clause to an IN clause averted gap locking, but that does not work with a nonunique index. In fact, InnoDB *adds* a gap lock in this case:

```
BEGIN;
UPDATE elem SET c='' WHERE a IN ('Ar', 'Au');


SELECT    index_name, lock_type, lock_mode, lock_status, lock_data
FROM      performance_schema.data_locks
WHERE     object_name = 'elem'
ORDER BY index_name;
+------------+-----------+--------------+---------------+------------------------+
| index_name | lock_type | lock_mode    | lock_status   | lock_data              |
+------------+-----------+--------------+---------------+------------------------+
| a          | RECORD    | X,GAP        | GRANTED       | 'Au', 2                |
...
```

I removed the original data locks from the output (they're identical) to highlight the new gap lock on tuple ('Au', 2). Strictly speaking, this gap lock is redundant with the next-key lock on the same tuple, but it does not result in incorrect locking or data access. Therefore, just let it be and never forget: InnoDB is full of wonders and mysteries. And what would life be without a few of those?

It's important to examine data locks because InnoDB is full of surprises. Although this section is detailed and meticulous, it's barely below the surface—InnoDB locking is deep, and in the depths hide secrets. For example, what data locks might InnoDB require if "Au" is changed to "Go"? Let's examine the data locks of that change:

```
BEGIN;
UPDATE elem SET a = 'Go' WHERE a = 'Au';
```

```
+------------+-----------+--------------+-------------+-----------------------+
| index_name | lock_type | lock_mode    | lock_status | lock_data             |
+------------+-----------+--------------+-------------+-----------------------+
| NULL       | TABLE     | IX           | GRANTED     | NULL                  |
| a          | RECORD    | X            | GRANTED     | supremum pseudo-record|
| a          | RECORD    | X            | GRANTED     | 'Au', 2               |
| a          | RECORD    | X,GAP        | GRANTED     | 'Go', 2               |
| PRIMARY    | RECORD    | X,REC_NOT_GAP| GRANTED     | 2                     |
+------------+-----------+--------------+-------------+-----------------------+
```

Figure 8-7 visualizes those four data locks.

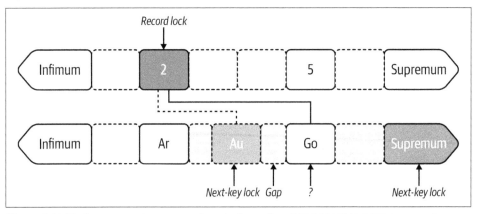

Figure 8-7. Update nonunique secondary index value, REPEATABLE READ transaction

The "Au" value is gone—changed to "Go"—but InnoDB still holds a next-key lock on the tuple: ('Au', 2). The new "Go" does not have record lock or next-key lock, only a gap lock before the tuple: ('Go', 2). So what's locking the new "Go" record? Is this some kind of REPEATABLE READ side effect? Let's change the transaction isolation level and re-examine the data locks:

```
SET TRANSACTION ISOLATION LEVEL READ COMMITTED;
BEGIN;
UPDATE elem SET a = 'Go' WHERE a = 'Au';
```

```
+------------+-----------+--------------+-------------+-----------+
| index_name | lock_type | lock_mode    | lock_status | lock_data |
+------------+-----------+--------------+-------------+-----------+
| NULL       | TABLE     | IX           | GRANTED     | NULL      |
| a          | RECORD    | X,REC_NOT_GAP| GRANTED     | 'Au', 2   |
| PRIMARY    | RECORD    | X,REC_NOT_GAP| GRANTED     | 2         |
+------------+-----------+--------------+-------------+-----------+
```

Switching to READ COMMITTED disables gap locking as expected, but where is the lock—any lock—on the new "Go" value? "Writes always lock rows," or at least that's what I said at the beginning of "Row Locking" on page 260. And yet, InnoDB reports no locks for this write…

What if I told you that InnoDB is so optimized that it can lock without locking? Let's use the next type of data lock, insert intention, to stare perilously deep into InnoDB locking and resolve this mystery.

Insert Intention Locks

An *insert intention lock* is a special type of gap lock that means the transaction will insert a row into the gap when the gap is not locked by other transactions. Only gap locks block insert intention locks. (Remember: *gap locks* include next-key locks because the latter are a combination of record lock and gap lock.) Insert intention locks are compatible with (do not block) other insert intention locks. This is important for INSERT performance because it allows multiple transactions to insert different rows into the same gap at the same time. How does InnoDB handle duplicate keys? I return to this question after demonstrating other facets of insert intention locks that make the answer more clear.

Gap locks *prevent* INSERT. Insert intention locks *allow* INSERT.

Insert intention locks are special for three reasons:

- Insert intention locks do not lock the gap because, as the term *intention* implies, they represent a *future* action: inserting a row *when* there are no gap locks held by other transactions.

- Insert intention locks are created and reported only when they conflict with gap locks held by other transactions; otherwise, insert intention locks are not created or reported by the transaction inserting the row.

- If an insert intention lock is created, it is used once and released immediately once granted; but InnoDB continues to report it until the transaction is complete.

In a sense, insert intention locks aren't locks because they don't block access. They're more like wait conditions that InnoDB uses to signal when a transaction can proceed with an INSERT. Granting the insert intention lock is the signal. But if a transaction doesn't have to wait because there are no conflict gap locks, then it doesn't wait, and you won't see an insert intention lock because none was created.

Let's see insert intention locks in action. Start by locking the gap between primary key values 2 and 5; then, in a second transaction, try to insert a row with primary key value 3:

```
-- First transaction
BEGIN;
UPDATE elem SET c='' WHERE id BETWEEN 2 AND 5;

-- Second transaction
BEGIN;
INSERT INTO elem VALUES (3, 'As', 'B', 'C');
```

```
+------------+-----------+------------------------+-------------+-----------+
| index_name | lock_type | lock_mode              | lock_status | lock_data |
+------------+-----------+------------------------+-------------+-----------+
| PRIMARY    | RECORD    | X,GAP,INSERT_INTENTION | WAITING     | 5         |
...
```

`X,GAP,INSERT_INTENTION` in column `lock_mode` is an insert intention lock. It's also listed as `X,INSERT_INTENTION` (not shown) when locking and inserting into the gap between the maximum record value and the supremum pseudo-record.

The first transaction locks the gap before primary key value 5. That gap lock blocks the second transaction from inserting into the gap, so it creates an insert intention lock and waits. Once the first transaction commits (or rolls back), the gap is unlocked, the insert intention lock is granted, and the second transaction inserts the row:

```
-- First transaction
COMMIT;

-- Second transaction
-- INSERT executes
```

```
+------------+-----------+------------------------+-------------+-----------+
| index_name | lock_type | lock_mode              | lock_status | lock_data |
+------------+-----------+------------------------+-------------+-----------+
| NULL       | TABLE     | IX                     | GRANTED     | NULL      |
| PRIMARY    | RECORD    | X,GAP,INSERT_INTENTION | GRANTED     | 5         |
+------------+-----------+------------------------+-------------+-----------+
```

As noted earlier, InnoDB continues to report an insert intention lock even though, once granted, it is used once and released immediately. Consequently, it looks like the gap is locked, but it's an illusion—a ploy by InnoDB to lure us in deeper. You can prove that it's an illusion by inserting another row into the gap at primary key value 4; it does not block. Why does InnoDB continue to report an insert intention lock that's not really there? Few mortals know, and it matters not. Look past the illusion to see it for what it *was*: in the past, the transaction blocked before inserting a row into the gap.

For completeness and a segue into deeper aspects of InnoDB locking, especially with respect to insert intention locks, here is what you see when an INSERT does not block on gap locks:

```
BEGIN;
INSERT INTO elem VALUES (9, 'As', 'B', 'C'); -- Does not block


+------------+-----------+-----------+-------------+-----------+
| index_name | lock_type | lock_mode | lock_status | lock_data |
+------------+-----------+-----------+-------------+-----------+
| NULL       | TABLE     | IX        | GRANTED     | NULL      |
+------------+-----------+-----------+-------------+-----------+
```

No record locks at all. That's how insert intention locks work on the surface, but we came here to stare perilously deep into InnoDB locking, so let's go deeper by asking the question that led us here: why is there no record (or next-key) lock on the newly inserted row? This is the same mystery from the previous section: no lock on the new "Go" value.

This is the secret: InnoDB has explicit and implicit locks and it only reports explicit locks.[2] Explicit locks exist as lock structures in memory; therefore, InnoDB can report them. But implicit locks do not exist: there is no lock structure; therefore, InnoDB has nothing to report.

In the previous example, INSERT INTO elem VALUES (9, 'As', 'B', 'C'), the index record for the new row exists, but the row is not committed (because the transaction has not committed). If another transaction attempts to lock the row, it detects three conditions:

- The row is not committed.
- The row belongs to another transaction.
- The row is not explicitly locked.

Then magic happens: the requesting transaction—the transaction attempting to lock the record—converts the implicit lock to an explicit lock *on behalf of* the owning transaction—the transaction that created the record. Yes, that means one transaction creates a lock for another transaction—but that's not the confusing part. Since the requesting transaction creates the lock that it's trying to acquire, at first glance InnoDB seems to report that the transaction is waiting for a lock that it holds—the transaction is blocked on itself. There's a way to see through this illusion, but we've gone too deep.

---

2 Thank you to Jakub Łopuszański for revealing and teaching me this secret.

I hope that, as an engineer using MySQL, you never need to descend to this depth of InnoDB locking to achieve remarkable performance with MySQL. But I led us down here for two reasons. First, despite the illusions, the fundamentals of InnoDB row locking with respect to transaction isolation levels are tractable and applicable. You are now fantastically well prepared to handle every common InnoDB row locking issue—and more. Second, InnoDB made me do it because I stared too deeply for too long; and when it all blurred into one, I knew that I had fallen from the precipice and could never return. Don't ask why it locks the supremum pseudo-record beyond the table condition range. Don't ask why it has redundant gap locks. Don't ask why it converts implicit locks. Don't ask; else the questions never cease. Go on; save yourself.

MVCC and the Undo Logs

InnoDB uses multiversion concurrency control (MVCC) and undo logs to accomplish the *A*, *C*, and *I* properties of ACID. (To accomplish the *D*, InnoDB uses a transaction log—see "Transaction log" on page 219.) *Multiversion concurrency control* means that changes to a row create a new version of the row. MVCC is not unique to InnoDB; it's a common method that many data stores use. When a row is first created, it's version 1. When it's first updated, it's version 2. The basis of MVCC is that simple, but it quickly becomes more complex and interesting.

 Using the term *undo logs* is an intentional simplification because the full structure of undo logging is complex. The term *undo logs* is sufficiently precise to learn what it does and how it affects performance.

Undo logs record how to roll back changes to a previous row version. Figure 8-8 shows a single row with five versions and five undo logs that allow MySQL to roll back changes to previous row versions.

That row harkens back to "InnoDB Tables Are Indexes" on page 41 in Chapter 2: it's the row with primary key value 2 in table elem, depicted as the primary key leaf node. For brevity, I include only the primary key value (2), the row version (v1 through v5), and column a value ("Au" for v5); the other two columns, b and c, are not shown.

Version 5 (bottom right in Figure 8-8) is the current row that all new transactions will read, but let's begin at the beginning. The row is created as iron ("Fe"): version 1 in the upper left corner. There's an undo log for version 1 because INSERT creates the first version of a row. Then column a is modified (UPDATE) to change iron to titanium ("Ti"): version 2. Upon creating version 2, MySQL also creates an undo log that records how to roll back version 2 changes, which restores version 1. (In the next paragraph, I explain why version 1 has a solid outline [and a camera icon] but version 2 has a dashed outline.) Then column a is modified to change titanium to silver

("Ag"): version 3. MySQL creates an undo log that records how to roll back version 3 changes, and this undo log is linked to the previous so that MySQL can, if needed, roll back and restore version 2. Two more row updates occur: silver to Californium ("Cf") for version 4, and Californium to gold ("Au") for version 5.

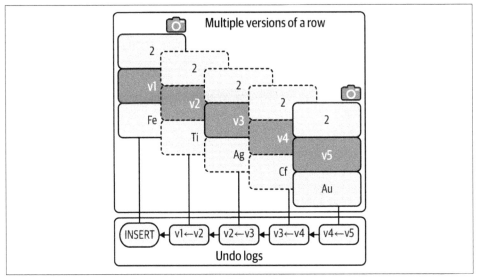

Figure 8-8. One row with five versions and five undo logs

There are two sets of undo logs: *insert undo logs* for INSERT and *update undo logs* for UPDATE and DELETE. For simplicity, I refer only to undo logs, which comprises both sets.

Version 1 has a solid outline and camera icon because an active transaction (not shown) holds a consistent snapshot at this point in the history of the database. Let me unpack that sentence. InnoDB supports four transaction isolation levels (*https://oreil.ly/xH5Gs*), but only two are commonly used: REPEATABLE READ (the default) and READ COMMITTED.

In a REPEATABLE READ transaction, the first read establishes a *consistent snapshot* (or *snapshot* for short): a virtual view of the database (all tables) at the moment when the SELECT is executed. The snapshot is held until the end of the transaction and used by all subsequent reads to access rows only at this point in the history of the database. Changes made by other transactions after this point are not figuratively visible within the original transaction. Presuming that other transactions are modifying the database, the snapshot of the original transaction becomes an increasingly old view of the database while the transaction remains active (does not COMMIT or ROLLBACK). It's like the original transaction is stuck in the 1980s and the only musicians it listens to are Pat Benatar, Stevie Nicks, and Taylor Dayne: old but still great.

Since version 5 is the current row, new transactions establish a snapshot from its point in database history, which is why it has a solid outline and camera icon. The important question is: why do versions 2, 3, and 4 still exist when there are no transactions holding snapshots at their respective points in database history? They exist to maintain the snapshot for version 1 because MySQL uses undo logs to reconstruct old row versions.

MySQL uses undo logs to reconstruct old row versions for snapshots.

It's easy to reconstruct Figure 8-8. First, immediately after inserting the row in Figure 8-8, start a transaction and establish a snapshot on version 1 of the row by executing a SELECT statement:

```
BEGIN;

SELECT a FROM elem WHERE id = 2;

-- Returns row version 1: 'Fe'
```

Since there's no COMMIT, that transaction is still active and holding its snapshot on the entire database, which is simply row version 1 in this example. Let's call this the *original transaction*.

Then update the row four times to create version 5:

```
-- autocommit enabled
UPDATE elem SET a = 'Ti' WHERE id = 2;
UPDATE elem SET a = 'Ag' WHERE id = 2;
UPDATE elem SET a = 'Cf' WHERE id = 2;
UPDATE elem SET a = 'Au' WHERE id = 2;
```

autocommit (*https://oreil.ly/nG8wa*) is enabled by default in MySQL, which is why the first (active) transaction needs an explicit BEGIN but the four UPDATE statements do not. Now MySQL is in a state represented by Figure 8-8.

If the original transaction executes SELECT a FROM elem WHERE id = 2 again, it reads version 5 (that's not a typo) but (figuratively) sees that that version is newer than the point in database history established by its snapshot. Consequently, MySQL uses the undo logs to roll back the row and reconstruct version 1, which is consistent with the snapshot established by the first SELECT statement. When the original transaction commits, and presuming no other active transactions are holding old snapshots, then MySQL can purge all the related undo logs because new transactions always begin with the current row version. When transactions are working well, the whole process is immaterial to performance. But you already know: problematic transactions can negatively affect the performance of the entire process. "Common Problems" on page 282 looks at how and why; but until then, there are more details to know about MVCC and the undo logs.

In a READ COMMITTED transaction, each read establishes a new snapshot. As a result, each read accesses the latest committed row version, hence READ COMMITTED. Since snapshots are used, undo logs are still created, but this is almost never an issue with READ COMMITTED because each snapshot is held only for the duration of the read. If a read takes a very long time *and* there's significant write throughput on the database, you might notice the accrual of redo logs (as an increase in history list length). Otherwise, READ COMMITTED is virtually free of undo logging.

Snapshots only affect reads (SELECT)—they're never used for writes. Writes always secretly read current rows, even if the transaction cannot "see" them with SELECT. This double vision averts chaos. For example, imagine that another transaction inserts a new row with primary key value 11. If the original transaction tries to insert a row with the same primary key value, MySQL will return a duplicate key value because the primary key value exists even though the transaction cannot see it with SELECT. Moreover, snapshots are very consistent: in a transaction, there is no way to advance the snapshot to a newer point in database history. If the application executing the transaction needs a newer snapshot, it must commit the transaction and begin a new one to establish a new snapshot.

Writes generate undo logs that are kept until the end of the transaction—regardless of transaction isolation level. Until now, I have focused on undo logs with respect to reconstructing old row versions for snapshots, but they are also used on ROLLBACK to revert changes made by writes.

One last thing to know about MVCC: undo logs are saved in the InnoDB buffer pool. You might recall from "Page flushing" on page 212 that "*Misc pages* contain miscellaneous internal data not covered in this book." Misc pages include undo logs (and many more internal data structures). Since undo logs reside in buffer pool pages, they use memory and are periodically flushed to disk.

There are a few system variables and metrics related to the undo logs; as an engineer using MySQL, you only need to know and monitor one: HLL, first introduced in "History list length (metric)" on page 205 and explained further in the next section. Otherwise, MVCC and the undo logs work flawlessly as long as the application avoids all "Common Problems" on page 282. One such problem is abandoned transactions, so let's avoid that by committing the original transaction:

```
COMMIT;
```

Goodbye, consistent snapshot. Goodbye, undo logs. Hello, history list length…

History List Length

History list length (HLL) gauges the amount of old row versions not purged or flushed.

Historically (no pun intended), HLL has been difficult to define because the full structure of undo logging is complex:

```
Rollback segments
└─ Undo slots
    └─ Undo log segments
        └─ Undo logs
            └─ Undo log records
```

That complexity obscures any simple relationship between undo logging and HLL, including the unit of measurement. The simplest functional (although not technically correct) unit of HLL is *changes*. If the HLL value is 10,000, you can read that as 10,000 changes. By understanding "MVCC and the Undo Logs" on page 276, you know that changes are kept (not purged) in memory (not flushed) in order to reconstruct old row versions. Therefore, it's accurate enough to say that HLL gauges the amount of old row versions not purged or flushed.

HLL greater than 100,000 is a problem—do not ignore it. Even though the true technical nature of HLL is elusive—even for MySQL experts—its usefulness is clear and undeniable: HLL is the harbinger of transaction-related problems. Always monitor HLL (see "History list length (metric)" on page 205), alert when it's too high (greater than 100,000), and fix the problem, which is undoubtedly one of the common problems discussed in the next section.

Although I caution against alerting on thresholds in "Wild Goose Chase (Thresholds)" on page 225, HLL is an exception: alerting when HLL is greater than 100,000 is reliable and actionable.

Alert on HLL greater than 100,000.

In theory, HLL has a maximum value, but MySQL performance is sure to crumble long before that value.[3] For example, just a few weeks ago as I write this, an instance

---

3 In *storage/innobase/trx/trx0purge.cc* of the MySQL 8.0 source code, a debug block logs a warning when HLL is greater than 2,000,000.

of MySQL in the cloud crashed at HLL 200,000, which took a long-running transaction four hours to amass before crashing MySQL and causing a two-hour outage.

Since undo logging is incredibly efficient, there is huge leeway in HLL with respect to the value at which MySQL performance will degrade or—worst case—crash. I have seen MySQL crash at 200,000, but I have also seen it run just fine well beyond 200,000. One thing is certain: if HLL increases unchecked, it *will* cause a problem: either noticeably slow performance, or MySQL will crash.

I want you to be the first engineer in history to use MySQL and never have a HLL problem. That's a lofty goal, but I encourage you to shoot for the stars. To that end, I intentionally flooded a MySQL instance with UPDATE statements to drive up the HLL—to amass thousands of old row versions. Table 8-2 shows the effect of HLL on query response time for a single row point-select: SELECT * FROM elem WHERE id=5 in an active REPEATABLE READ transaction.

Table 8-2. Effect of HLL on query response time

HLL	Response time (ms)	Baseline increase (%)
0	0.200 ms	
495	0.612 ms	206%
1,089	1.012 ms	406%
2,079	1.841 ms	821%
5,056	3.673 ms	1,737%
11,546	8.527 ms	4,164%

This example does *not* mean that HLL will increase query response time as shown; it only proves that HLL can increase query response time. From "MVCC and the Undo Logs" on page 276 and this section you know why: the SELECT in the active REPEATABLE READ transaction has a consistent snapshot on row 5 (id=5), but the UPDATE statements on that row generate new row versions. Each time the SELECT is executed, it slogs through the undo logs to reconstruct the original row version for the consistent snapshot, and that slog increases query response time.

Increasing query response time is proof enough, but we're professionals, so let's prove it irrefutably. At the end of "MVCC and the Undo Logs" on page 276, I mention that undo logs are stored as pages in the InnoDB buffer pool. As a result, the SELECT should access an inordinate number of pages. To prove this, I use Percona Server (*https://oreil.ly/OWUYR*) because its enhanced slow query log prints the number of distinct pages accessed when configured with log_slow_verbosity = innodb:

```
# Query_time: 0.008527
# InnoDB_pages_distinct: 366
```

Normally, the SELECT in this example accesses a single page to look up one row by primary key. But when the consistent snapshot for the SELECT is old (and HLL is large), InnoDB slogs through hundreds of undo log pages to reconstruct the old row.

MVCC, undo logs, and HLL are all normal and good trade-offs: a little performance for a lot of concurrency. It's only when HLL is inordinately large—greater than 100,000–that you should take action to fix the cause, which is almost universally one of the following common problems.

Common Problems

Transaction problems arise from the queries that constitute the transaction, how quickly the application executes those queries, and how quickly the application commits the transaction. Although a single query with autocommit (*https://oreil.ly/oQtD2*) enabled is technically a transaction that can cause the following problems (except for "Abandoned Transactions" on page 285), the main focus is multistatement transactions that begin with BEGIN (or START TRANSACTION), execute several queries, and end with COMMIT (or ROLLBACK). The performance impact of a multistatement transaction can be greater than the sum of its parts—the queries that constitute the transaction—because locks and undo logs are held until the transaction commits (or rolls back). Remember: MySQL is very patient—almost too patient. If the application does not commit a transaction, MySQL will wait even until the consequences of that active transaction ring its death knell.

Fortunately, none of these problems are difficult to detect or fix. HLL is the harbinger of most transaction problems, which is why you should always monitor it: see "History list length (metric)" on page 205 and "History List Length" on page 280. To keep the details of each problem uncluttered, I explain how to find and report problematic transactions in "Reporting" on page 286.

Large Transactions (Transaction Size)

A large transaction modifies an inordinate number of rows. How many rows is *inordinate*? That is relative, but engineers always know when they see it. For example, if you see that a transaction has modified 250,000 rows and you know that there are only 500,000 rows in the whole database, that's inordinate. (Or at the very least, it's a suspicious access pattern: see "Result Set" on page 139.)

 Generally, *transaction size* refers to the number of rows modified: the more rows modified, the larger the transaction. For MySQL Group Replication (*https://oreil.ly/wH10S*), *transaction size* has a slightly different meaning: see "Group Replication Limitations" (*https://oreil.ly/cJhWF*) in the MySQL manual.

If the transaction is running in the default isolation level, REPEATABLE READ, then it's safe to presume that it has locked a greater number of records than modified rows because of gap locking—as detailed in "Row Locking" on page 260. If the transaction is running in READ COMMITTED isolation level, then it's only acquiring record locks for each modified row. Either way, a large transaction is a large source of lock contention that can severely degrade write throughput and response time.

Don't forget replication (see Chapter 7): large transactions are a main cause of replication lag (see "Transaction Throughput" on page 240) and decrease the effectiveness of multithreaded replication (see "Reducing Lag: Multithreaded Replication" on page 246).

Large transactions can be noticeably slow to commit (or roll back) as previously addressed in "MVCC and the Undo Logs" on page 276, "Binary Log Events" on page 237, and Figure 6-7. It's quick and easy to modify rows because the data changes happen in memory, but commit is the reckoning when MySQL does significant work to persist and replicate the data changes.

Smaller transactions are better. How small? That, too, is relative and complicated to calibrate because, as I just noted, transactions cause a reckoning on commit, which means you have to calibrate several subsystems. (It's even more complicated when you factor in the cloud, which tends to limit and tweak little details, like IOPS.) Except for bulk operations which require calibrating a batch size (see "Batch Size" on page 115), calibrating transaction size is not commonly needed because, although the problem is common, it's typically a one-off problem: found, fixed, and doesn't reoccur (for awhile, at least). "Reporting" on page 286 shows you how to find large transactions.

The fix is to find the query (or queries) in the transaction that modify too many rows, and change them to modify fewer rows. But that depends entirely on the query, its purpose in the application, and why it's modifying too many rows. Whatever the reason, Chapters 1–4 equip you to understand and fix the query.

Finally, if you closely follow the principle of least data (see "Principle of Least Data" on page 97), transaction size may never be a problem.

Long-Running Transactions

A long-running transaction takes too long to complete (commit or roll back). How long is *too long*? That depends:

- Longer than acceptable for the application or users
- Long enough to cause problems (likely contention) with other transactions
- Long enough to cause a history list length alert

Unless you're proactively addressing performance, the second and third points are more likely to bring a long-running transaction to your attention.

Presuming that the application isn't waiting between queries (which is the next problem: "Stalled Transactions" on page 284), long-running transactions have two causes:

- The queries that constitute the transaction are too slow.
- The application executes too many queries in the transaction.

You fix the first cause with the techniques from Chapters 1–5. Remember: undo logs and row locks for all queries in a transaction are held until the transaction commits. On the upside, this means that optimizing slow queries to fix a long-running transaction has collateral benefits: the individual queries are faster *and* the transaction as a whole is faster, which can increase overall transaction throughput. The downside is that a long-running transaction might be quick enough for the application but too long for other transactions. For example, let's say that a transaction takes one second to execute, which is fine for the application, but during that second it holds row locks needed by another, faster transaction. This creates a tricky problem to debug because the fast transaction might run slowly in production but quickly in isolation when analyzed in the laboratory (on your laptop, for example). The difference, of course, is that the concurrency and contention of transactions in production is largely or completely absent in the lab. In this case, you must debug data lock contention, which is not easy for several reasons, the least of which is that data locks are fleeting. See the note following Table 8-1, and talk with your DBA or a MySQL expert.

You fix the second cause by modifying the application to execute fewer queries in the transaction. This occurs when the application attempts a bulk operation or programmatically generates queries inside a transaction without limiting the number of queries. Either way, the fix is to reduce or limit the number of queries in the transaction. Even if the transaction isn't long-running, this is a best practice to ensure that it won't accidentally become long-running. For example, maybe when the application is new it only inserts 5 rows per transaction; but years later, when the application has millions of users, it's inserting 500 rows per transaction because a limit wasn't built in from the beginning.

"Reporting" on page 286 shows you how to find long-running transactions.

Stalled Transactions

A stalled transaction is waiting too long after BEGIN, between queries, or before COMMIT. Stalled transactions are likely to be long-running transactions, but the causes are different: time waiting between queries (stalled) rather than time waiting for queries (long-running).

In practice, a stalled transaction appears as a long-running transaction because the end result is the same: slow transaction response time. Analyzing the transaction is required to determine if the response time is due to stalls or slow queries. Absent that analysis, engineers (and MySQL experts) often refer to any slow transaction as long-running.

Granted, there's always some wait time between queries (at least due to network latency required to send queries and receive result sets), but as in the previous two problems, you'll know a stalled transaction when you see it. To put it figuratively: the whole is much greater than the sum of its parts. To put it technically: the transaction response time from BEGIN to COMMIT is much greater than the sum of the query response times.

Since stalled transactions are waiting *between* queries (including after BEGIN and before COMMIT), MySQL is not culpable: the waits are caused by the application, and the reasons are limitless. A common reason is doing time-consuming application logic while a transaction is active, instead of before or after the transaction. But sometimes this can't be avoided; consider the following example:

```
BEGIN;
SELECT <row>
--
-- Time-consuming application logic based on the row
--
UPDATE <row>
COMMIT;
```

The solution in this case depends on the application logic. I'd begin by asking the most fundamental question: do these queries need to be a transaction? Can the row change after reading and before updating? If the row changes, does that break the logic? If nothing else, can the READ COMMITTED isolation level be used to disable gap locking? Engineers are clever and find ways to fix cases like this; the first step is finding them, which is covered in "Reporting" on page 286.

Abandoned Transactions

An abandoned transaction is an active transaction without an active client connection. There are two main causes of abandoned transactions:

- Application connection leaks
- Half-closed connections

An application bug can leak database connections (like leaking memory or threads): the code-level connection object goes out of scope, so it's no longer used, but it's still referenced by other code, so it's neither closed nor freed (probably resulting in a small memory leak, too). Apart from application-level profiling, debugging, or leak detection to verify this bug directly, you can verify it indirectly if restarting the application fixes (closes) the abandoned transactions. In MySQL, you can see what are likely to be abandoned transactions (as shown in "Reporting" on page 286), but you cannot verify this bug in MySQL because MySQL doesn't know that the connection has been abandoned.

Half-closed connections do not happen under normal circumstances because MySQL rolls back a transaction when the client connection closes for any reason detectable by MySQL or the operating system. But problems outside MySQL and the operating system can cause the client side of the connection to close without closing the MySQL side—that's why it's called a *half-closed* connection. MySQL is especially prone to half-closed connections because its network protocol is almost entirely command and response: the client sends commands, and MySQL sends a response. (If you're curious, clients send a query to MySQL with a COM_QUERY (*https://oreil.ly/I4RjE*) packet.) Between command and response, the client and MySQL observe total silence—not a single byte is transmitted. As peaceful as that sounds, it means that half-closed connections go unnoticed until wait_timeout (*https://oreil.ly/zP2bf*) seconds have passed, which defaults to 28,800 (8 hours).

Whether an application bug causing connection leaks or a half-closed connection mistaken for meditative network silence, the end result is the same if either occurs while a transaction is active (not committed): the transaction stays active. Any consistent snapshot or data locks stay active, too, because MySQL doesn't know that the transaction has been abandoned.

Truth be told, MySQL likes the silence; as do I. But we're paid to work, so let's examine how to find and report all four transaction problems.

Reporting

The MySQL Performance Schema (*https://oreil.ly/fgU04*) makes detailed transaction reporting possible; but at the time of this writing, there are no tools that make it easy. I wish I could tell you to use existing open source tools, but there are none. The following SQL statements are the state of the art. When new art is developed, I'll let you know at MySQL Transaction Reporting (*https://hackmysql.com/trx*). Until then, let's get the job done the old-fashioned way: *copy-paste*.

Active Transactions: Latest

The SQL statement in Example 8-2 reports the latest query for all transactions active longer than 1 second. This report answers the question: which transactions are long-running and what are they doing right now?

Example 8-2. Report latest query for transactions active longer than 1 second

```
SELECT
  ROUND(trx.timer_wait/1000000000000,3) AS trx_runtime,
  trx.thread_id AS thread_id,
  trx.event_id AS trx_event_id,
  trx.isolation_level,
  trx.autocommit,
  stm.current_schema AS db,
  stm.sql_text AS query,
  stm.rows_examined AS rows_examined,
  stm.rows_affected AS rows_affected,
  stm.rows_sent AS rows_sent,
  IF(stm.end_event_id IS NULL, 'running', 'done') AS exec_state,
  ROUND(stm.timer_wait/1000000000000,3) AS exec_time
FROM
        performance_schema.events_transactions_current trx
  JOIN performance_schema.events_statements_current    stm USING (thread_id)
WHERE
        trx.state = 'ACTIVE'
  AND trx.timer_wait > 1000000000000 * 1\G
```

To increase the time, change the 1 before \G. Performance Schema timers use picoseconds, so 1000000000000 * 1 is one second.

The output of Example 8-2 resembles the following:

```
*************************** 1. row ***************************
     trx_runtime: 20729.094
       thread_id: 60
    trx_event_id: 1137
 isolation_level: REPEATABLE READ
      autocommit: NO
              db: test
           query: SELECT * FROM elem
   rows_examined: 10
   rows_affected: 0
       rows_sent: 10
      exec_state: done
       exec_time: 0.038
```

The following is a bit more information about the fields (columns) of Example 8-2:

trx_runtime
: How long the transaction has been running (active) in seconds with millisecond precision. (I forgot about this transaction, which is why it's been active for almost six hours in the example.)

thread_id
: The thread ID of the client connection that is executing the transaction. This is used in "Active Transaction: History" on page 291. Performance Schema events

use thread IDs and event IDs to link data to client connections and events, respectively. Thread IDs are different than process IDs common to other parts of MySQL.

trx_event_id

The transaction event ID. This is used in "Active Transaction: History" on page 291.

isolation_level

Transaction isolation level: READ REPEATABLE or READ COMMITTED. (The other isolation levels, SERIALIZABLE and READ UNCOMMITTED, are rarely used; if you see them, it might be an application bug.) Recall "Row Locking" on page 260: the transaction isolation level affects row locking and whether or not SELECT uses a consistent snapshot.

autocommit

If YES, then autocommit is enabled and it's a single-statement transaction. If NO, then the transaction was started with BEGIN (or START TRANSACTION) and it's most likely a multistatement transaction.

db

Current database of query. The current database means USE db. The query can access other databases with database-qualified table names, such as db.table.

query

The latest query either executed by or executing in the transaction. If exec_state = running, then query is currently executing in the transaction. If exec_state = done, then query is the last query that the transaction executed. In both cases the transaction is active (not committed), but in the latter case it's idle with respect to executing a query.

rows_examined

Total number of rows examined by query. This does not include past queries executed in the transaction.

rows_examined

Total number of rows modified by query. This does not include past queries executed in the transaction.

rows_sent

Total number of rows sent (result set) by query. This does not include past queries executed in the transaction.

`exec_state`
> If done, then the transaction is idle with respect to executing a query, and `query` was the last query that it executed. If `running`, then transaction is currently executing `query`. In both cases, the transaction is active (not committed).

`exec_time`
> Execution time of `query` in seconds (with millisecond precision).

The Performance Schema tables `events_transactions_current` and `events_state ments_current` contain more fields, but this report selects only the essential fields.

This report is a true workhorse because it can reveal all four "Common Problems" on page 282:

Large transactions
> Look at `rows_affected` (row modified) and `rows_sent` to see the transaction size (in terms of rows). Experiment with adding a condition like `trx.rows_affected > 1000`.

Long-running transactions
> Adjust the `1` at the end of condition `trx.timer_wait > 1000000000000 * 1` to filter for longer-running queries.

Stalled transactions
> If `exec_state` = `done` and stays that way for a while, the transaction is stalled. Since this report only lists the latest query of active transactions, the query should change quickly—`exec_state` = `done` should be fleeting.

Abandoned transactions
> If `exec_state` = `done` remains for a long time, it's possible the transaction is abandoned because it stops being reported after commit.

The output of this report should be volatile because active transactions should be fleeting. If it reports a transaction long enough for you to see it multiple times, then the transaction is probably exhibiting one of the "Common Problems" on page 282. In this case, use its `thread_id` and `statement_event_id` (as in "Active Transaction: History" on page 291) to report its history—past queries—which helps reveal why the transaction is a problem.

Information Schema INNODB_TRX

Using the MySQL Performance Schema is the best practice and the future of MySQL performance reporting. But the MySQL Information Schema (*https://oreil.ly/2AOhC*) is still widely used and it can report long-running transactions by querying table information_schema.innodb_trx:

```
SELECT
  trx_mysql_thread_id AS process_id,
  trx_isolation_level,
  TIMEDIFF(NOW(), trx_started) AS trx_runtime,
  trx_state,
  trx_rows_locked,
  trx_rows_modified,
  trx_query AS query
FROM
  information_schema.innodb_trx
WHERE
  trx_started < CURRENT_TIME - INTERVAL 1 SECOND\G


*************************** 1. row ***************************
        process_id: 13
trx_isolation_level: REPEATABLE READ
       trx_runtime: 06:43:33
         trx_state: RUNNING
    trx_rows_locked: 4
  trx_rows_modified: 1
             query: NULL
```

In this example, query is NULL because the transaction is not executing any query. If it were, this field would contain the query.

I advise using the Performance Schema because it contains significantly more detail— essentially everything there is to know about what happens inside MySQL. All the examples in this book use the Performance Schema when possible; in rare cases, some information is still only available in the Information Schema.

To learn more about table information_schema.innodb_trx, read "The INFOR-MATION_SCHEMA INNODB_TRX Table" (*https://oreil.ly/jqVNx*) in the MySQL manual.

Active Transactions: Summary

The SQL statement in Example 8-3 reports the summary of queries executed for all transactions active longer than 1 second. This report answers the question: which transactions are long-running and how much work have they been doing?

Example 8-3. Report transaction summary

```
SELECT
  trx.thread_id AS thread_id,
  MAX(trx.event_id) AS trx_event_id,
  MAX(ROUND(trx.timer_wait/1000000000000,3)) AS trx_runtime,
  SUM(ROUND(stm.timer_wait/1000000000000,3)) AS exec_time,
  SUM(stm.rows_examined) AS rows_examined,
  SUM(stm.rows_affected) AS rows_affected,
  SUM(stm.rows_sent) AS rows_sent
FROM
       performance_schema.events_transactions_current trx
  JOIN performance_schema.events_statements_history    stm
    ON stm.thread_id = trx.thread_id AND stm.nesting_event_id = trx.event_id
WHERE
       stm.event_name LIKE 'statement/sql/%'
  AND trx.state = 'ACTIVE'
  AND trx.timer_wait > 1000000000000 * 1
GROUP BY trx.thread_id\G
```

To increase the time, change the 1 before \G. The fields are the same as in "Active Transactions: Latest" on page 286 but this report aggregates past queries for each transaction. A stalled transaction (not currently executing a query) might have done a lot of work in the past, which this report reveals.

When a query finishes executing, it's logged in table perfor mance_schema.events_statements_history but also remains in table performance_schema.events_statements_current. There- fore, the report only includes completed queries and should not be joined to the latter table unless active queries are filtered out.

This report is better to find large transactions—"Large Transactions (Transaction Size)" on page 282—since it includes past queries.

Active Transaction: History

The SQL statement in Example 8-4 reports the history of queries executed for a single transaction. This report answers the question: how much work did each query transaction do? You must replace the zeros with thread_id and trx_event_id values from the output of Example 8-2.

Example 8-4. Report transaction history

```
SELECT
  stm.rows_examined AS rows_examined,
  stm.rows_affected AS rows_affected,
  stm.rows_sent AS rows_sent,
```

```
    ROUND(stm.timer_wait/1000000000000,3) AS exec_time,
    stm.sql_text AS query
FROM
    performance_schema.events_statements_history stm
WHERE
        stm.thread_id = 0
    AND stm.nesting_event_id = 0
ORDER BY stm.event_id;
```

Replace the zeros with values from the output of Example 8-2:

- Replace the zero in `stm.thread_id = 0` with `thread_id`.
- Replace the zero in `stm.nesting_event_id = 0` with `trx_event_id`.

The output of Example 8-4 looks like:

```
+---------------+---------------+-----------+-----------+--------------------+
| rows_examined | rows_affected | rows_sent | exec_time | query              |
+---------------+---------------+-----------+-----------+--------------------+
|            10 |             0 |        10 |     0.000 | SELECT * FROM elem |
|             2 |             1 |         0 |     0.003 | UPDATE elem SET ... |
|             0 |             0 |         0 |     0.002 | COMMIT             |
+---------------+---------------+-----------+-----------+--------------------+
```

Apart from the BEGIN that started the transactions, this transaction executed two queries, then COMMIT. The SELECT was the first query, and the UPDATE was the second query. It's not a riveting example, but it demonstrates the query execution history of a transaction, plus basic query metrics. History is invaluable when debugging problematic transactions because you can see which queries are slow (exec_time) or large (in terms of rows), as well as the point at which the application stalls (when you know that the transaction will execute more queries).

Committed Transactions: Summary

The previous three reports are for active transactions, but committed transactions are also revealing. The SQL statement in Example 8-5 reports basic metrics for committed (completed) transactions. It's like a slow query log for transactions.

Example 8-5. Report basic metrics for committed transactions

```
SELECT
    ROUND(MAX(trx.timer_wait)/1000000000,3) AS trx_time,
    ROUND(SUM(stm.timer_end-stm.timer_start)/1000000000,3) AS query_time,
    ROUND((MAX(trx.timer_wait)-SUM(stm.timer_end-stm.timer_start))/1000000000, 3)
        AS idle_time,
    COUNT(stm.event_id)-1 AS query_count,
    SUM(stm.rows_examined) AS rows_examined,
    SUM(stm.rows_affected) AS rows_affected,
```

```
    SUM(stm.rows_sent) AS rows_sent
FROM
     performance_schema.events_transactions_history trx
 JOIN performance_schema.events_statements_history   stm
   ON stm.nesting_event_id = trx.event_id
WHERE
     trx.state = 'COMMITTED'
  AND trx.nesting_event_id IS NOT NULL
GROUP BY
  trx.thread_id, trx.event_id;
```

The fields of Example 8-5 are:

trx_time
> Total transaction time, in milliseconds with microsecond precision.

query_time
> Total query execution time, in milliseconds with microsecond precision.

idle_time
> Transaction time minus query time, in milliseconds with microsecond precision.
> Idle time indicates how much the application stalled while executing the queries
> in the transaction.

query_count
> Number of queries executed in the transaction.

rows_*
> Total number of rows examined, affected, and sent (respectively) by all queries
> executed in the transaction.

The output of Example 8-5 looks like the following:

```
+----------+----------+-----------+---------+-----------+-----------+-----------+
| trx_time | qry_time | idle_time | qry_cnt | rows_exam | rows_affe | rows_sent |
+----------+----------+-----------+---------+-----------+-----------+-----------+
| 5647.892 |    1.922 |  5645.970 |     2   |      10   |      0    |      10   |
|    0.585 |    0.403 |     0.182 |     2   |      10   |      0    |      10   |
+----------+----------+-----------+---------+-----------+-----------+-----------+
```

For this example, I executed the same transaction twice: first manually, then copy-pasted. The manual execution took 5.6 seconds (5647.892) and was mostly idle time due to typing. But a transaction programmatically executed should be mostly query execution time, as shown in the second row: 403 microseconds of execution time, and only 182 microseconds of idle time.

Summary

This chapter examined MySQL transactions with respect to avoiding common problems. The major takeaway points are:

- Transaction isolation levels affect row locking (data locks).
- The fundamental InnoDB data locks are: *record lock* (locks a single index record), *next-key lock* (locks a single index record plus the record gap before it), *gap lock* (locks the range [gap] between two records), and *insert intention lock* (allows INSERT into a gap; more like a wait condition than a lock).
- The default transaction isolation level, REPEATABLE READ, uses gap locking to isolate the range of rows accessed.
- The READ COMMITTED transaction isolation level disables gap locking.
- InnoDB uses *consistent snapshots* in REPEATABLE READ transactions to make reads (SELECT) return the same rows despite changes to those rows by other transactions.
- Consistent snapshots require InnoDB to save row changes in undo logs to reconstruct old row versions.
- History list length (HLL) gauges the amount of old row versions not purged or flushed.
- HLL is a harbinger of doom: always monitor and alert on HLL greater than 100,000.
- Data locks and undo logs are released when a transaction ends, with COMMIT or ROLLBACK.
- Four common problems beset transactions: large transactions (modify too many rows), long-running transactions (slow response time from BEGIN to COMMIT), stalled transactions (superfluous waits between queries), and abandoned transactions (client connection vanished during active transaction).
- The MySQL Performance Schema makes detailed transaction reporting possible.
- Transaction performance is as important as query performance.

The next chapter enumerates common MySQL challenges and how to mitigate them.

Practice: Alert on History List Length

The goal of this practice is to alert on history list length (HLL) greater than 100,000. (Recall "History List Length" on page 280.) This depends on your systems for monitoring (collecting metrics) and alerting, but fundamentally it's no different than alerting on other metrics. Therefore, the needed work is twofold:

- Collect and report the HLL value.
- Create an alert on HLL greater than 100,000.

All MySQL monitors should be able to collect and report HLL. If your current monitoring cannot, seriously consider a better monitor because HLL is a fundamental metric. Read the documentation for your monitor to learn how to make it collect and report HLL. HLL can change quickly, but there's leeway before MySQL is at risk due to high HLL. Therefore, you can report HLL slowly: every minute.

Once your monitor is collecting and reporting HLL, set an alert on HLL greater than 100,000 for 20 minutes. But recall "Wild Goose Chase (Thresholds)" on page 225: you might need to adjust the 20 minute threshold, but note that HLL greater than 100,000 for longer than 20 minutes is quite abnormal.

In case you need to query the HLL value manually:

```
SELECT name, count
FROM   information_schema.innodb_metrics
WHERE  name = 'trx_rseg_history_len';
```

Historically, HLL was parsed from the output of SHOW ENGINE INNODB STATUS: look for "History list length" under section header "TRANSACTIONS" in MySQL.

I hope that you're never alerted for HLL, but having the alert is a best practice, and it has saved many applications from an outage. An HLL alert is a friend.

Practice: Examine Row Locks

The goal of this practice is to examine row locks for real queries from your application and, if possible, understand why the query acquires each lock. *If possible* is a necessary disclaimer given that InnoDB row locking can be inscrutable.

Use a development or staging instance of MySQL; do not use production. Also, use MySQL 8.0.16 or newer because it has the best data lock reporting using the Performance Schema table data_locks, as shown in "Row Locking" on page 260. If you can only use MySQL 5.7, then you'll need to examine data locks using SHOW ENGINE INNODB STATUS: refer to MySQL Data Locks (*https://oreil.ly/f9uqy*) for an illustrated guide to mapping data lock output from MySQL 5.7 to MySQL 8.0.

Use real table definitions and as much real data (rows) as possible. If possible, dump data from production and load into your development or staging MySQL instances.

If there are particular queries or transactions that you're curious about, begin by examining their data locks. Otherwise, begin with slow queries—recall "Query profile" on page 9.

Since locks are released when a transaction completes, you need to use explicit transactions, as shown in "Row Locking" on page 260:

```
BEGIN;

--
-- Execute one or several queries
--

SELECT index_name, lock_type, lock_mode, lock_status, lock_data
FROM   performance_schema.data_locks
WHERE  object_name = 'elem';
```

Replace elem with your table name, and remember to COMMIT or ROLLBACK to release the locks.

To change the transaction isolation level for the next (and only the next) transaction, execute SET TRANSACTION ISOLATION LEVEL READ COMMITTED before BEGIN.

This is expert-level practice, so any effort and understanding is an achievement. Congratulations.

## CHAPTER 9

Other Challenges

This chapter is a short but important laundry list of common MySQL challenges and how to mitigate them. These challenges don't fit into other chapters because most are not directly related to performance. But don't underestimate them: the first two challenges, for example, can ruin a database. More importantly, these challenges are not special cases that only happen when the stars align and The Fates conspire to ruin your day. These are common challenges. Take them seriously, and expect to face them.

Split-Brain Is the Greatest Risk

Split-brain requires two conditions to occur at the same time, in the same replication topology:

- More than one MySQL instance is writable (`read_only=0`)
- Writes occur on more than one MySQL instance

Neither of those should ever happen—especially not at the same time—but life is full of surprises, and you cannot avoid bugs or accidents forever. When it happens, it's called *split-brain*: instead of all MySQL instances having the same data, they're figuratively split because data is no longer identical (consistent) on every instance. Not only is inconsistent data fundamentally wrong, it can break replication or—worse—have a ripple effect that causes more data to become inconsistent, which causes the next challenge: data drift.

Split-brain does not apply to MySQL replication topologies intentionally designed to have multiple writable instances.

If split-brain occurs, you must detect and stop it *immediately*. Why? Because a single write can affect any number of rows. Mere seconds of split-brain can produce an avalanche of inconsistent data, resulting in *weeks* of data forensics and reconciliation.

To stop split-brain, disable writes on *all* instances: `SET GLOBAL read_only=1`. Do not leave one instance writable; that will make the problem worse. If you cannot disable writes, then kill MySQL or the server—seriously. *Data integrity is more important than data availability.*

Data integrity is more important than data availability.

Ideally, you should take the entire database offline until all inconsistent data is found and reconciled. But realistically, if a prolonged database outage will kill the business and you're absolutely certain that reading potentially incorrect data will not cause further damage, then you can run MySQL in read-only mode (`read_only=1`) while you fix data using `super_read_only` (*https://oreil.ly/JrqIs*) mode.

There are only two ways to find inconsistent rows: run `pt-table-sync` (*https://oreil.ly/Dr10P*), or check manually. Manually entails whatever you can do to compare and verify rows given your understanding of the application, the data, and what changes were likely to have occurred during the split-brain. `pt-table-sync` is an open source tool that can find, print, and synchronize data differences between two MySQL instances, but use it with caution because any tool that changes data is inherently risky.

`pt-table-sync` is a dangerous tool unless you wield it carefully. Do *not* use its `--execute` option: only use `--print`, and reads its manual thoroughly.

Reconciling rows is the difficult part, and you should work with a MySQL expert to ensure that it's done correctly. If you're lucky, you'll determine that one MySQL instance is authoritative—all rows have the correct data—and you can rebuild rather than reconcile: rebuild all replicas from the authoritative instance. If you're not lucky, then work with a MySQL expert to determine your options.

Data Drift Is Real but Invisible

Data drift refers to inconsistent data: one or more rows have different values on different MySQL instances in the same replication topology. (*Drift* is figurative for the values drifting further apart as changes to the inconsistent data cause further inconsistencies.) Whereas inconsistent data from a split-brain scenario is expected, inconsistent data from data drift is unexpected: you don't know or have any reason to suspect that there is inconsistent data. Although data drift is invisible in the sense that it does not seem to cause a problem, it is nevertheless a real problem because the application could return wrong values.

Fortunately, data drift is easy to detect: run `pt-table-checksum` (*https://oreil.ly/mogUa*). This tool is safe: it only reads and compares data. Unfortunately, data drift is no easier to reconcile than inconsistent data due to split-brain. But that probably won't be an issue because data drift tends to be limited and isolated in scope—not an avalanche of inconsistent data—because it's not caused by a serious failure like split-brain.

The fascinating aspect of data drift is that, to my knowledge, no one has ever found or proven the root cause of data drift in the wild (in a real production database). In theory, it's caused by nondeterministic queries and statement-based replication, or writes on replicas. In a laboratory, those two would surely cause data drift, but they never seem to be the cause in the wild. Instead, engineers and DBAs alike are certain that nothing was done to cause or permit data drift. And yet, it exists.

 Check for data drift every few months (or once a year at the very least) by running `pt-table-checksum` (*https://oreil.ly/mogUa*). If you find data drift once, don't worry about it: reconcile the rows, and check again in a month. If data keeps drifting (which is very unlikely), then you have an exotic problem worth a detailed investigation to find and fix the root cause.

Don't Trust ORM

The purpose of object-relational mapping (ORM) is to aid programmers by abstracting data access into programming terms and objects. ORM is not inherently bad or inefficient, but you should verify queries generated by an ORM library because performance is not its purpose. For example, since ORM treats rows as objects, an ORM library might select all columns, which is contrary to what you saw in the efficient data access checklist (Table 3-2). Another example: some ORM libraries execute other queries (SHOW WARNINGS, for example) before or after the actual application query. When striving for maximum performance, every query is important; other queries are unacceptable waste.

There are high-performance applications that use ORM, but the engineers are careful not to trust ORM: they verify ORM-generated queries in the query profile and query report (see "Query profile" on page 9 and "Query report" on page 10, respectively). If an ORM-generated query is too inefficient, read the ORM library documentation to learn how to configure it to generate a more efficient query.

Schemas Always Change

You probably already know this challenge, but in case you're brand new to life with any relational database: schemas always change. (More specifically, table definitions always change, but tables constitute a schema.) The challenge is doing an *online schema change* (OSC): changing a schema while it's in use, without affecting the application. As mentioned in previous chapters, there are three great solutions for MySQL:

- pt-online-schema-change (*https://oreil.ly/brtmM*)
- gh-ost (*https://oreil.ly/ZKQAd*)
- ALTER TABLE (*https://oreil.ly/GRQuf*)

Each solution works very differently, but all of them can alter a table definition online without affecting the application. Read the documentation for each to decide which one works best for you.

There's another aspect to this challenge: integrating schema changes into the software development process. You can run an OSC manually, but engineering teams don't do that because, like other code changes, schema changes need to be a part of the development process so they are reviewed, approved, tested in staging, and so forth. Since development processes are team-specific, your team will have to create its own solution. But there is currently one open source solution: Skeema (*https://www.skeema.io*). For a thorough read on how renowned MySQL expert Shlomi Noach solved this challenge at GitHub, read his blog post "Automating MySQL Schema Migrations with GitHub Actions and More" (*https://oreil.ly/9cEJi*).

MySQL Extends Standard SQL

If you use only MySQL, then perhaps you can skip this challenge. But if you're coming from (or going to) another relational database, then be aware that MySQL has many extensions to standard SQL enumerated in "MySQL Extensions to Standard SQL" (*https://oreil.ly/gLN1l*) in the MySQL manual. And MySQL does not support some standard SQL features, like full outer joins. There are other restrictions and limitations cataloged in the aptly named excerpt "MySQL Restrictions and Limitations" (*https://oreil.ly/x3xro*), and you will find other mentions and oddities throughout the MySQL manual.

Any database with a history as long and storied as MySQL is bound to be equally eclectic. What's uniquely MySQL about MySQL is something that experts have come to know and trust so naturally that it's rarely pointed out: the MySQL Manual (*https://oreil.ly/IXARN*) is comprehensive and authoritative. Software documentation can be sparse, out of date, or nonexistent, but not the MySQL manual. There are arcane bits of information about MySQL not in the manual, but those aside, MySQL experts rely heavily on the MySQL manual—and so should you.

Noisy Neighbors

On a physical server, a *noisy neighbor* is a program that degrades performance for other programs by using inordinately more system resources. For example, if a server is running 20 separate MySQL instances, but one of them uses all the CPU and disk I/O, then it's a noisy neighbor. This is a common challenge because a *shared server* (or *multitenancy*) is the norm: running multiple virtualized environments on a single physical server. (The opposite, a *dedicated server* [or *single-tenancy*], is rare and expensive, especially in the cloud.) A noisy neighbor is a perplexing challenge because the performance impact is not your fault, but it is your problem.

If your company runs its own hardware, then the problem is tractable: measure the resource usage of each program or virtual environment on the shared server where you suspect a noisy neighbor. Noisy neighbors are easy to spot because they're noisy. Then move the noisy neighbor (or your database) to another, quieter server. If that's not possible, then buy another copy of this book for the noisy neighbor so they can learn how to optimize MySQL performance.

In the cloud, you cannot see or prove the existence of a noisy neighbor. For security, cloud providers maintain strict separation of tenants (customers like you) on shared servers. And they are unlikely to admit the existence of a noisy neighbor because it would imply that they are not balancing the server load, which should be included in the cost. Consequently, the standard practice is to reprovision a cloud database when you suspect a noisy neighbor. Some companies benchmark a cloud resource before using it and only keep it if performance meets a baseline; else, the resource is destroyed, another one is provisioned, and the process repeats until—by chance—the resource is provisioned on a quiet server.

Applications Do Not Fail Gracefully

Netflix originated *chaos engineering*: intentionally introducing problems and failures into a system to test its resiliency and necessitate that engineers design for failure. This philosophy and practice is bold because it *truly* tests the mettle of an application. Writing software that works correctly when everything around it also works correctly is an expectation so basic and obvious that it counts for nothing. The challenge is to write software that works—in some capacity—even when everything around it is failing. As engineers, we often think that we have accounted for failure in our software, but how do we know until something fails for real? Plus, not all failures are binary: working or not working. The most insidious problems are not outright failures but, rather, edge cases and outliers: the kind of problem that requires a story to explain it, not a simple failure statement like "the hard drive died."

The same is true for applications with respect to MySQL. However, chaos engineering is not standard practice in the MySQL industry because trifling with a database is risky and few engineers are so bold. But fortune favors the bold, so here are 12 database chaos scenarios to test the mettle of your application:

- MySQL is offline
- MySQL is very slow to respond
- MySQL is read-only
- MySQL has just started (cold buffer pool)
- Read replicas are offline or very slow
- Failover in the same region
- Failover to a different region
- Database backup is running
- DNS resolution is very slow
- Network is slow (high latency) or saturated
- One hard drive in a RAID array is degraded
- Free disk space on an SSD is less than 5%

Some of those 12 database chaos scenarios might not apply to your infrastructure, but most are standard and yield interesting results depending on the application. If you have never engineered chaos, then I encourage you to start because chaos doesn't wait until you're ready.

High Performance MySQL Is Difficult

If you earnestly apply all the best practices and techniques in this book, I am confident that you will achieve remarkable performance with MySQL. But that does not mean it'll be quick or easy. High-performance MySQL requires practice because resources—books, blogs, videos, conferences, and so on—teach you theory, which is different than reality. Consequently, when you begin to apply what you've learned from this book to your application, you might run into the following two challenges.

The first challenge is that real application queries can be—and usually are—more complex than the pithy little examples strewn throughout these pages. Add to that the additional challenge of remembering and applying so much knowledge at once: query metrics, indexes and indexing, EXPLAIN output, query optimizations, table definitions, and so forth. It can be overwhelming at first, but take it one query at a time, and remember "North Star" on page 3 and "Indexing: How to Think Like MySQL" on page 80. Even experts need time to unravel and understand the full story of a query.

The second challenge is that real application performance rarely depends on a single aspect of the workload. Fixing slow queries will undoubtedly help, but it might not help enough. The more performance you need from MySQL, the more you have to optimize the entire workload: each query, all data, and every access pattern. Eventually you will need to apply knowledge from every chapter of this book. (Except Chapter 10 if you're not using MySQL in the cloud.) Start small (Chapters 1–4), but commit to learning and applying everything in this book because you will need it.

There is more to MySQL performance than I present in this book, but I assure you: the knowledge imparted in these chapters is comprehensive and effective. Moreover, there are no secrets known only to experts that unlock amazing MySQL performance. I know that from my own experience and also from having worked with many of the best MySQL experts in the world. Plus, open source software is terrible at keeping secrets.

Practice: Identify the Guardrails that Prevent Split-Brain

The goal of this practice is to identify the guardrails that prevent split-brain. There are two parts: detailing the guardrails so that every engineer understands what they are, where they are (probably in tools), and how they work, and then carefully reviewing tools that manage or change MySQL instances, especially failover tools.

If you do not manage MySQL, then schedule time with the engineers who manage MySQL to have them detail how they prevent split-brain during operations, especially failover. This should be an easy request because preventing split-brain is fundamental to managing MySQL.

If you use MySQL in the cloud, the details vary. Cloud providers have undisclosed methods to prevent split-brain depending on the internal setup and management of MySQL. For example, split-brain is theoretically not possible with a standard multi-AZ instance of Amazon RDS for MySQL because, although it's multi-AZ, multiple instances of MySQL do not run at the same time. (It's a single running instance of MySQL in one availability zone [AZ]. If that instance fails, another instance is started in another AZ.) But if you add read replicas, then you have multiple running instances of MySQL in the same replication topology, and Amazon does not make any guarantees about split-brain with respect to read replicas. In the cloud, presume that you are responsible for the guardrails that prevent split-brain, but also know when the cloud provider does and does not prevent split-brain.

If you manage MySQL on your own hardware, then I advise you to contract a MySQL expert to help you identify the guardrails that prevent split-brain. (It shouldn't take long, so it should be a short and affordable contract.) There is one foundational guardrail that you must implement: configure MySQL (in its *my.cnf* file) to start in read-only mode: `read_only=1`. Always start MySQL in read-only mode. From this foundation, other guardrails detail how read-only mode is toggled such that it's guaranteed to be off (MySQL is writable) on only one instance at a time.

 Always start MySQL in read-only mode (`read_only=1`).

Once the guardrails are understood by engineers, the second part is to carefully review tools that manage or change MySQL instances, especially failover tools, to ensure that the guardrails are implemented and working as expected. Of course, all code should be unit tested, but preventing split-brain is so important that it warrants manual code review, too. There are issues in code that might not surface when identifying the guardrails; for example: race conditions, retries, and error handling. The last—error handling—is especially important: can (or should) a tool roll back changes on error? Remember: data integrity is more important than data availability. When toggling MySQL read-only, tools should err on the side of caution: if an operation has a nonzero chance of causing split-brain, don't do it; leave MySQL in read-only mode, fail, and let a human figure it out.

Bottom line: be 100% clear on the guardrails that prevent split-brain.

Practice: Check for Data Drift

The goal of this practice is to check for data drift using pt-table-checksum (*https://oreil.ly/mogUa*). You're in luck: this tool was purposely written to be easy and automatic. Simply download and run the tool, and it automates the rest in most cases. If not, a quick read through its documentation will answer any questions.

 Most MySQL tools need special configuration to work with MySQL in the cloud.

pt-table-checksum does only one thing: check for and report data drift. It can run for hours or days depending on data size and access load. By default, it's slow to avoid interfering with production access. Therefore, be sure to run it in a screen or tmux session.

When pt-table-checksum finishes checking a table, it prints a one-line result for the table. The output looks like this:

```
            TS ERRORS  DIFFS  ROWS  DIFF_ROWS CHUNKS SKIPPED    TIME TABLE
10-21T08:36:55      0      0   200          0      1       0   0.005 db1.tbl1
10-21T08:37:00      0      0   603          0      7       0   0.035 db1.tbl2
10-21T08:37:10      0      2  1600          3     21       0   1.003 db2.tbl3
```

The last line of the output reveals a table with data drift because column DIFFS has a nonzero value. If any table has data drift, rerun with the --replicate-check-only option to print the replicas and chunks that are different than the source. (A *chunk* is a range of rows delineated by upper and lower boundary values for an index [usually the primary key]. pt-table-checksum verifies rows in chunks because checking individual rows is too slow and inefficient.) You will need to devise a plan to isolate and reconcile inconsistent rows. If there are very few, you might be able to isolate and reconcile them manually. If not, then I advise you to work with a MySQL expert to ensure it's done correctly.

Practice: Chaos

The goal of this practice is to test the mettle of your application. Chaos engineering is not for the faint of heart, so start with your staging database.

 This practice will cause outages.

For the following chaos, MySQL and the application should be running normally with some load, and you should have good metrics and observability into both to record and analyze how they respond.

I propose the following chaos, but pick and choose based on your level of risk:

Restart MySQL

Restarting MySQL tests how the application responds when MySQL is offline, and how it responds when MySQL buffers are cold (specifically, the InnoDB buffer pool). Cold buffers require disk I/O to read data into memory, which causes slower than usual response time. It also teaches you three things: how long it takes MySQL to shutdown, how long it takes MySQL to start up, and how long it takes the buffers to warm up.

Enable read-only mode

SET GLOBAL read_only=1 on the source instance to enable read-only mode and test how the application responds to being able to read data but not write data. Engineers often think that the application will continue working for reads and gracefully fail for writes, but chaos is full of surprises. This also effectively simulates a failed failover, which should never happen (because it would mean a failure of high availability), but "should never happen" is within the purview of chaos.

Stop MySQL for 1 hour

Most applications can weather a storm for seconds or minutes—maybe even tens of minutes—but at some point, queues fill up, retires are exhausted, exponential backoffs become very long, rate limits reset, and users give up and go to a competitor. MySQL should never be offline more than a few seconds—if properly managed—but again: chaos.

Back in 2004 when I worked in a data center, moments before I started my 2 p.m. to midnight shift, an engineer accidentally hit the emergency power off button—*to the data center*. Calm is the only answer to chaos, so I got a cup of coffee before sitting down to help reboot the data center.

## CHAPTER 10

MySQL in the Cloud

MySQL in the cloud is fundamentally the same MySQL that you know and love (or know and tolerate). In the cloud, the best practices and techniques detailed in the previous nine chapters are not only true but *eminently* true because cloud providers charge for every byte and millisecond of work. Performance is money in the cloud. To recap the previous nine chapters:

- Performance is query response time (Chapter 1).
- Indexes are the key to performance (Chapter 2).
- Less data is better—for both storing and accessing (Chapter 3).
- Access patterns allow or inhibit performance (Chapter 4).
- Sharding is necessary to scale out writes and storage (Chapter 5).
- Server metrics reveal how the workload affects MySQL (Chapter 6).
- Replication lag is data loss and must be avoided (Chapter 7).
- Transactions affect row locking and undo logging (Chapter 8).
- Other challenges exist—even in the cloud (Chapter 9).

If you embrace and apply all those details, MySQL will execute the application workload with remarkable performance regardless of location: in the cloud, on premise, or anywhere.

For the sake of saving you time, I wish it were that simple—optimize the workload and you're done—but MySQL in the cloud raises unique considerations. The goal is to know and mitigate these cloud considerations so that you can focus on MySQL, not the cloud. After all, the cloud is nothing special: behind the proverbial curtain, it's physical servers in a data center running programs like MySQL.

This chapter highlights what to know when using MySQL in the cloud. There are four major sections. The first cautions against compatibility: when MySQL is not MySQL. The second is a quick discussion about varying levels of MySQL administration in the cloud. The third discusses network latency and its relationship to storage I/O. The fourth is about performance and money.

Compatibility

MySQL in the cloud might not be MySQL, or it might be a highly modified (and proprietary) version of MySQL. Compatibility of MySQL in the cloud has two sides: code compatibility and feature compatibility.

 By *MySQL*, I mean MySQL published by Oracle: the official, open source MySQL source code. I also mean Percona Server published by Percona, and MariaDB Server published by the MariaDB Foundation: both are widely used, safe and stable, and considered to be MySQL in general.

Code compatibility is whether or not MySQL is the same open source code published by Oracle, Percona, or MariaDB. The following nine words and phrases are commonly used in product descriptions and documentation to allude to the fact that MySQL is not code-compatible but, rather, something slightly (or significantly) different:

- Built on
- Emulates
- Compatible
- Client compatible
- Protocol compatible
- Wire compatible
- Replacement
- Drop-in replacement
- Works with existing

Code compatibility is important because MySQL is complex and subtle, and we entrust it to store invaluable data. In this book, I focus discussions to narrow the scope of MySQL complexity, but sections like "Page flushing" on page 212 and "Row Locking" on page 260 hint at how deep the rabbit hole goes. When any company alters MySQL source code, the risks are fourfold: data loss, performance regressions, bugs, and incompatibilities. The greater the alterations, the greater the risks. I have seen the latter three in the cloud; fortunately, I have not seen a cloud provider lose data.

 If you have any doubts whether or not MySQL in the cloud is code-compatible, ask the cloud provider, "Is it the same open source MySQL published by Oracle?"

To present the whole argument, not just the negatives (the risks), cloud providers alter MySQL to provide additional value: improve performance, fix bugs, and add features that customers need. Some alterations are valuable and worth the risks. But if you use MySQL in the cloud that is not code-compatible, you need to understand the extent of the alterations. This is basic due diligence for professional engineers using MySQL in the cloud.

> Given enough eyeballs, all bugs are shallow.
>
> —Eric S. Raymond

Feature compatibility is whether or not MySQL includes features not available outside the cloud provider or the distribution of MySQL. For example, Oracle publishes two distributions: MySQL Community Server and MySQL Enterprise Edition. The former is open source; the latter includes proprietary features. Oracle Cloud Infrastructure (OCI) (*https://www.oracle.com/cloud*) uses the latter, which is good: more value for the cloud money. But it also means that if you rely on features specific to MySQL Enterprise Edition, you cannot directly migrate to another cloud provider or distribution of MySQL. The same is true for Percona Server and MariaDB Server: these distributions of MySQL have unique features, which is good, but it complicates migration to another cloud provider or distribution of MySQL.

Feature compatibility is important for the same reason open source software is important: freedom to change. Software—MySQL included—should empower engineers and users, not lock us into specific cloud providers or vendors. That reasoning is more philosophical than technical, which is why I'll present the whole argument again: some features are valuable and worth *not* changing to keep. But if you choose to use a feature that's not available outside the cloud provider or the distribution of MySQL, you need to document why, so that future engineers can understand what's at stake (and what needs to be replaced) if they use another cloud provider or distribution of MySQL. This, too, is basic due diligence for professional engineers using MySQL in the cloud.

Management (DBA)

We have successfully dodged MySQL administration (DBA work) from the very first pages of this book, so we're not about to fail now, but MySQL in the cloud raises an issue that you need to know and address: who manages MySQL? Ostensibly, the cloud provider manages MySQL, but it's not that simple because managing MySQL entails many operations. Brace yourself: I'm going steer this book dangerously close to DBA work in order to explain.

Table 10-1 is a partial list of DBA operations and who manages them: you or the cloud.

Table 10-1. DBA operations

Operation	You	Cloud
Provision		✓
Configure		✓
MySQL users	✓	
Server metrics	✓	
Query metrics	✓	
Online schema change (OSC)	✓	
Failure recovery		✓
Disaster recovery (DR)	✓	
High availability (HA)	✓	†[a]
Upgrading		✓
Backup and recovery		✓
Change data capture (CDC)	✓	
Security	✓	
Help	✓	
Cost	✓	

[a] Indicates some management.

Let me breeze through the 15 operations in Table 10-1 because being aware of the full scope—even at a high level—helps you avoid gaps in MySQL management that will become an issue if not addressed. Also known as *CYA*: cover your administration.

Provisioning MySQL is, of course, what a cloud provider must provide: the lowest level operation of running MySQL on a computer. Cloud providers use a decent MySQL configuration, but double check because no default configuration can suit every customer. Apart from a root user necessary to give you initial control of the MySQL server, cloud providers do not manage MySQL users. Server and query metrics are also your responsibility to collect and report. Granted, some cloud providers expose basic sever metrics, but none are even remotely close to the full spectra of metrics detailed in Chapter 6. OSCs—running ALTER statements without affecting the workload—are entirely your responsibility, and they tend to be a little more difficult in the cloud for various technical reasons outside the scope of this book. Cloud providers do handle failover: when hardware or MySQL dies, the cloud provider will failover to restore availability. But cloud providers do not handle *disaster recovery*: when an entire region fails and availability must be restored by running MySQL from a different geographic location. Given the previous two operations, high availability (HA) has mixed management (hence † in the cloud column). The full discussion of MySQL high availability in the cloud is too nuanced to cover here; let's just say that the cloud provides some amount of high availability. Cloud providers upgrade MySQL, which is really nice because this operation is tedious at scale. Cloud providers backup MySQL, provide long-term backup retention, and provide methods to restore backups—all of which are incredibly important. You are responsible for change data capture (CDC), which usually involves another tool or service acting like a replica to dump (or stream) binary logs from MySQL to another data store (often a big data store or data lake). Security of MySQL in the cloud is your responsibility— the cloud is *not* inherently secure. Cloud providers help with running MySQL in general, but don't expect much (or any) help with MySQL performance unless your company pays for that level of support. And finally, you must manage costs: the cloud is notorious for costing more than engineers anticipate.

 The three major cloud providers—Amazon, Google, and Micro- soft—have a 99.95% or 99.99% availability SLA for MySQL (as a managed service), but read the fine print—the full legal details. For example, maintenance windows usually do not count against the SLA. Or, the SLA might be voided if MySQL is not properly configured *by you*. There are always details and caveats to cloud provider high availability and SLAs.

Table 10-1 is descriptive, not prescriptive, because different cloud providers and third-party companies provide different levels of MySQL management in the cloud. For example, some companies *fully* manage MySQL in the cloud (or on-premise). As an engineer using MySQL, not managing it, you only need to know that all the operations are managed—all the boxes are checked—so that none of them interfere with your work. Once you know that, please forget everything you read in this section, else you'll wind up a MySQL DBA before you know it, twenty years will pass, and the next engineer to join your team will have been a newborn infant when —lo, the many years past—you were dealing with an inexplicable multi-range read performance regression after an innocuous point release upgrade.

Network and Storage...Latency

When running MySQL on-premise (in data center space that your company leases), the local network should never be a consideration or concern for you, presuming it was designed and wired by competent professional network engineers. Local networks are blazing fast and stable with submillisecond latency. The local network should be more boring than the database (recall "Normal and Stable: The Best Database Is a Boring Database" on page 180).

But the cloud is global, and wide-area networks have higher latency and lower stability (greater fluctuations in latency and throughput). For example, the network round-trip time (RTT) between San Francisco and New York City is approximately 60 milliseconds, plus or minus 10 milliseconds. If you run MySQL in San Francisco (or anywhere on the U.S. west coast) and the application is in New York City (or anywhere on the U.S. east cost), the minimum query response time is approximately 60 milliseconds. That is 60 times slower than a local network.[1] You will notice that slowness, but it will not show up in query response time because the delay is outside MySQL. For example, a query profile (see "Query profile" on page 9) shows that a query takes 800 microseconds to execute, but your application performance monitoring (APM) shows that the query takes 60.8 milliseconds to execute: 800 μs for MySQL, and 60 ms for network latency from sea to shining sea.

Network latency over long distances is physically limited by the speed of light and exacerbated by intermediate routing. Consequently, you cannot overcome this latency; you can only work around it. For example, refer to "Enqueue Writes" on page 145: enqueue locally, write remotely—where *remotely* is any process that incurs high network latency.

Switching back to local networks, it's a good thing they're blazing fast and stable because cloud providers typically store MySQL data on *network-attached storage*: hard drives connected to the server through a local network. By contrast, *locally-attached storage* (or *local storage*) is hard drives connected directly to the server. Cloud providers use network-attached storage for various reasons beyond the scope of this book. What's important to know is that network-attached storage is much slower and less stable than local storage. All three major cloud providers—Amazon, Google, and Microsoft—publish "single-digit millisecond latency" for network-attached storage (using SSD),[2] with one exception: Amazon io2 Block Express has submillisecond latency. The bottom line is, when using MySQL in the cloud, expect

---

1 Technically, all networks are equally fast: the speed of light. The problem is physical distance and intermediate routing over long distances.

2 See Amazon EBS features (*https://oreil.ly/NIly1*), block storage performance on Google (*https://oreil.ly/7Zxaj*), and premium storage with Microsoft Azure (*https://oreil.ly/LMg03*).

the storage to have single-digit millisecond latency, which is equivalent to a spinning disk.

Network-attached storage is an order of magnitude slower than local storage (with SSD; don't use spinning disks), but is it a problem that you should address? If you're migrating MySQL to the cloud from bare metal hardware with high-end local storage *and* the application heavily and consistently utilizes the local storage IOPS (see "IOPS" on page 208), then yes: verify that the increased latency of network-attached storage does not cause a ripple effect of performance degradation (because IOPS incur the latency). (Heavy and consistent utilization of IOPS is a hallmark of a write-heavy workload: see "Read/Write" on page 133.) But if you're already in the cloud, or starting a new application in the cloud, then no: don't worry or think about storage latency in the cloud. Instead, lay a foundation of highly optimized queries (indexes), data, and access patterns—as covered in Chapters 2, 3, and 4, respectively—and storage latency in the cloud may never be an issue.

If storage latency in the cloud is a problem, then you need to optimize the work-load further, shard (Chapter 5), or purchase better (more expensive) cloud storage. Remember: Netflix runs in the cloud, as do other very large and successful compa-nies. The performance potential for MySQL in the cloud is virtually unlimited. The question is: can you afford it?

Performance Is Money

Fittingly, the beginning of this book—"A True Story of False Performance" on page 2—mirrors the end. But in the cloud, customers sell themselves more RAM to "fix" MySQL performance. An engineer at one of the three major cloud providers told me that most MySQL instances are over-provisioned: customers pay for more capacity than the application needs or utilizes.[3]

Has the industry come full circle and now, with the ease of scalability in the cloud, performance is simply a larger instance? No, definitely not: *performance is query response time*; and in the cloud, every byte and millisecond of performance is billed hourly, which makes all the best practices and techniques in this book more impor-tant than ever.

If you have used any services in the cloud, then the following information probably won't surprise you. But if you're new to the cloud, then let me be the first to tell you: cloud pricing is complex, nearly intractable, and frequently underestimated (which means over budget). That's true when engineers make a concerted effort to estimate and control cloud costs; when they don't, I have seen six-figure surprises: more than

---

3 Due to nondisclosure agreements, I cannot cite the source.

$100,000 over budget. Following are the three most important things to know to avoid billing surprises when using MySQL in the cloud.

The first thing to know is that *the price doubles* for each level of the underlying compute (the virtual server that runs MySQL) because the resources (vCPU count and memory size) at each level double. For example, if the minimum level of compute is 2 vCPU and 8 GB RAM, the next level up is 4 vCPU and 16 GB RAM—and the price doubles, too. There are a few exceptions, but expect doubling. As a result, you cannot gradually increase costs; you double costs for each level of compute that you scale up. From an engineering point of view, scaling up from 2 vCPU to 8 vCPU is still a very small compute, but the price quadruples. To put this in perspective, imagine if your monthly mortgage or rent payment doubled, or your car payment doubled, or your student loan payment doubled. You would probably be upset—and rightly so.

The second thing to know is that everything in the cloud costs money. Compute costs are just the beginning. The following list includes common charges for MySQL in the cloud in addition to compute costs:

- Storage type (IOPS)
- Data storage (size)
- Backups (size and retention)
- Logs (size and retention)
- High availability (replicas)
- Cross-region data transfer (size)
- Encryption keys (to encrypt data)
- Secrets (to store passwords)

Moreover, those charges are per-instance. For example, if you create five read replicas, each replica is billed for data store, backups, and so forth. I wish it were simpler, but this is the reality: you need to investigate, understand, and estimate all costs when using MySQL in the cloud.

 Some proprietary versions of MySQL in the cloud (see "Compatibility" on page 308) have additional costs, or a completely different pricing model.

The third and final thing to know is that cloud providers offer discounts. Don't pay full price. At at minimum, costs can be significantly reduced with a one or three year commitment, rather than paying month to month. Other discounts vary by cloud provider: look for (or ask about) reserved instances, committed usage, and volume discounts. If your company relies on the cloud, then it has most likely negotiated a contract with the cloud provider. Find out if that's the case and whether any of the contract pricing details affect costs for MySQL in the cloud. If you're lucky, the contract might reduce *and* simplify costs, which allows you to focus on the fun details of using MySQL.

Summary

This chapter highlighted what to know when using MySQL in the cloud. The substantial takeaway points are:

- Code and feature compatibility of MySQL varies in the cloud.
- Your due diligence is to know any code or feature incompatibilities compared to open source MySQL.
- MySQL can be partially or fully managed, depending on cloud provider or third-party company.
- Network latency over wide-area networks increases query response time by tens or hundreds of milliseconds.
- Data for MySQL in the cloud is usually stored on network-attached storage.
- Network-attached storage has single-digit millisecond latency, which is equivalent to a spinning disk.
- The cloud charges for everything, and costs can (and often do) go over budget.
- Cloud providers offer discounts; don't pay full price.
- Performance is query response time in the cloud.

This is the last chapter, but don't \q yet: there's one more practice.

Practice: Try MySQL in the Cloud

The goal of this practice is to try MySQL in the cloud—just to see how it works, no DBA work required. On the one hand, I don't want to provide any of the following five cloud providers free marketing—this book is strictly technical. But on the other hand, using MySQL in the cloud is increasingly common, so I want you to be prepared and successful. Plus, this is a *free trial*: the following five cloud providers have a free tier or an initial account credit. Don't pay for anything yet: cloud providers must earn your business and money by proving the value of their services to you.

Try creating and using MySQL with any one (or several) of these cloud providers:

- MySQL Database Service (*https://oreil.ly/Z7ZA8*) by Oracle
- SkySQL (*https://oreil.ly/tn1KY*) by MariaDB
- Relational Database Service (RDS) (*https://oreil.ly/yNPfc*) by Amazon
- Azure Database for MySQL (*https://oreil.ly/Tj3Y1*) by Microsoft
- Cloud SQL (*https://oreil.ly/pnsVt*) by Google

If you find that one is easy to use and potentially valuable, investigate its pricing model and additional costs. I specifically use the verb *investigate* because, as I mention in "Performance Is Money" on page 313: cloud pricing is complex, nearly intractable, and frequently underestimated (which means over budget).

 Don't forget to destroy your MySQL instance in the cloud before the free trial ends or the initial account credit reaches zero.

This is the last practice in this book, but I encourage you to keep learning and practicing because MySQL continues to evolve—so does the cloud. For this reason, even MySQL experts must continue to learn and practice, and that reminds me of a Zen proverb on which I end this book:

Chop wood. Carry water.

Index

About the Author

Daniel Nichter is a DBA with over 15 years of experience with MySQL. He started optimizing MySQL performance in 2004 while working in a data center. Soon after, he created *https://hackmysql.com* to share information and tools about MySQL. Daniel is most known for the tools he published during his eight-year tenure at Percona, several of which remain the de facto standard and in use at the largest tech companies in the world. He is also a MySQL Community Award winner, conference speaker, and wide-ranging open source contributor. Daniel currently works as a DBA and software engineer at Square, a fintech company with thousands of MySQL servers.

Colophon

The bird on the cover of *Efficient MySQL Performance* is a crested barbet (*Trachyphonus vaillantii*), commonly known as "fruit salad" for their colorful plumage and fruit-based diet. Mostly native to Southern Africa, they are usually found in woodland areas, suburban gardens and orchards, and along riverbeds and are nonmigratory.

The adult crested barbet's coloration makes it easily identifiable. It has a red and yellow head, a large, stout, pale greenish-yellow bill, and a gray-black dot on its cheek. Its mantle, wings, tail, and thick breast band are black with white crescents or dots. The crested barbet's lower back is yellow with red upper tail coverts. There is more yellow and red on its underside, and its legs and feet are gray.

Crested barbets are highly vocal birds that have a shrill, drumming-like song that can last several minutes. They are territorial and aggressive, especially during the breeding season. Although small and clumsy in flight, they are strong and known to harass and even attack other birds, mammals, and reptiles that approach their nests. They are monogamous and usually seen in pairs. The pairs work together to dig cavity nests in rotted trees and breed year-round if conditions are right.

Because they eat small insects and snails, residential areas welcome the crested barbet, but on commercial farms, they seriously damage crops. Crested barbets face capture for this damage and for the pet trade but are not yet endangered. Many of the animals on O'Reilly's covers are endangered; all of them are important to the world.

The cover illustration is by Karen Montgomery, based on a black and white engraving from *English Cyclopaedia*. The cover fonts are Gilroy Semibold and Guardian Sans. The text font is Adobe Minion Pro; the heading font is Adobe Myriad Condensed; and the code font is Dalton Maag's Ubuntu Mono.

Milton Keynes UK
Ingram Content Group UK Ltd.
UKHW050046230924
448644UK00004B/14

9 781098 105099